OPIUM
NATION

OPIUM NATION

*Child Brides, Drug Lords, and
One Woman's Journey Through
Afghanistan*

FARIBA NAWA

HARPER ⬤ PERENNIAL

NEW YORK • LONDON • TORONTO • SYDNEY • NEW DELHI • AUCKLAND

HARPER ● PERENNIAL

This is a work of nonfiction. The events and experiences detailed herein are all true and have been faithfully rendered as I have remembered them, to the best of my ability. Some names, identities, and circumstances have been changed in order to protect the integrity and/or anonymity of the various individuals involved, and who have a right to tell their own stories if they so choose. Though conversations come from my keen recollection of them in my native language, Farsi, they are not written to represent word-for-word documentation in English; rather, I've retold and interpreted them in a way that evokes the real feeling and meaning of what was said, in keeping with the true essence of the mood and spirit of the event.

FIRST EDITION

Designed by Justin Dodd

Photographs courtesy of the author

Library of Congress Cataloging-in-Publication Data.

Nawa, Fariba.
Opium nation : child brides, drug lords, and one woman's journey through Afghanistan / Fariba Nawa.
    p. cm.
ISBN 978-0-06-193470-4
1. Opium trade—Social aspects—Afghanistan. 2. Drug traffic—Social aspects—Afghanistan. 3. Women—Social conditions—Afghanistan. 4. Afghanistan—Social conditions—21st century. 5. Afghanistan—Social life and customs—21st century. I. Title.
HD9675.O653A363 2011
958.104'7—dc23   2011028527

11 12 13 14 15   OV/RRD   10 9 8 7 6 5 4 3 2 1

To my parents, Sayed Begum and Fazul Haq,
who introduced me to the Afghanistan of the past,
and to my daughter, Bonoo Zahra,
who I hope will become a positive force in the country's future

Contents

Prologue

In the summer of 2003, I met a girl in an Afghan town straddling the desert who would become an obsession for me. I knew her for only a few weeks, but those few weeks shaped the next four years of my life in Afghanistan. What I remember most about her is her scared look, a gaze that deepened her otherwise blank green eyes. She was the daughter of a narcotics dealer who had sold her into marriage to a drug lord to settle his opium debt. Her husband was thirty-four years her senior, and even her threats to burn herself to death did not change her fate. A year after I met her, she was forced to go to a southern province as the wife of this man, a man who did not speak her language and who had another wife and eight children.

I met Darya on a quest to write a magazine story about the impact of the Afghan drug trade on women. Ghoryan, the Afghan district where she used to live, is two hours from the Iranian border, and the people there make their living on opium transport. In this vast district I met many men and women who were either victims or perpetrators in the worldwide multibillion-dollar drug trade, but none of them stayed in my heart as much as Darya. She had become a child bride and a servant, a casualty of the drug trade—an opium bride. Darya is a link in a long chain that begins on Afghanistan's farms and ends on the streets of London and Los Angeles. In order to understand what happened to her, I had to understand the drug trade. I chased clues from province to province to find out who was behind the business; who its victims were; how it was impacting Afghans; and what the world, and the Afghan government, were doing to stop it.

In 2000, I made my first trip back to Afghanistan in eighteen years, during Taliban rule, to search for something I had lost—a sense of coherence, a feeling of rootedness in a place and a people, and a sense of belonging. I had many unsettled emotions toward my homeland, which I had had to flee at the impressionable age of nine. The strongest feelings were aching nostalgia and lingering survivor's guilt, which my parents and siblings did not share. I was the youngest, with the fewest memories of the war-torn land, but I longed for it the most. All that my adopted home, the United States, offered me could not make up for the loss I felt in leaving Afghanistan.

In the process of finding ways to deal with my demons, I wanted to tell the world that the Afghan drug trade provided funding for terrorists and for the Taliban, who were killing Americans and strengthening corrupt Afghan government officials whom the United States supported. A former chief of the U.S. Drug Enforcement Administration called the Afghan opium trade "a huge challenge" in the world. Americans and the British are directly harmed by it. Afghan heroin is a favorite among addicts because it's a potent form of heroin, and increasingly available.

I spent 2000 through 2007 shuttling back and forth between Afghanistan and the United States, with detours to Iran and Pakistan. The majority of my time was spent traveling through Afghanistan. During that time, I witnessed the country's shift from a religious autocracy to a fragmented democracy and, finally, to a land at full-scale war. The result of that war has been dependence on an illicit narcotics trade, without which the Afghanistan economy would collapse. For the opium trade is the underground Afghan economy, an all-encompassing market that directly affects the daily lives of Afghans in a way that nothing else does.

Ghoryan district, Darya's childhood home, is full of individuals and families with stories few have heard. The Afghan women who live there are not the weak, voiceless victims they are so often made out to be in the Western media. Since they see themselves as part of their family units, Afghan women rarely demand individual rights, as women, something uncommon in the West. During my time in Ghoryan, these women, including Darya, showed me just how powerful they were, and how capable of overcoming their problems.

The effect of the opium trade in Ghoryan is very real. Yet Ghoryan is not the only place where the drug trade resides. In some places, the trade is destroying lives; in others, saving them. During my time in Afghanistan, I was drawn to cities and villages where some chose this illegal business while local warlords force others to dive into it. Opium is everywhere—in the addict beggars on the streets, in the poppies planted in home gardens, in the opium widows hidden from drug lords in neighbors' homes, in the hushed conversations of drug dealers in shops, in the unmarked graves in cemeteries, and in the drug lords' garish opium mansions looming above brick shacks and mounds of dust. The dust is a reminder of the destroyed land that opium money seems unable to transform into cement, asphalt, or water.

In this book, I've changed many of the names to protect the people I write about. In Afghanistan, revealing identities does not just invade privacy but also endangers lives. I also try not to focus on the ethnic rivalries in Afghanistan that have, to my mind, been overemphasized and overanalyzed in the West, though it is impossible to ignore them. After September 11, 2001, many Americans were anxious to know whether I was Pashtun, Tajik, or another minority group. I'd stare at them confused and say simply that I was from Herat.

The years I spent working in Afghanistan were the most dangerous and exciting of my life thus far. The action-packed sequence of events I experienced there tested my will to live and set me on a journey to see if the passion I held for my birthplace and its people was rooted in the present or lost in the past.

ONE

Home After Eighteen Years

Flies buzz and circle my face. I swat them away as I slowly look up to see a dozen men watching me outside the visa building. I'm standing in line at the Iranian border, waiting to cross into my home country, Afghanistan. Men stare at my face and hands. My hair and the rest of my body are covered in a head scarf, slacks, and a long coat, in observance of Iran's dress requirements for women.

I keep my eyes to the ground to avoid the ogling. An Iranian border agent calls out my name. My hands tremble as I give him my Afghan passport—perhaps the least useful travel document in the world. I've hidden my American passport in my bra; Iran restricts visas for American citizens, and the Taliban are wary of Afghan women returning from the United States.

"Where are you coming from?" the agent asks with a serious face.
"Pakistan."

"What are you doing there?"

"I work for a charity organization." I actually work for a Pakistani think tank as an English editor, and I'm a freelancer writing articles about Afghan refugees in Pakistan for American media outlets. I don't share these details with the Iranian border agent, though; they would only raise more questions and delay my journey.

"What were you doing in Iran?"

"Visiting my relatives."

He eyes me suspiciously and flips through the pages of my passport. Then he stamps the exit visa with "Tybad," the Iranian border city, and motions me to leave.

It is late morning and a cool fall breeze hits my face. My hands stop shaking but become clammy, my stomach churns with nausea, my head spins. In just a few hours I will be in Herat, my childhood home, for the first time in eighteen years. The anticipation feels a bit like the moment before I delivered my daughter: painful, frightening, yet exhilarating.

I am accompanied by Mobin. The Taliban require that women travel with a male relative, a *mahram*, but I didn't have a male relative willing to lead me to war-battered Afghanistan. In Iran, I stayed with Kamran, whose family were our neighbors in Herat. He is the son of Mr. Jawan, a retired opium smuggler, and a close friend of our family. He asked his friend Mobin to act as my *mahram*. Mobin, a merchant based in Herat, met me at Kamran's home in Torbat-e-Jam, Iran. He is shy and taciturn; he shows his expressions by raising or lowering his deeply arched dark eyebrows. Mobin imports buttons and lace from Iran to sell in Afghanistan, earning about $3,000 a year. He sees his wife and eighteen-month-old son in Herat one week out of every month. Shrewd and experienced on the road, he promised Kamran he would safely guide me from Iran to Afghanistan and finally back to Pakistan.

Mobin and I walk a few yards from the Iranian side of the border and onto Afghan soil, in the town of Islam Qala. We rent a taxi with two other women; Mobin is acting as their *mahram* as well. Each woman is dressed in a black chador, a one-piece fabric covering the whole body. The women whisper to each other and wrap one end of their chadors over their mouths. The Taliban have banned music everywhere in the country, but our driver, a tall, unassuming man, slips in a cassette of Farhad Darya, the most renowned Afghan pop singer, and turns up the volume as we head for Herat. He risks the destruction of his tapes and a beating if the Taliban catch him. (The Taliban usually rip out the ribbons from seized video- and audiocassettes and display them in town centers as a lesson to others.) But our driver is among many Afghans who take this risk.

The taxi rolls up and down over sand dunes, lolling me back to the past. The desert we are crossing was the front line in the war when I was a child. I was nine years old the last time I crossed the path of the ancient Silk Road, when my family fled Afghanistan in 1982, during the Soviet invasion. For six hours my parents and older sister walked while I rode on the donkey carrying our belongings until we safely reached Iran, and then Pakistan. We eventually sought asylum in the United States, where I grew up in California. I haven't stopped dreaming of returning to Afghanistan since I left. I cling to my memories of the nine years I spent there, a mixture of blissful childhood innocence ruptured by the bloodshed of war.

A bump in the road jolts me out of my reminiscences. I take out my journal and write under my black coat. The others in the car see the journal.

"How can you write on such a rough ride?" Mobin asks.

"My handwriting will be bad, but I'll be able to read it," I answer.

I scribble as the car jumps, rolling over a big rock. Where are we? Was it here that I cried for water for two hours under the scorching sun? Water had finally arrived, in a plastic oil container from a salty desert well. I drank and gagged, I remember, spitting the water on the donkey I was riding.

I put the journal away and look out the taxi's dust-covered window. My view is an endless desert dotted with boulders and thorns. The taxi's tires kick up more dust, and a rain of sand blocks the view for a moment.

Every time a man appears, either walking or in a car in the distance, the other women and I shield our faces with the edge of our head scarves.

"Don't worry. The Taliban are scared of women," Mobin says. "They usually stop cars with only men. The ones with women, they just turn their heads." He's not kidding. Many of the Taliban were orphans who grew up in Pakistani refugee camps, attending religious schools. Some have had little or no contact with women.

I close my eyes and listen to the voice of Farhad Darya.

> In this state of exile
> My beloved is not close to me
> I've lost my homeland
> I've lost my wit
> O dear God

The singer laments his distance from Afghanistan; he recorded this song in Virginia. Darya is loved for his original lyrics, which invoke the nostalgia and painful experience of exile. His songs are steeped in loss, longing, and the warmth the homeland gave him. His music speaks to those inside the country as well as to the Afghan diaspora. I usually become melancholy when I listen to his music, but this time I smile. I'm no longer in exile.

I think I'm getting closer to home.

The war was in its fourth year, and my mother, Sayed Begum; my father, Fazul Haq; and my sister, Faiza, lived in our paternal family property in downtown Herat. My brother, Hadi, had already fled the country. Our home consisted of two rooms and was one of three houses built on two acres of land. The land, once emerald with gardens of herbs and vegetables, was now dry, with only a few surviving pomegranate trees and a blackberry tree. The war, the shortage of water, and the absence of a caretaker—our caretaker, Rasool, died before the war—had led to the land's neglect. We shared the property with my father's youngest brother, a dozen of his in-laws, my paternal grandfather, Baba Monshi, and his wife, Bibi Assia.

Baba Monshi's name was Abdul Karim Ahrary. A renowned essayist and intellectual, he was an adviser on the drafting of Afghanistan's constitution in 1964 and pioneered the women's movement in Herat city in the 1960s. He established Donish (Knowledge) Publishers and was the editor of Herat's official newspaper, *Islamic Unison*. His protégé was his niece, my aunt Roufa Ahrary, who started *Mehri*, the first women's magazine in Herat. Our home was a meeting point for secular intellectuals to debate politics, play chess, and drink tea. Baba Monshi's opinions were ahead of their time. He believed that women should have the right to an education and he wrote against the injustices of British imperialism and the inequalities in the Afghan government. The government first jailed him in the early twentieth century, then exiled him from Herat to Kabul. His influence had spread in Herat, which made the Afghan monarchy nervous.

By the time I was born, Baba Moshi had lost his once-vibrant

capabilities for intellectual thought. When my blood grandmother Bibi Sarah died in 1967, my grandfather married Bibi Assia,
who became my step-grandmother. She was a plump and petite
woman, and hugging her was like wrapping my arms around a
soft pillow. She dedicated her time to caring for my ailing grandfather. In his later years, Baba Monshi spent most of his hours
roaming around the property, feeding his gray-and-black cat,
Gorba, and giving bread to the ants in the yard. Near the end, he
didn't recognize most of his family, except for his wife, whom he
sought out only when he was hungry. Bibi Assia's biggest gripe was
that Baba Monshi would not eat the meat on his plate; instead he
fed it to Gorba.

Two miles from our property on Behzad Road was my maternal grandfather's three-and-a-half-acre orchard home near Herat Stadium, on tree-lined Telecom Road. My mother would take me to
Haji Baba's house every weekend and on holidays. We would stay for
several nights at a time. I recall the cheerfulness of my childhood
in this home. I'd climb trees, pick fruit, and play with my dozen
maternal cousins. The orchard was replete with mulberry, cherry,
pomegranate, walnut, apple, peach, and orange trees, as well as grapevines. My grandparents also had a small barn in the back of the
land, with a few cows. A narrow creek cut through the trees, and
their eight-room redbrick house sat in the center of the land. The
rooms were full of people. Haji Baba's real name was Sayed Akbar
Hossaini and he was a financial adviser for the government who traveled to other districts and provinces for work. He also wrote essays,
which one of my maternal uncles, Dr. Said Maroof Ramia, compiled
into a book, published in Germany in 2006, titled *The Authorities of
Herat.* Haji Baba did not get to spend much time with his family, but
Bibi Gul, my maternal step-grandmother, was hardly alone with ten
children—my aunts and uncles—and a dozen grandchildren. Fewer

bombs dropped near Haji Baba's property than ours, because it was secure with the presence of the nearby police station and several government offices. The orchard there was my sanctuary.

Outside the gated properties was a lively city with horse wagons, public buses, shoppers, and a five-thousand-year history shared by the city where we lived. The city was surrounded by four-meter-high walls that hid the houses, most constructed from adobe or concrete. Five gates served as entrances and exits for the city. Herat's older homes, including the remains of the Jewish neighborhood, were two-story structures decorated with intricate tilework and carvings, and were designed with square courtyards and fountains. Among the houses and shops were numerous architectural wonders that made the city an outdoor museum of Afghanistan, including a centuries-old fort, spectacular minarets, shrines, and mosques.

Herat's history is wrought with peaks and valleys of war and conquest, of progress and destruction. Various eras have labeled Herat the cradle of art and culture and the pearl of the region. Prominent Sufi poets Khwaja Abdullah Ansari and Nuruddin Jami and medieval miniaturist Behzad all flourished in Herat. Two periods define extreme eras for the city: In the thirteenth century, Genghis Khan held the city under siege after his son was murdered by native rebels. The Mongol leader killed thousands, leaving only forty people alive. Nearly two centuries later, during the Turkic Timurid dynasty, Herat served as the capital of the Turkic Mongol empire and thrived with advancements in art and education. Under the leadership of Queen Gowhar Shad—who ruled for ten years but whose influence spanned generations—magnificent architecture was built that still stands today. The Muslim queen of Sheba, as Gowhar Shad is widely known, also focused her attention on scholarship and diplomacy.

This glorious past was forgotten when bombs rained on the city during the Soviet invasion and wealthy, educated residents began to flee in the thousands. The American-funded mujahideen rebels fought ferocious battles against a ruling Communist government aided by Soviet troops and airpower. The battles occurred a mile from our Behzad Road home, in neighborhoods such as Baraman, Houza Karbas, and Shahzadaha. Of the seven mujahideen factions, Jamiat-e-Islami fought in Herat under the leadership of Ismail Khan, an educated soldier and warrior. Khan was ally to the head of Jamiat, Ahmad Shah Massoud, who became famous in the United States after the Taliban employed two Arab suicide bombers to kill him two days before September 11. The United States gave weapons to the Pakistani intelligence agency, ISI, to hand over to the mujahideen, who numbered roughly 200,000. The mujahideen had guns, rockets, and Stinger missiles, but also knowledge of the terrain and, most important, local support. The Afghan Communist government had a shrinking army—Afghan soldiers deserted or defected to the mujahideen—but was reinforced by about 120,000 Soviet troops and Soviet helicopters, planes, tanks, missiles, and mines. The rebels attacked from behind hills, shrines, and even some houses; the Soviets sometimes carpet-bombed in response.

A normal day at our home included the rumble of gunshots and rockets. We ignored the sounds and carried on with life. My sister played volleyball with relatives, I played hopscotch, and my father took his daily walks around the property after coming home from his job as an administrative director at the National Fertilizer Company, an American-funded, Afghan government–owned project that offered chemical fertilizer to farmers. On some days, however, the shots and explosions barely missed members of my family.

One spring day, when I was eight years old, Bibi Assia was extracting rosewater from the pink roses that bloomed on our property when a stray bullet passed just above her four-foot-nine inches of height. (It was hard to place the origin of the bullets because there were always so many of them.) The bullet struck the brick wall of our house and burned a hole in it. After the incident, Bibi Assia hid in a room for a month, coming out only when necessary. And our family developed a morbid sense of humor.

"Assia Jan's height saved her life. Who said being short is a bad thing?" my father joked. That winter, he nearly met his own bullet. One day my mother (Madar), my sister, and I were playing cards around the *korsi*—a table warmed by a makeshift heater, with a charcoal barbecue lit up underneath it—with a big blanket covering our bodies, when a bullet fractured the window of our living room. The golden bullet rushed over our heads, ricocheted off a wall, and fell to the floor, just missing my father's hand—he had been pacing the room, as he often did out of habit. We all thought the Communist government soldiers or the mujahideen were raiding our house, but when my father ventured outside to investigate, he found there had been only the lone bullet.

One attack that still disturbs my dreams occurred at my school, Lycée Mehri, a year later, in July 1982, when I was nine years old. In provinces with heavy snowfall, such as Herat, schools are open in the summer and closed for the winter. Girls from kindergarten up through the twelfth grade attended my school, which was on an unpaved block about two football fields from our home. The day of the attack, Madar let me play hooky, and she and I went to take our weekly bath at the public bathhouse, a few miles from our neighborhood, while Faiza, who was in the tenth grade, went to school.

The bathhouse was a place to strip down, relax, and gossip, though the talk often turned to the war. One of the women there that day, with gold bangles and stringy hair, told my mom that her husband had heard that the mujahideen planned to attack Lycée

Mehri because girls were being taught Communist propaganda there. "Haven't you noticed how there are fewer cars and horse wagons on the road?" the woman said. "People are staying home because they are afraid of a big attack right here in town."

These rumors were too common to take seriously. Madar shrugged off the news and asked the woman why she had come out if she was so worried about an attack. Later, when we left the warmth of the bathhouse, a cool summer wind hit our faces and we noticed that the streets were empty and the shops that were usually bustling with customers were closed. We walked halfway home because we couldn't find a taxi, wagon, or bus any sooner, and then we finally hailed a horse wagon.

Madar seemed worried when we reached our house. "I hope that woman at the bathhouse was wrong about the school being attacked." I remained quiet and set about ironing my favorite fuchsia chiffon dress, which my mom had made for me. I brushed off my mother's concern and wondered what I was missing at school.

Just then, there was a boom, a much bigger and closer one than usual. Madar and I looked at each other.

"Faiza!" she screamed. She was wearing a colorful dress, without a burqa, so she grabbed a flower-printed sheet, wrapped it around her thin body, and ran out of the house. I left my dress half ironed and dashed out barefoot. It was the first time I'd seen my mother run on Herat's streets without her burqa and with her small feet in only house slippers. Her face was paler than usual, and her tiny hands were curled in fists. I struggled to keep up with her; I've never run faster.

At the gate of Lycée Mehri, an ambulance overflowed with injured students. The ground was deep red, and people were running in and out of the school grounds. I saw Maha—a classmate I often played hide and seek with—carried out by a man in a white coat; her arm was missing and she was bleeding from one eye. I recognized Jaber—the son of a teacher and the only boy in the school—from his clothes; his head had been blown off. But where was my sister? Faiza was skinny and petite, with platinum blond hair that she had to dye black, lest people mistake her for a Russian.

My mother and I frantically searched amid the debris and the dust, shouting Faiza's name. I found some of her classmates huddled in a corner outside. "She's okay, but she thinks you were also in school," Sadia, one of her friends, told me. "She went looking for you. They dropped the bomb over the elementary section."

Nearly three decades later, Faiza told me what she remembered of the attack:

"It was recess time in the morning for the elementary section, and we were in class. When the rocket hit, there was a huge noise, followed by darkness everywhere for a few minutes. We could tell that we were hit. Nobody could see anything. And all my classmates were screaming. Dust was all over the place. We were thinking we might get attacked again. People got hurt rushing out in a mob. My dress was full of blood and I didn't know whose it was.

"As soon as I got out of the building, I heard that the elementary school building was hit, and so I ran there looking for you, but the area was cordoned off. The stairway outside the buildings, even the ground and the walls, had blood on them. I saw people, injured hands and legs bleeding, you could see the fear in their eyes. All this occurred in ten minutes at the most."

Faiza was looking for me, and I was running to find her. I sprinted toward the elementary school building, which was fifty meters from the high school building, but before I got there, I heard her screaming my name. Suddenly the three of us—Madar, Faiza, and I—were embracing.

The violence I witnessed at my school defined the path I have taken in my adult life—the road to war. I became a foreign correspondent so I could keep going back to war zones, witnessing gory scenes again and again, to understand the extremism in humanity, something that both revolts and fascinates me. War can become an addiction for its victims because it provides them meaning at the same time that it strips them of decency.

The rocket at Lycée Mehri killed Jaber, his mother's only child, and injured dozens of others. The attack shook the neighborhood, and afterward some parents forbade their daughters to attend classes. The school closed for a few months, and my parents started to discuss fleeing the country.

"It's too dangerous. There are bullets flying everywhere, and our daughters are in danger," my mother told my father as we ate dinner one evening.

He didn't argue. "With the school closed, there's no education. I don't want illiterate children. I'm working on it. Give me some time."

My father sold his share of our property, dug a ditch in the ground near our house to hide $3,500 cash, and set about preparing travel documents for our family's escape.

Two months after the bombing of Lycée Mehri, in September 1982, my father, mother, sister, and I secretly crossed the desert to Iran, then journeyed to Pakistan, where we joined the millions of other Afghan refugees. We did not take any of our family photos or other memorabilia, for fear that, if confiscated as we were flee-ing, they would implicate the family members who'd stayed behind. Agha (Father) had no political affiliations, but we had friends and relatives involved on both sides of the war.

Mr. Jawan, our opium smuggler neighbor, was a mujahideen sympathizer. Before we left, he contacted his tribe, who were fight-ing the Communists on the border of Iran and Afghanistan, and told the men there that we were going to escape to Iran. His oldest son, Shafiq, escorted us to the border. A few of our relatives, mostly uncles, were Communists working for the government and they did not approve of our departure. They knew we would go to a capitalist country and be considered enemies of the Soviet Union.

By the time of my visit in 2000, the Soviet troops were long gone, having withdrawn in 1989, and the seven groups of the mujahideen government that replaced the Communist regime in 1992 had turned on one another and reduced Kabul to rubble. The rest of the country also fell to the mujahideen strongmen—many of whom Afghan civilians began referring to as warlords, because they extorted money and seized land from the poor. A few mujahideen commanders, such as Ismail Khan in Herat, focused on rebuilding their cities, but they were in the minority. Isolated for decades at war, many of the mujahideen commanders turned to pedophilia for sexual fulfillment and fought over young civilian boys in their communities.

In 1994 a group of young Pashtun men trained in Islamic seminaries on the borders of Pakistan paraded into Kandahar and defeated the mujahideen commanders. Some of them were former mujahideen themselves, or sons of the mujahideen. They referred to themselves as *Taliban*, which in Arabic means "students." The Taliban bribed their way to Kabul and Herat and fought hard to seize central and northern Afghanistan. In response, the mujahideen reunited under Ahmad Shah Massoud, but they now controlled only 10 percent of the country, in the northeast.

Beginning in the early 1990s, the Taliban, aided by drug traffickers, the Pakistani government, and rich Gulf Arabs such as Osama bin Laden, ruled the country under a mysterious one-eyed leader, Mullah Omar. In the mid-1990s, Afghanistan was facing a severe drought, and the threat of starvation. From 1994, when they seized Kandahar, until 1999, the year with the highest opium output under their control, the Taliban gave carte blanche to the drug business, permitting processing labs to refine opium into heroin, thereby allowing poppy cultivation and trafficking to flourish. The four thousand tons of opium produced in 1999 flooded the illicit narcotics market worldwide, and demand for the drug dropped.

This was bad news for the Taliban, who had up until this time survived primarily on taxing opium farmers. The Taliban were fighting to gain international legitimacy, though only Saudi Arabia, the United Arab Emirates, and Pakistan accepted them as the official government of Afghanistan. (Other countries, including the United States, still recognized Ahmad Shah Massoud and the mujahideen.) In July 2000 the Taliban banned poppy cultivation. The ban was a response to the market and a bid to create more demand, yet the Taliban claimed it was for moral reasons—a political move to gain international recognition that failed: the Afghan farmers who had formerly farmed poppies now faced severe hardships and could not afford to pay their debts to lenders. Even after the ban, the Taliban continued to take a cut from opium and heroin traffickers.

The Taliban also focused their attention on enforcing a new code of law that was horrifying to educated Afghans. In the name of religion, they forbade women from going to school or working in most fields, and they forced men to pray. (Until the 2000 opium ban, one of the few jobs women could still perform was to work on poppy farms.) They also closed public bathhouses, outlawed kite flying, and forced men to grow long, scraggly beards. The Taliban government performed public executions of accused adulterers, homosexuals, and killers. Thieves' hands were severed, as in Saudi Arabia.

This is the Afghanistan I am about to enter in a taxi with Mobin as my *mahram*.

In pitch dark we pass through Herat's city gates. My heart is throbbing. Designed like wedding cakes, shiny four-story concrete houses with tinted windows tower over white-painted walls. Downtown is lit up with neon-colored lights. Men ride their bicycles on the unpaved roads. It is ten PM, and there is not a woman in sight.

The taxi stops in front of Mobin's house, and he hurries to inform his family that they have a guest. I stay behind and kiss the ground, hoping no one on the street will see me. It is a private moment I imagined throughout my years in exile. Jalaluddin Rumi, the thirteenth-century Farsi poet who was born in what today is Afghanistan, expresses the emotions I feel at that moment in the poem "Call of Love":

> At every instant and from every side, resounds the call of Love:
> We are going to the sky, who wants to come with us?
> We have gone to heaven, we have been the friends of the angels,
> And now we will go back there, for there is our country ...

I look up at the unpolluted sky. The night breeze blows dust in my eyes, but I can still see the constellations, the Big Dipper, shooting stars, and the moon. The sky looks the same as it did when I was seven and slept on the roof next to my mother on summer's hottest nights. We were alone on the roof. I used to count the stars while she slept peacefully. Few people dare to sleep on their roofs anymore. The bombs and bullets flying through the night sky have driven them inside.

Bibi Assia, who still lives on the same property we once did with my ailing grandfather, is my closest relative in Herat. My mother has many extended relatives here, including her stepuncle Ahmed and her cousin Sattar Agha.

I spend my first night in Herat with Mobin and his wife,

Farida, a young woman with full lips and sharp cheekbones,
who is hospitable but visibly uncomfortable that I am traveling
with her husband. She is not bothered by my surprise appearance. People visit without warning in Afghanistan; calling ahead
suggests that the guest wants to stay for a meal and is therefore
considered rude. The couple leave me alone in a rectangular room
whose floor is covered by a red silk carpet and red spongy mats.
Carpeted cushions are arranged against all four walls. The room's
twenty-seven-inch television set is covered by embroidered pink
fabric. Farida has left me a large, round tray bearing a plate of
steaming rice, lamb stew, and potatoes, and a can of orange soda.
I hear Mobin explain to her in the next room that I am here to
work and will stay with my relatives for a week. But he has to take
me back to Pakistan, because he promised Kamran that he would
protect me from the Taliban.

"Why did you make such a promise?" Farida asks. "Don't you
have enough danger traveling by yourself?"

"I stay with Kamran every time I'm in Iran. I couldn't say no.
She's a nice girl who only has her mind on her work. Don't be scared.
I have no interest in her," he reassures her in the same tone with
which he told me not to fear the Taliban.

I savor the tender lamb and tangy potatoes, wondering if I
should go to Uncle Ahmed's house right away so that Farida will
sleep easier. But it is too late; once the sun has set, women are allowed out of the house only in the case of an emergency, to go to
the hospital.

My mother's uncle Ahmed knows I'm coming to Herat, because
Kamran called him from Iran to inform him.

"Is she coming to work as a reporter?" Uncle Ahmed asked him.

"No, she just wants to see her birthplace again. Relax. She will
not get you in trouble," Kamran told him.

My first morning in Herat, I take out the blue burqa Kamran's wife, Abida, lent me in Iran and place its round hat on my head. The Taliban force women to wear the burqa in public or risk a beating. What if I fall and the covering drops? I am carrying underneath it a handbag filled with illicit equipment: a camera, a notebook and pen, a U.S. passport, and a few hundred dollars.

Mobin drives me to Uncle Ahmed's house, where his two wives, five daughters, and only son come out to greet me. I kiss Uncle Ahmed's hand and kiss his wives three times on the cheek, as is customary. The entire family is grinning.

"We're so glad you're here. How are your mother, father, brother, and sister? How come you came alone?" Uncle Ahmed's older wife, Aunt Maria, asks.

The five daughters each take turns kissing my cheeks and squeezing me tightly. "*Kheily khosh amadid* [welcome, we're so happy to see you]," the eldest daughter, Sadaf, says.

Uncle Ahmed lives on a small property on Telecom Road that includes a house with two bedrooms, a basement, and an indoor bathroom. There is a separate quarter for his older wife, Aunt Maria, who lives by herself. Across the street from his property is my grandfather Haji Baba's orchard. Uncle Ahmed owns a bus service, transporting Afghan passengers to and from Iran. His second wife, Aunt Zulaikha, is a schoolteacher who teaches young girls clandestinely in their house. The family is fairly well off; they eat and wear what they want. Their only son, Bahram, is a capricious fifteen-year-old who bosses his older sisters around. He goes to school but says he does not learn anything in the classroom. He studies English and science in the increasing number of private courses offered to boys his age in Herat.

Because of its location on the border, Herat province is the Taliban's most lucrative area. The Afghan government benefits from customs fees charged for goods entering the country from Iran. The province is home to hundreds of wealthy merchants who profit from importing goods such as clothes and cars. But being rich in Afghanistan means merely that families have enough to eat.

This prosperity, compared with the rest of the country, gives Herat's residents more leeway to break the law. For example, though women are officially banned from leaving their homes without a *mahram*, I see dozens of them walking the streets without men. The Taliban soldiers leave them unharmed. (In Kabul, the ragtag moral police beat women caught in public without a man.) The Taliban's strict rules are constraining for my uncle's family, and for many others in urban Herat, but a quiet rebellion is unleashed inside homes in response to the laws that limit education and mobility. Uncle Ahmed's family disobeys the Taliban every day. My cousins scoff at the ban on music and television, and the girls show me their satellite dish propped up on their porch, the family's television, and the musical instruments in the basement.

Despite the disobedience, the Taliban have instilled fear in Herat's women and young men. True, Heratis take advantage of their more permissive situation, but they go about it in a schizophrenic manner. My first night at Uncle Ahmed's, my cousins drum on their tambourines at midnight, cursing the Taliban as they play. All five girls raise their voices in chorus to sing a famous folk song, "Sabza":

The tan-skinned beloved is coming coquettishly.
The holder of secrets is coming.
Listen to my heart full of pain
Love burns my heart.

Habiba, ten years old and the youngest girl, with a plump round face and a thick mane of hair, sings louder than the others, and Nazaneen, fair skinned and stout, who is five years older than Habiba, admonishes her.

"Shameless! Lower your voice! Do you want the Taliban to come to our door?"

"Allow me to shit on the beard of the Taliban's father," Habiba shoots back, invoking a common Herati expletive.

The next day, the girls speak in hushed voices, afraid the Taliban are coming to punish them. They have heard too many stories of the moral police raiding homes, even those of their neighbors, to remove musical instruments, satellite dishes, and television sets. One way of appeasing certain high-ranking members of the local Taliban is to invite them to parties, where they join in on the festivities. Uncle Ahmed sees that his daughters are afraid now and thinks of sending out an invitation.

"I can invite over the chief of our police district tonight if you girls cook him a big dinner," he says. "He likes to watch the Hindi film songs."

"They don't deserve to eat, Haji Agha," the outspoken Habiba responds.

On the second day of my visit, I stroll through the streets for the first time with my cousins. I walk more slowly than the girls, embarrassed that I might trip on the flowing fabric of my burqa. There is power in being invisible. Men on the street notice my ankles and hands but do not look at my face, do not see my eyes watching them. I stare at their expressions, reading them without the interruption of their gaze. I see in their eyes a devilish curiosity about the opposite sex.

The main streets have been paved since my childhood. There is a new market for computers and software, and a sparkly building has replaced the cinema where my parents used to watch Hindi movies.

The biggest difference is the rise in the number of beggars. Maimed children, women in torn, dirt-covered burqas, and old men with white beards lower their heads and hold out their hands as my cousins and I walk past them. I recall beggars from when I was young, but they dotted the streets then; they didn't line them.

"Let's go back home," I tell the girls after an hour. I need to digest the changes I've seen.

After lunch, my cousin Bahram escorts me to my family home in downtown Herat. It's two miles from my uncle's house, and we take a taxi—a Toyota Corolla with red-velvet-covered seats, an ornament with "Allah" inscribed inside dangling from the rearview mirror, and spotless windows. Halfway through the ride, I see a horse wagon and become nostalgic. Bahram and I step out of the taxi and board the wooden wagon. The driver, an old man with a turban, holds a whip. He slaps the horse once with it, and I protest. "It's okay if the horse goes slow. Please don't hit him."

"Okay, sister," he replies, and the horse trots behind the rickshaws, taxis, and buses. A few minutes later we reach Baba Monshi's property. Behzad Road is wider, with a new market of small variety shops, but the same dusty pine trees I tried to climb as an eight-year-old. I knock at the home's old brass gate. A child opens the door and leads me to my ailing grandmother, who is praying. I lift the front of my burqa as she turns her head. Bibi Assia screams in disbelief, as if I am a ghost. She seems to pass out for a few seconds, before hugging me and sobbing on my shoulder. She still feels like a cushion when I hug her. Her hair is completely gray now, but her eyes are still a warm blue. She gives me a tour of the old property, most of which has been sold off by my family. The new owners built several smaller houses and walls, which divide the land. The only part of the property that remains the same is the *saracha*, the guesthouse, where Bibi Assia lives. Baba Monshi died in 1984, and all my aunts and uncles moved to Europe and the United States. The *saracha* is nearly in shambles—the bathroom roof has collapsed, the paint is chipping off the walls, and the doors are rotting. My paternal family also owns farmland in the village of Abdi, in Herat province, and Bibi Assia receives her share of profits from the harvest, plus portions of rice and flour that come from our land. She has enough to survive, but I never expected to find her living in these squalid conditions. She sees the concern on my face and says she plans to move.

"I'm going to sell this place and use the money to buy a quieter house in the city," she says reassuringly. "Businesses want this property so they can add to the row of shops being built on the block. It's time for me to shut the doors here. Then you can come and stay with me in the new house."

My memories of this place are riddled with the violence of the Soviet war, the stray bullets, the school bombing, and the blood—painful reminders of a past I wish I could forget. But I cannot, and it's these same memories that have brought me here. Two decades later, with Bibi Assia next to me, I now stand on the ground where I once played hopscotch. I scatter some dirt with my shoe and a knot ties itself in my throat. I want to leave. I take Bibi Assia to Uncle Ahmed's house to spend the next few days with me.

When we get there, Aunt Zulaikha greets us with a long face. When I ask her why she looks upset, she says she's just found out that her brother has been imprisoned in Iran for smuggling opium from Herat. She isn't sure he'll make it out alive. "He searched for legitimate work, but narcotics trafficking was the only option he found. I hope they don't hang him." I haven't seen her brother, and it's the first time I've heard about the dire consequences of opium smuggling for Afghans.

"Hanging? That's terrible, Khala Jan," I say. "The only stories about opium I know are the ones that our neighbor Mr. Jawan told us as kids. The worst punishment back in those days was a few nights in jail."

"Fariba Jan, there's a lot more opium and a lot more misery now," she says, smiling at my naïveté.

I want to know more about the drug trade and how Aunt Zulaikha's brother was arrested, but asking questions will only endanger Uncle Ahmed's family.

The next five days pass quickly. The few times I go out with my female cousins, I shop at the dozens of jewelry shops with gaudy gold earrings and necklaces displayed in the windows. The Taliban do not allow women to enter the shops; all transactions have to be made outside the store. We visit the crowded mausoleum of Sufi poets Ansari and Jami. Frequenting shrines seems to be the only outing for families besides shopping. One day I walk down the street of my old school, Lycée Mehri. The main door appears locked, which I expected, since it was an all-girls school and girls are now banned from education. I do not cross the street to get a closer look. The memories of the attack are still vivid.

On the sixth day of my visit to Herat, I return to my maternal grandfather's orchard home for the first time in eighteen years. I could have visited the orchard on my first day, because Uncle Ahmed has the key and lives only a few houses away, but I wanted to save the best for last. The property is empty because my grandparents and ten aunts and uncles now live abroad. This is the place I have been longing to see all these years.

I throw my burqa on the ground as soon as the rusted red gate closes and I sprint toward the living quarters, imagining my family's laughter ringing inside the hallways. But there is no one there; the place is silent. The doors of each of the eight rooms are locked shut; some of the windows are broken. I run out to the field, look-

ing for the mulberry and pomegranate trees under which we used
to have picnics. I find the trees—but no fruit, due to the drought.
The small creek is parched. The house, the barn, and the land seem
much smaller. Then I recall that my uncles sold an acre of the land
a few years ago. Both my paternal and maternal family properties
have undergone the same transformation. I had no expectations
with regard to the Behzad Road property, where Bibi Assia lives. But
here, in my refuge, I envisioned ripe, colorful fruits, verdant fields,
and water flowing through the creek.

I climb the roof overlooking Herat and find even more changes
caused by the war. A dust bowl covers the once-green stadium
nearby. During my childhood, festivals were held there. Now the
stadium has become the Taliban's execution site. I bury my face in
my hands and cry. The tears are cathartic.

My distance from Herat for these nearly two decades left a void
in me. Now, ten thousand miles away from my parents and family
in California, I feel comforted; I've been indulging the past, but
now that I have returned I'm able to look ahead to Afghanistan's
future—a future I hope to witness close up.

On the seventh day, when I am due to leave, Mobin picks me up
from Uncle Ahmed's home. My uncle, aunts, cousins, and I hold and
kiss one another; we promise to keep in contact. I'm returning to
Pakistan, but I'm not going back to Iran. Mobin and I fly to Kabul
on Ariana Afghan Airlines. In Kabul, we take a taxi to the border
of Pakistan. For thirteen hours I sit huddled next to Mobin and
two other men in the taxi's backseat while, up front, two men share
the passenger seat. The driver is the only one sitting comfortably
as the taxi dodges boulders and potholes on the treacherous road.
The only sound is the Hindi music, all but drowned out by the
crackle of gravel underneath the tires. No one speaks, other than

to ask what time we're arriving. The driver turns off the music at checkpoints.

Mobin and I spend the night in a seedy hotel in Jalalabad city, and the next day we take another taxi, this time to Torkham, the town where we will cross the border into Pakistan.

At five AM, we come upon a sea of women in blue burqas and men with long beards in *pirahan tomban* (a long tunic with loose pants) squatting on the ground near the border gates. I count more than five hundred people. From a restaurant loudspeaker, a man sings religious hymns set to no music. The restaurant is divided by a wide curtain to separate the men from the women. Most of the customers just drink tea. Mobin says that crossing will be difficult if he stays with me. "You can cross easier as a lone woman, because the Pakistanis allow women to enter without too much trouble." I agree.

He hires an emaciated man with a wagon to carry my bags across. He gives the man forty thousand Afghanis, the equivalent of one U.S. dollar. When the gates open, the mob lurches forward, pushing to cross the border. I have never seen such chaos—the Pakistani or tribal border police lash at the men with steel-tipped whips to keep them from moving forward. The women push, pull, kick, and yell to reach Pakistan. No one checks passports. A Pakistani policeman hits my porter with his whip.

"*Paisa, paisa* [money]!" the porter yells at me.

I hand him some small Afghan notes. He hands them to the police. Then comes another lash, and then another, until the porter is bleeding near his right eye. All the while the mob is pushing us forward. I feel paralyzed but continue to push as well. "Why is he hitting you?" I ask in Farsi. The porter speaks only Pashto, which I do not. He repeats the one word we both understand: *money*. I let loose some more notes. The porter grabs them and throws them at the policeman.

"Stop hitting him, you motherfucker. Beat me!" I shout at the top of my lungs in broken Urdu, Pakistan's official language. Finally, in what seems like hours but is closer to a few minutes, we reach the other side of the border. The religious hymns on the Afghan side are tuned out by loud Hindi Bollywood songs. Shops display AK-47s and advertise hashish for sale.

A few steps farther on, I see Mobin hailing a taxi to take me to Peshawar.

"How could you leave me alone in that environment?" I say. "I had no idea what to expect. The porter was bleeding, and it was a mob. How did you get here faster than me?"

"I also pushed my way through," he said. "It's always like this, every morning."

"I want to make sure the porter's okay."

"He'll be fine. I see he's gotten you all worked up. That's what they hope to do, so they can take your money. After the border closes, they split the money the police get from you. It's all a show. The police beat them to make you feel sorry for them and pay up. Then they divide up the profits."

"That's how desperate people are—to allow themselves to be beaten for a few bucks? I probably gave just a dollar in that exchange. How awful."

"Fariba Jan, you remember the beginning of war in Afghanistan. What do you think happened all these years you've been gone? Life became bloodier and more miserable. I guess you won't be coming back to Afghanistan again."

He was wrong. Although I'd lived a peaceful life in exile, I not only endured emptiness, but also carried the guilt that comes with survival. The only way I could absolve myself of that guilt, redeem myself, was to return and document the stories of those who were left behind, to make sure their experience of war would not be erased or forgotten.

TWO
Four Decades of Unrest

In Fremont, California, where we have made our new home, my family gathers around the television to watch the rebels entering Kabul. A convoy of hardened fighters in beards and turbans wave their arms at the crowd of proud Afghans, who welcome them with shouts of "God is great!" The uniformed, clean-shaven Soviets left in 1989, and in the spring of 1992, Najibullah, the last ruler of the Communist regime, surrendered to the mujahideen. It's a moment we, the exiled diaspora, have been anticipating for a decade. We feel victorious, avenged. I'm a teenager boiling over with political fervor, anxious to travel back to Afghanistan to see what I left behind. Some of our family friends plan their repatriation; celebratory parties are held.

My father knows better. "What are these mujahids capable of doing when they can't even get along with each other?" he says. "It's no time to go back." He's cynical and believes that inevitably the underreported ethnic, linguistic, and religious disagreements among the seven main factions of the mujahideen will surface.

My mother doesn't argue, even though she misses home. "Too much has been destroyed for us to return," she says, her eyes fixed on the television. "Maybe someday, but not now."

Disappointed, I leave the living room and take refuge in my room. I lie on my bed and stare at the ceiling, thinking of how I could return on my own without my parents. But I'm too young, only nineteen, and too broke.

Afghanistan was the last proxy conflict in the Cold War between the United States and the Soviet Union. The country does not fit into any regional categories—it's not South Asia, Central Asia, or the Middle East. The British carved out present-day Afghanistan in the nineteenth century as a buffer zone between British-controlled India and czarist Russia, and to keep its neighboring empires from attacking each other. The most contentious segment of the current border is the Durand Line, the 1,610 miles between Pakistan and Afghanistan that divides the Pashtun tribes who live in both countries. The Durand Line was drawn in 1893 under an agreement between Afghan and British leaders, but contemporary Afghan leaders refuse to recognize that agreement, claiming the tribal territories of Pakistan as the property of Afghanistan. Many of the Pashtuns in Pakistan have separatist sentiments, wishing to reunite with Afghanistan, which gives Pakistan reason to want to control Afghanistan's affairs. Some political analysts say that buffer zones fail as states and that Afghanistan is destined to fall apart because of its geography. Since Afghanistan's inception as an empire in 1747, the area has been plagued by battles and wars, the latest of which is that between the United States/U.S. allies and the Taliban/al Qaeda.

That armed conflict is supported by another war: the opium trade. The Taliban and al Qaeda are funding their war with arguably half a million dollars annually from Afghanistan's illicit narcotics operation. In the 1980s the United States spent more than $3 billion funding the mujahideen's overthrow of the Soviet-backed Communist regime. Ronald Reagan's government disregarded—some historians say actually *encouraged*—the guerrillas to collect the benefits of the heroin trade to bankroll the larger cause of defeating the Soviets. Peter Dale Scott, a former Canadian diplomat and a sharp critic of U.S. policy in Afghanistan, wrote, "The United States was not waging a war on drugs, in short, but a war helped by drugs."

Three thousand years ago, opium was traded along the Silk Road, which included modern-day Afghanistan. But it was Genghis Khan who introduced poppy farming to Afghanistan, when the Mongol conqueror built an empire there in the thirteenth century. For centuries poppy cultivation remained limited to medicinal use and was locally consumed. Its trade, however, flourished in the 1800s after Afghanistan ruler Abdur Rahman Khan relocated—by force, in some cases—Pashtun tribes to the non-Pashtun borders of Afghanistan with Iran and Central Asia. The king's motives were twofold: to disperse Pashtun tribes who were rebelling against his nationalist policies, and to place an ethnic division between his neighbors to the west and north, who claimed rights to lands inside Afghanistan inhabited by Tajiks, Uzbeks, and Turkmen. Abdur Rahman Khan's most detrimental pact was the Durand Line. The displaced Pashtuns had little access to resources or legitimate jobs. Many of the tribes therefore turned to smuggling goods across the borders. In Iran, Afghans found a growing market for opium, hashish, and other narcotics among the many commodities, including green tea and spices, they smuggled across the border on donkeys or on their own backs to avoid import and export taxes.

In 1958, King Mohammed Zahir outlawed the cultivation and consumption of opium but did not enforce the ban, perhaps because it was a contained problem. In the 1960s and early 1970s, Afghanistan produced one hundred to one hundred fifty tons of opium consistently to meet Iran's demand. Still, cannabis farming was more popular; 30 percent of the global hashish supply was cultivated in Afghanistan in the same time period. Afghanistan was on the hippie trail then, with tourists arriving partly to smoke hashish and opium.

Antinarcotics policies did not challenge drugs in Afghanistan until 1971, when the United States confronted hashish trafficking syndicates in Kabul and provided aid for the Afghan government to fight the trade. In 1973, in one of the last royal decrees before Daud Khan ousted King Zahir, the ban on opium and hashish was reissued, and forced eradication cleared out the cannabis farms. But Afghanistan's economy did not depend solely on drug exports then. It was the Communist coup of 1978 and the subsequent Soviet invasion that changed the magnitude of the drug trade.

As happened in Laos, Burma, Vietnam, Colombia, and other parts of the world, in Afghanistan illicit drugs began to finance war. (The other similarity with the conflicts in the aforementioned countries is that they were proxy wars fought between the United States and the Soviet Union.) In Afghanistan, the CIA chose to support the most radical guerrilla leader, and a known trafficker, Gulbuddin Hekmatyar, in the war against the Soviets. Pakistanis who had become experienced in farming and smuggling opium inside their own country helped Afghans learn the techniques. Seeds were loaned to poor Afghan farmers to start the process. If they made a profit, they could pay back the loan and keep some of the revenue. If there was no harvest, farmers still had to repay the loan, in cash. If they didn't have the cash, they bartered their belongings and property.

The Soviet invasion destroyed traditional farming and replaced it with poppy cultivation. But it wasn't just the war that increased the drug trade. In Helmand province, American agricultural aid projects from the 1950s had advocated modern farming techniques on incompatible soil. These techniques led to eroded soil, which made it possible for only a few crops to grow—the most lucrative of which was poppy. Also in Helmand, mujahideen commander Mullah Nasim forced farmers to grow opium. The mujahideen and their cohorts discovered the lucrative benefits of heroin. As poppy farming took root across the country—in the east in Nangarhar province and in the north in Badakhshan and Balkh provinces—Afghanistan eventually turned into a one-stop shop for drugs: the opium was cultivated there, processed into heroin, and then trafficked. When the mujahideen were in power in the early 1990s, most of the opium was processed into a crude form of heroin in Pakistan, but under the Taliban, heroin labs moved to Afghanistan. Once the Soviets left, the mujahideen and then the Taliban continued to reap the profits.

The opium trade prospers in lawless countries, and thirty years of strife in Afghanistan turned that country into a major producer of opium in the mid-1980s. It's now labeled a narco state in which drug lords and traffickers control both the economy and law enforcement. The United Nations estimates that the Afghan opium trade supplies fifteen million addicts worldwide and kills one hundred thousand people a year. More Russians die from addiction to Afghan opiates every year than the total number of Soviet soldiers killed (fifteen thousand) during the Soviet-Afghan War. In 2010, Russia reported thirty thousand deaths caused by drugs that originated in Afghanistan. About 6.4 percent of Afghanistan's population is involved in the drug trafficking chain, and the overall international trade in Afghan opiates is worth $65 billion annually. With each border crossing heading west, the price of the drug rises. A kilo of heroin, an extract of opium, which sells for $3,000 in Afghanistan, can be worth as much as $50,000 by the time it reaches the United States.

The year I was born, 1973, was the end of forty years of relative peace in Afghanistan, one of the longest in the country's contemporary history. King Zahir, the reigning monarch, had managed a sporadically centralized government that focused on modernizing the country. Since Zahir was only nineteen when he was crowned in 1933, he turned his authority over to two paternal uncles until the 1960s. In 1964 his government drafted a new constitution, the same document that my grandfather Abdul Karim Ahrary (Baba Monshi) approved with a group of Afghanistan's progressive thinkers. The constitution made primary education obligatory for all children; gave women the right to vote, attend school, and work; and called for democratic elections for a national parliament. The first institute of higher education, Kabul University, had been established in 1932, but it excelled in academic achievement during Zahir's rule.

Zahir's critics say there was peace during his tenure but little progress. Afghanistan remained poor and fragmented, and ethnic tensions brewed between Pashtuns, the ethnic group to which Zahir belonged, and other ethnic factions. Nepotism, inefficiency, class differences, and ethnic isolation paved the way for the king's ouster in 1973.

Foreign intervention for strategic interests has continually fueled ethnic tensions inside Afghanistan. No reliable statistics exist on the current population's ethnic makeup, partly because so many Afghans, especially in urban centers, have mixed ethnic backgrounds. (For example, I'm a mix of Tajik and Pashtun.) But in Afghanistan, perception is more important than fact, and it is the *perception* of ethnicity and ethnic loyalty that drives relations.

Pashtuns consider themselves the majority, but they could very well be the biggest minority in the country. Some Afghanistan experts say no majority ethnic group exists in the country, while others argue that Pashtuns comprise the largest population. The consensus is that Tajiks, Uzbeks, Hazaras, and Turkmen are minority groups. Whatever the case may be, throughout Afghanistan's history the ruling class has been Pashtun, with the exception of one leader, who was on the throne for only four months, in 1929. As a result, other ethnic groups have been marginalized.

My eighty-year-old father remembers his early years in school, from 1936 to 1946, when, under Zahir, the language instruction across the country changed suddenly from Farsi to Pashto. "The teachers didn't speak Pashto in the north and Kabul, so education stopped," he told me. "It made no sense. It was stubbornness on the part of the ruling elite to enforce their language, despite the fact that even the king spoke Farsi at home."

Mohammed Daud Khan, Zahir's cousin, thought of the king as ineffectual and weak. Zahir fired Daud from the position of prime minister a decade before Daud rallied support from Afghan leftists and military conservatives to oust the king in a bloodless coup: in July 1973, while Zahir was in Italy receiving eye treatment, Daud seized power. Instead of fighting back, Zahir abdicated and stayed in exile until 2002. When he returned, he was named the honorary father of the nation. When he passed away in 2007, he was one of the few contemporary Afghan leaders who died of old age. The majority were murdered.

In 1965 the People's Democratic Party of Afghanistan, the first Communist Party in the country, formed and held regular meetings. Before the coup, Daud befriended them, but after he was in power, he purged the growing number of Soviet-educated Afghan Communists from his government. He established one party and declared Afghanistan a republic. Though Daud was a nationalist who opposed foreign intervention, Afghanistan received aid from both the Soviet Union and the United States—however, during Daud's five years in power it was more dependent on, and closer to, the Soviet Union. Daud's closeness to Moscow made Washington, Tehran, and Islamabad—all allies at the time—nervous. Daud's vision of a united Afghanistan with a strong central government was not in the interests of Pakistan or the United States.

Beginning in the 1960s, students at Polytechnic University and Kabul University, where my paternal uncle Fazel Ahmed Ahrary taught pharmacy, were becoming highly politicized, influenced by various international ideologies. While thousands of students turned to communism, the most famous leaders of the mujahideen, Gulbuddin Hekmatyar and Ahmad Shah Massoud, were inspired by Egypt's Muslim Brotherhood and began their Islamic activism during their years at the university.

Pakistan welcomed the two Islamic agitators and assigned a Pakistani general known as Colonel Imam (born Sultan Amir Tarar), who had been trained by the American Green Berets, to train them. At the time, Pakistan was hurting from the loss of East Pakistan, which had declared independence in 1971 as Bangladesh and was struggling with its own Baloch and Pashtun ethnic groups, who also wanted independence.

With President Richard Nixon in the throes of a losing war in Vietnam, Daud's friendly relations with the Soviet Union were causing a quiet uproar in Washington, which led to support for the Islamists being groomed in Pakistan. In 1975, Pakistan returned Hekmatyar and Massoud to Afghanistan, where they tried to rally uprisings against Daud in the Panjshir Valley and Laghman. But the locals refused. Afghans enjoyed peace, and the dearth of religious motivation at the time—no infidels or foreign powers were on Afghan soil—delayed the inevitable coup that the Afghan Communists would execute. After the failed attempt, Daud threw the two Islamists out of Afghanistan—he believed in the separation of church and state and had no tolerance for religious militancy. The pair went back to Pakistan.

The Communist People's Democratic Party of Afghanistan (PDPA) broke into two factions, the Khalq and the Parcham. The former consisted of primarily Pashtun laborers and farmers, and the latter included elites and intellectuals from the various Afghan ethnicities. Khalq believed in building a strong working class to achieve a Marxist revolution, and Parcham thought Afghanistan was not ready for a traditional Marxist revolution; Afghans had to be patriotic and anti-imperialist first. However, the ideological differences were merely a front for the personality clash between the two leaders who headed the parties. Nur Mohammed Taraki was the leader of the Khalqis, and Babrak Karmal was the head of the Parchamists.

In 1978 the two parties set aside their differences and united to kill Daud and force a socialist revolution in Afghanistan.

On April 27, 1978, I'm with my family at a wedding in Lashkargah city, in the southern province of Helmand, where my dad works for the fertilizer company. Dressed in a frilly spaghetti-strap dress, I'm digging my fingers into a frosty piece of wedding cake when the music suddenly stops and there are whispers among the women guests.

"The president has been killed. The Communists are in the palace," the whispers echo.

My five-year-old fingers freeze, and I search for my mother. "Don't worry. Everything's okay," she says, hugging me.

But it isn't okay. My father is abruptly transferred by his new Communist bosses to Kandahar province, and we have to move. He works in Kandahar for only a year, then puts in a request to be transferred to our home province, Herat.

In April 1978, Taraki became the Afghan president and exiled Karmal, assigning him the ambassadorship in Czechoslovakia. Hafizullah Amin, known for being the most wicked and ambitious member of the Khalq Party, was named foreign minister and, later, prime minister. Over the next year, Taraki and Amin enforced a series of changes that upset Afghans. The government killed the feudal landowners, or buried them alive with bulldozers, to seize their properties. Any opposition to the government was quelled with imprisonment or execution. Every large family in the diaspora that my family knows is missing a member who was jailed and then vanished—and that's just from April 1978 to December 1979. My uncle Fazel Ahmed Ahrary, who taught at Kabul University, disappeared in 1979.

The Afghan secret police, guided by the Soviet KGB, were responsible for rounding up the opposition in Afghanistan. Assadullah Sarwary, a key member of the Khalq Party, who later became the head of the brutal secret police, tells me in a jailhouse interview in Kabul in 2007 that Afghan Marxists could not commit to their ideology. "Afghans are not capable of breaking away from their nationalist sentiments, so we were never true Communists." Sarwary is the only man in jail for war crimes from the Soviet era in Kabul. He is on death row.

My Uncle Fazel disappeared during the time Sarwary controlled the secret police. My uncle's wife and five children now live in the United States and Japan. Fazel was not a Communist, but he had friends who were Maoists, a faction banned altogether by the Khalq government. Guilt by association may have been the reason he was jailed.

"Did you know Fazel Ahmed Ahrary?" I ask Sarwary.

He pauses for a minute and shakes his head. I tell Sarwary that Fazel was my uncle and that he disappeared during his tenure as chief of the secret police. "Do you know where those who disappeared are buried?"

"I don't know anything. If I killed anyone, slaughter me," he responds angrily, gesturing with his finger as if using a knife to cut his own throat.

I find out through my uncle's students at Kabul University that Sarwary's secret police most likely tortured my uncle to death.

In March 1979 the Khalqis tried to enforce women's liberation in Herat. The government's campaign for literacy obliged women to participate alongside men. The action offended conservatives in Herat enough for them to launch the first serious uprising against the regime, which came as a shock to everyone. Heratis are known as polite, small-statured Afghans with an affinity for literature and trade.

A division of the Afghan Army mutinied and joined the mujahideen rebels, who stole weapons stockpiles and murdered government officials, Soviet diplomats, advisers, and their families. People tortured the accused in public and displayed their bodies on pikes. Taraki called for help from the Soviet military, but Moscow refused. For seventy-two hours Kabul could not control Herat. Taraki responded by ordering the Afghan military to bomb from the air and shoot from the ground. An estimated five thousand people died.

At the time of the attacks, my father, mother, sister, and I were in Lashkargah, but my brother, Hadi, a charming musician disinterested in politics, was visiting our relatives in Herat, on holiday from Kabul University. Hadi, now a fifty-seven-year-old businessman in Fremont, California, recounts his memory of those nightmarish three days:

"At nine AM, villagers poured into the city from all sides. There were rumors that people would protest, but few thought it would be so organized and violent. Farmers held their shovels and pickaxes, ready to strike. First they seized the governor's office. The Khalqis in the offices ran away or hid in the Friday Mosque. They killed who they could find. The government announced martial law, but that's when the army mutinied and the violence worsened, because now the mob had guns. Then the planes began bombing."

Hadi went to Haji Baba's, our maternal grandfather's orchard home, and hid there with the family for a week. Families in the area climbed onto their roofs after the bombings stopped, to talk and exchange food and supplies. Some houses in Herat were connected to each other, with no divisions. The roofs provided open access to communication. After three days, the violence lessened. People picked up their dead, and heavy rains washed away the blood. Then the regime began to round up anybody who had participated in the uprising. My brother returned to Kabul as soon as the siege ended.

In Kabul, Amin plotted a coup against Taraki and his ministers. In August 1979 he persuaded enough officials inside the government to proceed with an overthrow. Taraki was arrested, then smothered to death with a pillow in Kabul's notorious Pul-e-Charkhi prison.

Moscow was outraged by Taraki's death, seeing Amin as too brash and power hungry. The Soviet leadership wanted him deposed. They planned a large operation, executing Amin and his family inside the historic Tajbeg Palace on December 27, 1979, and deploying eighty thousand troops to Afghanistan. They then repatriated Karmal and installed him as president of Afghanistan.

When the initial bloodbath was over, the Soviets released thousands of political prisoners as a goodwill gesture. But it was too late. The Soviet invasion spurred Afghans across all sectors to take up arms and join the guerrillas under the banner of jihad, or holy war. The seven mujahideen factions divided by ethnicity and language who had earlier banded together to battle the Communists now had a tougher enemy, the "infidel Russians," and a stronger devotion to defeating them.

Washington became heavily involved during the Reagan administration, with lobbying from Senator Charlie Wilson. Guns, Stinger missiles, mines, grenades, and a cocktail of other weapons were channeled through Pakistan and its intelligence service, the ISI. Mules were provided to transport the weapons to the rebels. Arabs and other Muslim militants, including Osama bin Laden, traveled to the mountains of the Afghan-Pakistani border to train and fight against the Soviets. The ISI provided training, while China, Egypt, Saudi Arabia, the United Arab Emirates, and the United States donated money for what became a pan-Islamic cause. The rebels were smuggling opium and heroin to make money, and the CIA, well aware of this fact, ignored it. By some accounts, the CIA helped the mujahideen smuggle out narcotics and fund heroin laboratories. The U.S. attorney general gave the CIA legal exemption from reporting drug smuggling by its agents, officers, or assets as the mujahideen found ways to hook Soviet troops on fine-grade heroin. Russian soldiers had to be sent back to the Soviet Union due to addiction. According to authors Amir Zada Asad and Robert Harris, President Reagan approved Operation Mosquito, a French-hatched plan to distribute heroin and fake Russian newspaper articles emphasizing Soviet losses in the war to Soviet troops in the battlefield. The motives were to lower morale and encourage addiction to heroin, similar to what the Viet Cong did to Americans during the Vietnam War. Asad and Harris write that the CIA executed the plan with the aid of a mujahideen leader and French journalists who had access to the troops inside Afghanistan.

The current burgeoning opium economy in Afghanistan is the product of these wars. In the 1980s, provinces under mujahideen control—Helmand, Kandahar, Nangarhar—grew more and more poppy. Opium production, which was 75 tons in 1932, the first year estimates are available, had jumped to 8,200 tons by 2007. Before the wars in the 1970s, about 85 percent of the country's population lived in rural areas, and agriculture accounted for 68 percent of employment. But the continued conflict destroyed two-thirds of all villages and damaged the rural economy. The consequences were a 77 percent fall in livestock production, the destruction of a quarter of the irrigation system, and the abandonment of one-third of all farms. A third of the population fled Afghanistan, and 11 percent became internally displaced. By 1988 there had been a 45 percent decrease in food production since the 1979 Soviet invasion.

In September 1982, after the school bombing, my family flees across the desert to Iran, a donkey bearing the weight of our belongings—clothes, shoes, toiletries, and a carpet. We reach Iran safely, but after a month we must leave. Afghans cannot obtain visas to the United States or Europe from Iran. The 1979 Iranian Revolution has hindered Iran's relationship with the United States and Europe. Afghans who stay in Iran end up becoming laborers and are treated as second-class citizens: they are not allowed to own homes or businesses, get a higher education, or become citizens. Afghan refugees who want to go to a developed nation head for Pakistan, the transition country.

In Pakistan, my father exchanges his slacks and collared shirt for the traditional Pakistani cotton tunic and loose pants; my mother and Faiza wear the black Iranian chador; and I wear a long dress with white pants and a large scarf. My mom sews some of her collection of gold around the edge of my scarf. The rest of our fortune—$3,500 in cash, a reference letter from an American Peace Corps serviceman who worked with my father, and my mother's remaining gold—are in a leather wallet wrapped around my mother's neck and tucked under her dress. We take Iranian public buses to Zahedan, at the border, then ride on various private Pakistani buses that smuggle Afghans across the southern tip of the Iranian-Pakistani border. At one point the Pakistani bus we are on stops and uniformed tribal Pakistani soldiers board it with a heavyset woman. The woman searches the females, including me, and finds the gold around my light green scarf. She takes off my scarf. I feel naked and want to cry, but I hold back and gain strength by looking at my father. He smiles at me. The woman also takes my mom's wallet. My father steps outside the bus with the police and settles on a bribe: five dollars to get back all our belongings.

A few hours later we reach safety in Quetta, Pakistan, and a few days later, we are in Pakistan's verdant capital, Islamabad. We spend eighteen months in Islamabad awaiting a visa to the United States or Germany, where my brother fled after his college graduation. We are now officially refugees, part of the mass exodus of Afghan technocrats and intellectuals. But we, the well-to-do diaspora, do not live in camps as the poor do. We rent big, shady houses and enroll in the mujahideen-run schools. Afghans organize daily demonstrations against the Soviets on the streets of Pakistani cities. My mother and I go out shopping one day and see hundreds of demonstrators shouting, *"Allahu Akbar* [God is great]!" and *"Marg bar Rus* [Death to the Russians]!" It's in Pakistan where the mujahideen become our heroes. They are going to save us and Afghanistan. I tug on my mom's skirt to push her to join the demonstration and revel in the power of crowds—the solidarity of feeling as one, chanting and marching all together. We forget that the mujahideen bomb our schools and kill our children as collateral damage just like the Soviets. Distance allows us to form an idealized version of the truth. The memories powered by our nostalgia will become reality.

Afghans in Pakistan seek political asylum through a U.S.-funded refugee office established in Islamabad in 1980 to serve the mass of Afghan refugees who want to flee to the United States. If Afghans want to apply for asylum in other developed countries, they go to those countries' respective embassies. Most countries they apply to require some form of evidence to grant asylum, but obtaining a visa to the United States, where American churches and nonprofit groups sponsor refugees, is easy for Afghans. Some Iranians and Pakistanis even forge Afghan identities to seek entry to the United States. We apply to both the United States and Germany, but my father's reference letter from the Peace Corps serviceman ensures us a visa to the United States faster than one to Germany. From the plane, I wave good-bye in the direction of Afghanistan, unaware of the changes that lie ahead.

The relatives we leave behind endure seven more years of the Soviet invasion and then a civil war among the mujahideen. One of my mother's brothers, Uncle Rostam, was conscripted as a soldier in the Afghan military. He managed to work at a base near home, until he, too, fled with his wife and children in 1988.

From his new home in Germany now, Uncle Rostam, fifty-one, tells me about life in Herat after my family escaped:

"The city deteriorated every year as the war ensued. There was no security. We had no fun, no real work or education. Our wives were teachers, and we all had government jobs and survived on the meager government salary, but the teachers could not teach fairly because a Khalqi student would force them to give a good grade or risk death. We could not leave our homes past the eight PM curfew. The younger women who had never worn burqas began to wear them out of fear. We would come home to watch the one channel run by the government on TV when there was electricity."

The thunder of cluster bombs, rockets, and grenades got louder and closer. Some of the soldiers in my uncle's unit were working for both the government and the rebels. By day they would guard the city as soldiers, but at night they'd steal ammunition and weapons for the mujahideen. The Soviets were losing the war, and the Afghan military was deserting by the thousands. "We couldn't kill our own people," my uncle explained.

Uncle Rostam, an unassuming, lanky man with a wide smile, was deployed to battle a few times. "There were hundreds of us armed with tanks, helicopters, and guns marching toward the rebels, but they were usually the winners, because they got to hide and ambush in small packs of a dozen. Toward the end of the war the Soviets would bribe the mujahids to surrender and join the army. They were called *taslimis* [surrenderers], and this began the disease of warlordism in the country. These illiterate *taslimis* were criminals. They had been in the mountains fighting, and the government let them keep their arms and gave them more power. They trafficked drugs, stole, extorted money, and raped women."

One of them came to a tailor friend of Uncle Rostam's and ordered him to sew seven outfits for his men in two days. He didn't give him money, even for the fabric.

"It's impossible for us to finish this in so little time," the tailor told him.

"Well, then I'll have to finish a round of these on your shop and your family," the *taslimi* threatened, showing the tailor the necklace of bullets wrapped around his shoulder. "Would you like that?"

The tailor called all his employees and made sure the outfits were done in time.

Uncle Rostam says drug trafficking became more common during the war, but there was little heroin then. It was mostly opium being transported to Iran. Since the mujahideen controlled most of the borders, they also controlled the trafficking, taking cuts from any transactions they could track. Addicts within Afghanistan were few and far between, and poppy planting was unknown in Herat. The drugs came from the south, the east, and from Pakistan, he says.

Mr. Jawan, our neighbor in Herat, was a man with a big heart and a head covered in coarse, shiny hair. He liked to shop at the stores that did not have many customers, to help the struggling shopkeepers. The people who worked for him were the poorest and neediest. His driver, Kako, was night blind, but Mr. Jawan hired him because no one else would. Mr. Jawan's second wife, Sitara, complained to him about the driver's limitations. "Why can't you hire a driver who can drive day and night?"

"Try to go to the places you want during the day, because he has kids and needs a job, and nobody else will hire him," Mr. Jawan replied.

Mr. Jawan was not related to us, but since they lived next door, his family was like family to us. My memories of him in Herat revolve around food. When his family invited us to his ten-bedroom house for a meal, the housekeeper laid out a *sofra*, a tablecloth, on the floor and Mr. Jawan's four children gathered around, mouths watering, hands washed. The children sat cross-legged, the women bent their knees and tucked their feet under, and Mr. Jawan leaned on a pillow, half of his body plopped on the floor. He was not fond of exercise or diet food. Servants filled the *sofra* with large china platters wafting the aromas of freshly cooked delicacies: *qabuli palau* (rice mixed with carrots, raisins, and mutton), *borani banjan* (fried eggplant with yogurt and tomatoes), and *bolani* (fried stuffed potato and leek pancakes).

"Don't take too long digging in, because I'm going to eat all of this," he used to warn my father.

Mr. Jawan liked the servants to sit next to him, eat, and finish the food on their plates. He also insisted that women join in with the men in conversation. The telephone had to be near him at all times. It allowed him to communicate with relatives and colleagues without getting up, which he preferred. He liked to tell stories, and when he retired from opium smuggling and moved to Italy in 1992, many of those stories were about his escapades in the drug trade.

In the summer of 2005, I visit Mr. Jawan in the one-bedroom apartment he shares with Sitara in Rome. His hair has turned white, and he complains of fatigue and a pain in his left arm. He is in his eighties. He sits up on a twin brass bed as he holds his cup of boiling black tea in his right hand and talks.

"It was a business like any other. I made money, but I made sure anyone who needed my money got it as well. Most people at that time used opium to treat the pain they had from illnesses, because they didn't have access to other medicines. So I helped people in that way.

"I almost got caught during the Soviet invasion, but God was with me because I escaped . . . with some help from contacts in law enforcement," he chuckles, his light brown eyes sparkling.

Friends, relatives, and Mr. Jawan himself recall his adventures as endearing comic mishaps, not tragic tales of death and destruction. But when the stories are unraveled, beyond the humor lie corruption, violence, and the various misfortunes of drug smuggling. The main difference is the level of violence then and now. Mr. Jawan had an automatic rifle, but he never shot people when he transported drugs. The smugglers I encounter today have shot their machine guns and rockets at authorities and rival smugglers numerous times.

Mr. Jawan was a *kerakash*, a middleman, in the drug trade. Rich merchants paid him a few hundred dollars to transport sealed boxes of drugs to Iran, but he rarely carried them across the border himself. He had a network of couriers he paid to traffic. He would transfer the drugs in a Jeep from Herat city to his village, Tirpul, on the border. In the village, the men had dug several deep ditches to store the contraband, which they covered with wooden boards. Several armed guards patrolled on rooftops to protect the hidden drugs.

The couriers would take small amounts of drugs to Iran. As in the United States, Iran punished smugglers according to the number of kilos seized. Iranian merchants paid Mr. Jawan to smuggle gold coins and gold bricks to China. If they transported the gold legally through Afghanistan, they had to pay high tariffs.

Even before the 1978 coup, battles and skirmishes killed smugglers in the desert; one of Mr. Jawan's brothers was killed in a tribal dispute over drugs. Often the instigating clan had to give a daughter in marriage to settle the argument. Two of Mr. Jawan's attractive sisters were bartered as opium brides.

My late maternal grandfather, Sayed Akbar Hossaini, was the district governor of Ghoryan in 1957 when he received reports that

Mr. Jawan was about to transport large quantities of opium to the border. "Even a migrating bird traveled with smuggled goods in Ghoryan," my grandfather used to say. But like today, the district governor did not have the manpower or the weapons to fight the smugglers. He took five of his police officers to block the road that Mr. Jawan was due to use on his way to Tirpul. The officers with my grandfather, whose guns had no ammunition, nervously waited for Mr. Jawan, terrified he would shoot them.

But when Mr. Jawan saw my grandfather and the police, he stopped driving, raised his arms, and exited his Jeep. He greeted the authorities with respect.

"Governor, sir, here is my gun, my Jeep, and my goods hidden in the back of the Jeep," he told my grandfather. "Please take them. I can take your old car to go to my village, if you allow me, and we can forget this ever happened."

My grandfather's hands shook as he took Mr. Jawan's gun. He could not believe that Mr. Jawan was being so accommodating.

"*Khair bini* [bless you]," he said to the smuggler. Haji Baba agreed to let Mr. Jawan take his car and carry on to Tirpul. Then he proudly brought Mr. Jawan's surrendered items to his boss, the provincial governor of Herat, who told my grandfather that Mr. Jawan must come see him.

"I want to convince him to stop drug smuggling," he told Haji Baba.

My grandfather relayed the message to Mr. Jawan, who promptly obeyed. He conveyed his apologies and kissed the Herat governor's hands. He said in front of the governor's staff that he would cease smuggling. Later the truth came out—some of the drugs he'd been carrying that day belonged to the provincial governor.

"It was how things were done," Mr. Jawan tells me. "The governor could not make that kind of money as a government official, but he needed to show that he had a luxurious life as a person of power. He did what was necessary."

Mr. Jawan became our neighbor in the 1950s, shortly after this incident, when he married a respected city girl, Sitara, in Herat. His first wife, Narinji, was his first cousin, and she could not bear children. He married a second time to have children, especially a son. Sitara bore three sons and a daughter. Traditionally Afghans prefer to marry first cousins, and if such a marriage proves problematic, a man can take on another wife if he has the means. Some interpretations of Islam allow men to marry up to four wives, if they can treat them equally.

After the Soviet invasion, Mr. Jawan's smuggling business became riskier. The fighting on the borders and in the deserts kept him away from his village. In his Herat city home, he built an underground storage facility for drugs and arms. One day, outside his house, he and another smuggler fought, and the smuggler reported Mr. Jawan to the police.

"The godless liar accused me of shortchanging him," Mr. Jawan says, smirking and taking a sip of his cooled tea. "I slapped him. He took his revenge, but he didn't succeed."

When the police showed up at his home, Mr. Jawan climbed the wall in his yard and crawled through a hole to his next-door neighbors' house, the Faruqis. He fell on his round belly and injured it. The neighbors helped him hide behind a stack of folded mats and blankets in one of their rooms. The police raided his house and found the drugs. His wife Sitara and daughter, Nadia, sat huddled in their chadors inside the house.

"Where is your husband?" one of the officers asked Sitara.

"He's out of town," she answered with a confident, straight face.

Then one of Mr. Jawan's friends, who worked in the police station, appeared and tried to defuse the situation.

"He's gone, and these women are innocent. We should get out of here," he told the lead officer.

When the police left, Mr. Jawan's wife and daughter lifted their chadors to reveal the guns and ammunition Mr. Jawan had been storing to give to the mujahideen. His clan had become mujahideen members, and Mr. Jawan had found a side business smuggling arms. If the police had found the weapons on the women, it's likely they would've killed the entire family. The Communist government allowed drug smugglers to go free, but not mujahideen supporters.

The neighbors helped dress Mr. Jawan in a turban and a long coat, which he had to struggle to fit into, and a pair of eyeglasses. They put him in a taxi, and he left town for more than a month. He continued to smuggle after this incident, but on a much smaller scale. "It wasn't worth the money anymore," he tells me. "I had children who needed me. But the business did not have a good end, so I left it and my homeland. Now I just live with my memories."

By the end of the war in 1989, the Afghan Army had shrunk from ninety thousand men to thirty thousand. The Soviets carpet-bombed villages, killing civilians, and mined the countryside with toy mines, which have left Afghanistan with thousands of maimed men, women, and children. A change of guard in Kabul put Mohammed Najibullah, a former secret police chief, in charge of the country in 1987. He established a nationalist party and invited debate and participation in the government. Some Kabulis remember his time as the most peaceful and prosperous of the Soviet invasion. In Moscow, Mikhail Gorbachev, the new charismatic leader interested in openness and change, wanted the Soviets to leave Afghanistan. The Stinger missiles Washington was sending had demoralized the Red Army and tipped the war greatly against the Soviets. Withdrawal was long overdue.

In 1989, with 15,000 Soviet soldiers dead and 1.5 million Afghans killed, the Red Army pulled out the last of its troops. Najibullah continued to rule the country, opening it up economically and so-cially. The war still raged in the countryside, though, with Afghan forces fighting the rebels. The mujahideen wanted power, and Na-jibullah's new nationalist rhetoric still sounded like secular hypoc-risy to them. Najibullah agreed to step aside, and in 1992 the rebels marched to Kabul and declared victory.

After the rebels take over Kabul, my family in Fremont monitors the Afghan news regularly. The relatives who wanted to return to Afghanistan have gone back to their American jobs, to paying their mortgages. I see my father listening to the news on the Afghan dias-pora radio program. He shakes his head at the report of the ensuing civil war he predicated.

"You were right, Agha. It's no time to go back," I tell him, sitting next to him to hear the news.

"I wish I had been wrong," he replies.

The Soviet enemy that had united Afghanistan's various ethnic and political factions was now gone, and these groups turned against one another for control of Kabul. The United States stopped aiding rebel groups, but those groups now had a stockpile of weapons to kill one another with, and a downtrodden population. The civil war among the mujahideen was the bloodiest time in the capital, which had been left intact during Communist rule. In the four years Hekmatyar, Massoud, and other commanders pummeled Kabul, casualties rose to sixty thousand. In other cities, the commanders looted homes and businesses and terrorized the civilian population. In Herat, however, Commander Ismail Khan began rebuilding the city and brought some level of security, albeit under an authoritarian theocracy similar to that in Iran. In the north, Abdul Rashid Dostum also brought order. But most of the country fell into general chaos.

The Islamist mujahideen now in power countered the country's traditional tribal structures; the heroes now became the enemy. Afghans waited for yet another savior. It came in the form of the Taliban, who, like the Islamist mujahideen, emerged from a modernist revolutionary movement that focused on a radical pan-Islamist vision. Although the next heroes in the epoch of Afghanistan, the Taliban also terrorized. They had no real education, no expertise, and no skills to run a country—but they did not need those. They had God, guns, and opium.

THREE

A Struggle for Coherency

The few passengers on the British Airways plane keep getting up to look out the large window near the bathroom at the back of the plane. I watch some of the passengers staring with suspicion at the man or woman sitting next to them. A collective fear weighs down the aircraft. Even the flight attendants seem on edge, making more rounds than usual to check on passengers. The summer sky is an ocean of blue, no clouds to dream upon. I close my eyes, trying to catch up on a week of lost sleep. Seven days ago, the demons of Afghanistan struck New York City and Washington, D.C.

After my trip to Afghanistan in 2000, I return to the United States to attend graduate school at New York University, to further my studies of the Middle East and journalism. Classes have just begun when, on the morning of September 11, 2001, a loud knock wakes me up. I look at the clock. It's 9:05 AM.

I lift my head up from under my pillow. "Yes?"

Osama, my roommate Rona's cousin, opens my bedroom door a crack. Osama is visiting us temporarily in our Brooklyn brownstone near Atlantic Avenue. "You need to come to the roof," he says urgently.

The tone in his voice tells me something is very wrong. I jump up and sprint to the stairs in my pajamas. There is a billow of black smoke across the East River, blocking our enviable view of the city.

"Was there a fire?" I ask Osama.

"No. Two airplanes crashed into the World Trade Center."

"Oh my God!" I gasp for breath. I hold my hand over my forehead to block the sun and look as far as I can see across the river. The sky is all blackness and smoke. Our television is not working, so the three of us go to a bar and join a crowd of dozens watching the TV there. The cameras zoom in on the people trapped and jumping to their deaths from the top floors of the two towers. On the ground, a storm of debris and dust covers a mass of people running in all directions. Fleeing New Yorkers cover the Brooklyn Bridge, some crying, others looking frightened and confused. The news report shows President Bush cursing enemies of the United States.

Two days before, two Arabs had assassinated the mujahideen leader Ahmad Shah Massoud, the only challenge to the Taliban's final victory in Afghanistan. It is clear to me that the Taliban will protect al Qaeda and its leader, Osama bin Laden, who allegedly masterminded the attack on the United States. In exchange for the Taliban's cooperation, Bin Laden sponsored the killing of Massoud. I predict the next chapter in Afghanistan's history: it will be bombed again, and more names will be added to the list of three thousand

American lives lost in the September 11 attacks as U.S. troops gear up to head east.

The two countries that form the basis of my dual Afghan American identity, the identity I have been struggling to merge, will finally go to war. I am numb.

Osama, Rona, and I walk along the Promenade by the Brooklyn Bridge in a daze. We hear people cursing Arabs and Muslims.

"It's the clash of civilizations!" one man shouts. "It's time we show these bastards who's the winner."

What clash? Believers of scholar Samuel Huntington's theory that conflicts in culture and religion will dictate future wars are now vindicated. Huntington wrote that the Islamic and Western civilizations will collide due to the differences in Islam and Christianity and in the identities that arise from those religions. The Bush administration invokes these ideas to push its war on terror. But the theory dismisses the fact that culture is fluid and multifaceted. It ignores the interdependence and harmony of cultures and religions in various parts of the world, such as among Muslims in the United States. It dismisses identities such as mine—mixed, mired, and myriad. I am constantly struggling to combine Afghan and American, but that struggle has created a stronger individual in me, and it has allowed me to see the world from a more nuanced perspective. It's scholar Edward Said's response to Huntington that considers identities like mine. Said posits in his "clash of ignorance" theory that current conflicts are based on misinterpretations of religion, and he recognizes the complexities of identities and cultures.

Atlantic Avenue is in the most well-known Arab neighborhood in New York. I fear a backlash; our friend Osama has already asked us to call him Aziz instead. I can blend in because I have blond hair and fair skin; no one can tell I'm Afghan.

Afghanistan becomes hot news—a month before I'd had to explain to a woman that Afghan is also a nationality, not just a breed of dog. Now I hear on TV and from people on the street explanations of who we Afghans are and what we believe—a simplified version of our country. After I write an article about a possible backlash against Muslims, there's a barrage of journalists at my house to interview me about Afghanistan. I'm a white face Americans can trust. They want me to be the speaker for the disenfranchised Afghans, but I want to tell my own story as a journalist.

In the journalism department at NYU, students have no context or history of Afghanistan. In the Middle Eastern studies department, professors and students dissect and analyze, but they have no solutions. I feel useless sitting in a classroom. A friend who works with Agence France Presse in Islamabad calls and offers me a temporary job covering the expected Afghan—U.S. war from Pakistan. I take leave from school to fly to Islamabad once again. The only person who knows I'm leaving is my brother, Hadi. My parents cannot know, because they will worry. They gave up everything in their country to make sure their children were safe, and now I am headed straight into the war my mother and father risked their lives to take me out of nearly twenty years ago.

On June 14, 1983, my feet touch American soil. After two days of traveling on three airplanes, my family and I finally land in Dallas, Texas, home of the U.S. nonprofit that sponsored our journey. The couple who works for the nonprofit drives us to a garage behind a house in a suburban area in Fort Worth, which becomes our home for the next three months. One of our few possessions is a black-and-white TV. When I turn it on, I watch—for the first time—a man and woman French-kissing. My mother is mortified and turns off the television.

"How can they show such dirty things so openly!" she shouts.

My family finds Texas lonely and hot. After three months there, the four of us take a Greyhound bus to the San Francisco Bay Area, where my dad's cousin Uncle Turfa resides. Uncle Turfa helps us rent a two-bedroom apartment in a Mexican neighborhood in Union City. My father goes out and buys a Mazda station wagon with money my brother sends us from Germany. My parents enroll in English-language classes, Faiza takes classes at the local community college and works in retail full time, and I'm placed in the local elementary school. I'm ten years old and incredibly curious about the new world we've entered. Unfortunately, I know how to say only "thank you" in English. The garbled *rs* and *vs* of English words hurt my tongue when I try to pronounce them. My mother tongue is genderless. Everything is an "it," and when we refer to a girl or boy, we actually say the Farsi word for *girl* or *boy*. But English has the "he" and "she" complications I must learn. When people speak to me, it sounds like baby gibberish. I nod my head as if I'm mute.

I like my teachers but not the students. They're rude and disrespectful. A few weeks into the fourth grade, I make an observation. "How come they don't wear uniforms here?" I ask my mom.

"I don't know. They should, though," she says.

"Well, I will from now on. I can choose one of my dresses that you made me and wear it every day. That will be my uniform," I decide. I feel more organized and focused with a uniform. It just seems like the right thing to do, since that's what we did in Herat. Besides, we don't have the money to buy the stylish clothes my classmates wear.

I choose a simple blue-and-red-checked dress with white socks and black shoes. My hair is always in twin braids. The second week I wear the outfit, Sarah, a loudmouthed classmate, tugs on my sleeve.

"You must be really poor, because you wear the same outfit every day. Is your family homeless?"

My English is good enough now for me to understand this, and her words prick me. Tears well up in my eyes, and I go home and throw the dress in the garbage. From that day on I wear a different outfit every day, selecting from the sundry dresses my mother has sewn for me. I am out of style, but at least no one will think less of me.

As the years go by I often think back to those first weeks at my unfamiliar American school and how my ill-fated attempt to impose order there would eventually have meant social suicide. Throughout my adolescence, I try to fit in as a misfit. I want to make up my own rules for conformity. I'm disinterested in and critical of the kids who are popular and apathetic. In my middle school, it seems half of the boys are on drugs and many of the girls become pregnant before going to high school. They are in gangs called Norteños and Sureños, and they wear red or blue to mark which gang they belong to. One day in the sixth grade, I'm doing my homework in the school library when I see an eighth-grade boy pull up his sleeve to scratch an itch. I glimpse red marks scarring the inner part of his arm.

I ask my friend Carmela, who's sitting across from me, if the boy's sick.

"He's shooting up heroin," she explains. "I guess that means he's sick, 'cuz he's an addict."

"What's heroin? Doesn't *heroine* mean the woman character in a book or movie?" I am sure I read that in *Webster's* dictionary.

"No, silly," Carmela says. "It's a drug that makes you high and then you die if you take it too much. I heard that worms come out of your brain and spirits take over your heart if you inject heroin." Her eyes are wide and she gestures emphatically.

"That's so scary. What's it made of?"

She shrugs her shoulders. "Bad stuff, I guess."

I look up *heroin* in the encyclopedia and am fascinated by the drug. Its base is opium—I know the Farsi word for opium is *tariak*. My parents used to talk about our neighbor Mr. Jawan in Herat and his forays in opium smuggling.

"Mr. Jawan is trying to get his family out of Afghanistan," my mom informs my dad. "He lives such a comfortable life that I'm not sure he would be happy outside his country."

"Well, he works in the international business of illegal narcotics. I'm sure he could transfer his business to wherever he goes with the contacts he has," my father jokes.

Another person my parents reminisce about around the dinner table is the gypsy musician Ozra, a legendary beauty and opium addict who left her husband to marry another man of status and wealth in Herat.

"I was a young boy and had trouble with pain in my eyes," my father recalls. "When Ozra came to our property to sing, she always brought her opium pipe. She would light up the opium, take a whiff, and then blow the smoke in my eyes. The pain went away."

"I remember her eyes were magical, but always yellowed from the drugs," my mom says. "Men fell in love with her. Good thing you were a young boy then," she jokes to my dad. "She was famous in Herat for her music, beauty, and opium. She would go into an empty room, draw all the curtains to make it dark. She preferred to smoke her opium alone."

"Well, it must have been that beauty that convinced Said [the wealthy man] to marry a drug addict from a lower class," my dad says, then chuckles. "Or Said was also smoking opium."

The next day in school I tell Carmela that heroin is refined opium and that opium comes from my country. I'm somehow proud. Heroin is something about Afghanistan that she can relate to, even if it feeds addicts like the boy I saw in the library.

"That's cool," she says. "Are there a lot of people with worms in their brains and spirits in their hearts in your country?"

"I don't know." We both go back to doing our homework.

I stay away from the gangs, the drugs, and trouble; my role models are the nerds, who, like me, do not fit in. In high school, I choose a group of culturally eclectic girlfriends—a Nicaraguan, an African American, and a Caucasian—and we indulge in being different from our classmates and families. We talk about boys, sex, politics, race, and our families and conflicts. But I wish I had an Afghan friend with whom I could share my duality, someone who could feel the warm sensation when the word *Afghanistan* was mentioned, someone who listened to the famous deceased Afghan pop singer Ahmed Zahir and who ate *shiriakh*, the creamy Afghan ice cream. But I also want that friend to be someone who can discuss existentialism or feminism and enjoy partying like I do.

Sixty thousand Afghan refugees have made their homes in the San Francisco Bay Area. Most of the refugees receive public benefits. They've moved from other states to California partly because of the government resources, but also for the area's rolling green hills, small lake, and large streets, which are reminiscent of Kabul's landscape. We live among the largest Afghan community in the United States, followed by Washington, D.C., and Virginia, then New York City. Despite the diverse members of the community, I feel poles apart when I socialize with Afghans in high school. My ideas are too liberal—I believe in gay rights, women's liberation, and the freedom to choose one's religion.

My beliefs are markedly different from those of mainstream Afghans. Even the Afghans in the San Francisco Bay Area believe that gays are sick and must be treated for their illness; women should learn how to cook and clean in order to find good husbands, their most important goal in life; and Islam should be the only religion everyone follows. The Afghan girls I know have to go home after school and tend to guests. The Afghan boys, however, can loiter in the school courtyard and whistle at pretty girls. They can even bring their (non-Afghan) girlfriends home, while the Afghan girls are not even allowed to have male friends.

Lina and I are opening our lockers in the school hall one day when two openly gay boys pass by. Lina is an Afghan girl who was three when her family immigrated to the United States. She sees the gay boys and sneers. "They gross me out, damn *coonies*!" she says, using one of the most offensive Farsi expletives, the equivalent of *faggot*; the word is meant to emasculate a man and shame his honor.

I'm angry and make sure she knows it. "You're so prejudiced and ignorant. They have the right to be and love who they want. They don't hurt you, so why is it your business? Lina, get your head out of your ass and look up the word *equality*." I slam my locker shut and run off to class. Lina refuses to acknowledge me for the rest of our high school years.

My family's social life revolves around dinner parties, funerals, and weddings. Guests are a daily disruption in my life, and my mother wants me to spend time with the countless relatives and friends who drop by from the next block or fly in for seasonal visits from Europe.

"Badeh, it's improper," she says, "when you walk in and say a cold hello and go to your room. You need to be respectful, Fariba."

"Why? All your guests do is sit around, eat, and gossip. They haven't earned my respect. I hate the fake kissing and pleasantries. We're so fake, I hate it!" I shout and throw myself on my bed, burying my head under a pillow.

"Whatever we are, we are Afghan, and even if you don't believe in the customs, you need to do it for me. I care what the guests think, even if you don't," she says in her usual calm, pleading tone.

"And I wish you wouldn't wear such short skirts," she adds. "It's sinful for a Muslim girl—"

"Go away, please," I cut her off in an American teenage voice. The double standard regarding girls and boys also frustrates me, and I argue with my mother when she demands that I follow the rules and be a good Afghan girl.

My father, on the other hand, leaves me alone and is happy as long as I do well in school. My parents know I'm not going to come home pregnant or on drugs.

Unlike other Afghan girls my age, I don't go home until I'm done with all my afterschool activities. I fight for the freedom to spend the night at friends' homes, to go out as late as I want on the weekends, and to dress as I please. Sometimes I want to disown my Afghan identity when I see the inequalities between men and women, but I cannot. Being Afghan is deeply rooted in my soul, but it's something I'm constantly trying to define. I seem to find the most in common with men my father's age, who talk about politics and ideas. They also have a connection to our homeland that I share. The men, dressed in suits, visit our two-bedroom apartment and waste little time on small talk. They drink their tea and lose themselves in debate.

"Islam is not the antidote to communism," says Mr. Saboor, an engineer with expressive eyebrows. "Look at what the Islamic Revolution did to Iran—it's where we went on vacation, and now it's the last place I want to visit. The mujahideen are not going to offer us a better alternative."

My father nods his head in agreement. He is a believer in Islam but advocates for a secular government, just as his father, Baba Monshi, did.

Mr. Aria, however, a descendant of a respected Sufi family, scratches his disheveled mustache and disagrees. "Islam is our heritage and the only ideology that is legitimate among the people. Nationalism and communism have failed, and this American democracy will not work in Afghanistan. The only viable and righteous option is Sharia and Islam."

These men indulge in their nostalgia and dream up scenarios for a peaceful Afghanistan. A lament I hear often from them is "Perhaps if we had stayed and tried to find a solution, things would not have gotten so bad." I share their guilt for leaving, and I chastise my parents for not caring as much as they should have. The Afghan community in California stays connected to Afghanistan through extended family who still live there. But for my family, making a call to Afghanistan is too expensive (and the postal system in Afghanistan is too unreliable). The only time I recall my mother phoning Herat is when she asked for my now sister-in-law's hand in marriage for my brother. "We would be honored to have your daughter Lila as our bride," she said to the girl's father, whom I call Uncle Zarif Khan. That day, the telephone connection was crackly and occasionally broke up.

So my family stays connected by reading and listening to news about Afghanistan. The only way I can express my identity angst and biculturalism is in writing. When I am in the seventh grade, after my English teacher, Mrs. Lockhart, tells me I can write well, I decide I want to be a journalist. I love to travel, to write, and to get to know people. I pursue my journalism career beginning in high school, by writing a column about cultures in the school newspaper and joining a youth newspaper in San Francisco. One of the stories I do for the paper focuses on gangs, and when I go out to report, I see heroin addicts lying in corners of the Tenderloin district in San Francisco, a city with one of the highest rates of drug addiction in the country. A couple lies in each other's arms, their skin marked with needle punctures. They are pale, lifeless, and skeletal. I stare at them and the girl holds out a can. I have no change and walk away, but their image is imprinted in my head. Then I recall the boy I saw in my middle school library. These two have the same hopeless look on their faces. I wonder if the heroin they are taking comes from Afghanistan.

At ten PM, on October 7, 2001, in Islamabad, I'm awakened by a knock on my hotel room door. It is what I've been expecting for days.

"The U.S. started bombing," Rasheed, a colleague from Agence France Presse, tells me. "You need to come down and work." I do not tell Rasheed how sad I am to hear the news; I don't share my feelings of ambivalence about the war. I want the Taliban defeated, but without any civilian casualties, which I know is naïve. I simply say okay, slip on my shoes, and walk out the door.

For the next two months I spend my days on a satellite phone with Afghan mujahideen commanders who are on the front line fighting the Taliban and al Qaeda in Afghanistan. The United States and its allies bomb from the air, while the mujahideen, re-united temporarily under the name United Front, fight on the ground. Afghan experts warn that empowering the mujahideen again will revive hostilities and may result in corruption and civil war. But the United States needs them on the ground—it's not pre-pared to risk too many American lives, and besides, the mujahi-deen know the terrain. The commanders go back to their former territories, to the caves and hideouts they used when they fought the Soviets.

So the next anticipated heroes for the citizens of Afghanistan are the Americans—most Afghans think they will be saved by them. I call my relatives in Herat and talk to Uncle Ahmed's son,

Bahram, for a minute. "We're so happy the Americans are coming. We're standing on our roofs to watch the bombs. It's like fireworks here," he says before the line goes dead.

I'm living on coffee and cigarettes in an office with half a dozen male journalists from Europe, Australia, and Pakistan. We work seventeen-hour days covering the war. There's no time to ponder the situation or allow my personal feelings about Afghanistan to affect my reporting. I know that the commanders I'm interviewing are professional killers without much regard for human rights. In late November 2001 my most informative source, Mohammad Ashraf Nadeem, a spokesman for the commander Atta Mohammad Noor in Balkh province, says the Taliban are surrendering in large numbers. "But we have some issues with the prisoners. They've staged a riot and we're trying to regain control."

"Were they being treated with dignity?" I ask cynically.

"Commander Atta Mohammad's men have been fair to them, but others in the United Front are not so kind."

The extent of Nadeem's understatement is revealed a year later by Physicians for Human Rights: fighters under Abdul Rashid Dostum, another powerful northern commander and rival to Atta Mohammad, trapped hundreds of Taliban prisoners in metal truck containers and let them suffocate, then buried their bodies in a mass grave.

No matter how much I dislike the Taliban, I realize the mujahideen are not a reliable alternative government. The Taliban brought draconian rules to an anarchic country and successfully banished poppy. I wonder what the new U.S.-sanctioned government will do if farmers replant poppy. The world knows that the Americans and their allies will be the victors, but the real battle will begin after the triumph. The smuggling of illicit narcotics is just one of a hundred issues the new government will face.

After the mujahideen head back to Kabul in November, flanked by American troops, and the United States declares victory, I head to Bonn, Germany, where a new Afghan government will be cobbled together by the victors of war. Hamid Karzai, an English speaker from Kandahar who comes from a respected Pashtun family, is posted as the interim president; three of Ahmad Shah Massoud's sidekicks become ministers; and a women's ministry is born. A five-year plan to rebuild Afghanistan is mapped out, and both Afghans and Americans celebrate the ouster of the Taliban. Refugees in Pakistan and Iran repatriate in the millions, and thousands in the diaspora in the West pack their bags, ready to serve their homeland. The doors to Afghanistan are open again.

Even my disillusioned father is hopeful. "If anyone has the resources and ability to help Afghanistan, it's the United States," he tells me when I call home from Germany. "But the question is how long will it stick around and tolerate our ignorant mullahs? The U.S. is looking out for its own interests. We shouldn't expect too much."

I'm more excited about the future than he is.

FOUR

My Father's Voyage

My father and his male cousins all bear nicknames they chose for themselves as young men, names to represent who they wanted to be. Their fathers were writers and they wanted their sons to continue in the same tradition. The nicknames their sons chose were meant to be pen names, but they evolved into their identities: Mr. Lamay (light), Mr. Turfa (new), Mr. Shaheer (famous), and my father's, Mr. Nawa (tune, voice, or solution). In his teenage years, when he began to write letters and essays, my father asked to be called Nawa. Now few people know his actual given name. His first cousins—some poets, some historians, nearly all of them gifted wordsmiths—wrote for pleasure and signed their writings with these monikers. My father's work was not published inside Afghanistan, but coworkers and relatives who communicated with him in writing still praise his Farsi calligraphy and his prose. The only essay I have read of his is an account of our last few weeks in Afghanistan, which he wrote for his Fremont literary association's publication in 1997. He describes a trip from Kabul to Herat during the Soviet invasion in this passage:

> Several other travelers and I boarded one of the only passenger buses [headed for Herat]. We were driving toward the city near Pashto Bridge and at a check post where many Russians and tanks stood, the bus stopped. Two of their soldiers came next to the bus and the other passengers and I thought we were going to be searched. But one of the soldiers approached the driver and said, "Hashish," and the driver handed him some amount of hashish. Then the soldiers waved to us and left while the bus continued toward the city. The driver, who I was sitting next to, told me he has never used hashish in his life but in order to appease these soldiers, he has to carry the drug with him in the bus.

Afghans do not refer to my dad as a writer; they know him as a personality. Mr. Nawa can make anybody laugh in painful situations, especially me. Once, while on a visit to Fremont during my travels, I sat with my father on the couch drinking hot black tea. He was recounting for me the follies of kings in the history of Afghanistan, scratching his clean-shaven face, a habit he has when in serious conversation. I picked up my just-poured cup of tea to take a sip, but I was so engrossed by his words that I spilled the scalding tea on my chest. He drove me to the emergency room, waited five hours while I was treated for first-degree burns, and then carried me to the car to drive me back home. When I woke up after twelve hours woozy from Demerol, he sat next to my bed with a cup of hot tea.

"You want some? Or have you forgotten altogether where the path to your mouth is?"

I forgot my pain and hid my head under the blanket in hysterical laughter.

My father's not an extraordinary achiever, or the hardest working family member, but he is an avid reader and harbors an unquenchable desire for knowledge. In Afghanistan, from the age of sixteen, he held many positions, mainly as an administrator, in various government jobs. He ran the literary club in Herat, and worked closely with hippie American tourists at the government tourist office. His last and most lucrative job was at the fertilizer company. He taught himself English and Russian, becoming a translator of Russian in the 1960s, and read and understood Arabic. He married my mother when he was twenty-one and she was fifteen (their generation married young).

"Mr. Nawa was a person whom you wanted to work with," says Mr. Herawi, one of my father's closest friends and former colleagues, who now lives in Fremont. "He had several employees working under him, and he dealt with them with respect, and dealt with problems with a sense of humor. He never took anything too seriously."

My father was fond of what were considered forbidden vices in Afghanistan, including alcohol and cigarettes. Mr. Herawi recalls, "He would light one cigarette, place it on the ashtray, and then forget about it and light another, especially while he was writing something."

Parties with live music, alcohol, and a four-course meal prepared by hired cooks made our home a revolving door for my father's friends on weekends. The most serious issue on his mind was how to spend money. To my mother's dismay, my father's paycheck often didn't last through the month, because he liked to buy what he wanted when he wanted it. My mother says he rarely thought about saving for a future. Life was now—until the Communist coup.

Then Mr. Nawa met the agony of war.

He lost his closest brother, Fazel Ahmed. His son, Hadi, had to flee the country. His job became a dangerous chore. Communist Party members put daily pressure on him and other employees of the fertilizer company to pay allegiance to communism. The employees collectively refused, despite threats to their lives. Even during the Communist takeover, my father continued to wake up at seven AM; put on his wrinkle-free slacks, shirt, and blazer; shine his shoes; and go to the office. With his country disintegrating, the routine was a comfort to him. Still, his mass of dark hair turned gray, and the defined lines on his forehead deepened. After my school was bombed, my father began to think about a future without a homeland. He had no illusions that at age fifty-two he would find a better life elsewhere. But life wasn't about him anymore—it was for his children.

Two real estate textbooks lay on the coffee table in our California apartment. My father walked around the table, smoking a cigarette, and opened one of the books, read a page, then closed the book again. "Could you bring me a cup of tea?" he asked my mother, who was cooking dinner in the small kitchen. I was thirteen and confused as to why my father wanted to study real estate. He was not a salesperson.

"Agha, why don't you study something you like?" I asked.

"Because I did what I liked in Afghanistan. Now I have to make money," he explained.

But he did not finish reading the books, and he did not take an interest in any other subjects or long-term jobs. He spent his days riding around in his Mazda station wagon, buying groceries, helping my mother with housework, watching TV, listening to the radio, and reading. He also dedicated his time to Faiza and me. He drove me to and from school, taught me how to ride a bike, taught us both how to drive, and was there to listen if we needed him. The burden of providing fell on my siblings and the American government. My mother sewed clothes for my teachers, but she was too ill to work full time. With a slipped disc in her back, she could barely do the housework. At age thirteen I started working as a babysitter, for two dollars an hour.

Aside from a two-year stint as an assistant at a nonprofit for Afghan refugees in Fremont, Mr. Nawa became homebound and reclusive. He no longer cared for parties or entertainment. The skills he had could not get him a job in the United States. His respected family and intellectual background, both so important in Afghanistan, did not matter anymore. During our first decade in the United States, his cousins and other relatives who lived nearby gathered with him to talk poetry and politics. Some of the intellectuals from Herat even formed a literary association, with its own publication. But over time, as they became older, the men, like my father, dispersed and began battling various illnesses, including depression. For my father's generation of Afghan men, America was not the land of opportunity but a place to die. Exile was the end.

But after the U.S.-led coalition ousted the Taliban in 2001, my father showed a desire to return home for a visit. I quickly responded and bought us both tickets. In May 2002, after a twenty-year separation from his homeland, Mr. Nawa returned to his birthplace.

For the second time, I stand in line at the Afghanistan-Iran border. I keep my Iranian hijab on, happy not to have to wear a burqa this time. My father wears his signature slacks and collared shirt. The Taliban have been gone for six months, U.S.-backed Karzai is president, and eleven thousand international troops have occupied the country. Ismail Khan, the mujahideen leader, has returned to power in Herat. The changes made since the fall of the Taliban are immediately obvious at the border. The visa representatives and guards do not have beards, but some of them have an untanned shadow of skin on their faces, where their beards once grew. Afghans tend to smile often, and whoever we talk to is eager to express his ideas. A sense of hope—no, euphoria—is omnipresent among the people, the feeling that life will change now that the United States has come to save them.

"Welcome to the new Afghanistan, where you don't have to cover your face and live in fear," the woman who searches my purse chimes. "Look at me, I can laugh again."

My father cannot contain his excitement; the grin on his face seems tattooed there. He hands out big Iranian bills that amount to a dollar each to the children gathering around him. They are the daily border beggars who rely on the generosity of returning Afghans. "Agha, stop giving away all your money," I tell him as if I'm his guide. "There are people inside Afghanistan who are much more needy."

"I'll give the needier kids bigger bills. Stop fussing. Let's get to Herat."

We hail a taxi. When it pulls up, one of Ismail Khan's armed soldiers asks if he can hitch a ride with us. On the highway to Herat, the view of desert and dust remains unchanged from my last visit, in 2000. But on this ride, the adventurous taxi driver, Eraj, speeds thirty miles faster than his car can take. I ask the soldier, Dastoor, a stocky, gregarious former guerrilla fighter, about the opium trade.

"The Taliban were able to get rid of poppy planting so fast," I say. "Can the new government keep it up?"

"We're definitely going to stop this evil business from expanding," Dastoor shouts through the noise of the fierce wind and the cracking of rocks under the tires. "The Taliban were only doing it because the prices of opium had gone down. It's *haram* [forbidden by religion], and we must get rid of it. Afghanistan is going to be known for better things than opium and war from now on."

Eraj claps in agreement. "Yes, life is going to change, *Inshallah*. America is going to help rebuild Afghanistan, because it is in its interest to do so."

My father and I look at each other skeptically as if to say, "They don't know the United States very well."

The American government is in Afghanistan to oust the terrorists who allegedly engineered the September 11 bombings, none of whom were Afghan. The reconstruction of the country is a burden the international community is willing to bear in order to fight the terrorists, but it's not a priority. The new Afghan government the United States has helped install is filled with ruthless warlords and corrupt officials who know only how to resist. Neighboring countries such as Iran and Pakistan will continue to support rivaling factions of the mujahideen and Taliban who serve their interests. The dearth of infrastructure and education in the last two decades is a formidable challenge that will take decades to overcome. Still, I push my cynicism to the back of my mind.

The happiness that Afghans inside the country radiate is contagious, and despite my reservations about the new government and foreign involvement, I begin to believe that Afghanistan may come out of its decades-long coma. If educated Afghans return and partake in rebuilding Afghanistan, then a chance for security and a stable government exists. Perhaps a firm leader with will and vision can revive the country.

"Mr. Nawa, where should I drop you off?" the driver asks. "You're welcome to come to our house."

"We're going to my wife's cousin's house," my father replies. "His name is Sayed Sattar Agha." On my trip to Herat in 2000, I formed a bond with my step-grandmother Bibi Assia and Uncle Ahmed's family. For that week at Uncle Ahmed's house with his two wives, five daughters, son, and my grandma, we disobeyed the Taliban and played cards and music, shopped, and visited shrines. My cousins watched me stand on the roof of my childhood home and cry. But on this trip, Bibi Assia is on holiday in Iran, and my mother has suggested that we stay with her first cousin Sattar Agha, so that I have a chance to get to know my other relatives in Herat.

"He has seven daughters," my father explains to the driver. "I'm not sure what their address is, except that he lives in an orchard home."

"There's no need for the address," the driver says. "He's famous in Herat for having seven daughters and no sons. He lives in the best part of Herat, near downtown. I'll take you to his doorstep."

Once we arrive at Sattar Agha's house unannounced, his wife, Aunt Masooda, and four of the daughters welcome us with hot thermoses of tea and plates of pistachios, walnuts, and raisins. The other three daughters live in Germany and Russia with their families. The daughters in Herat inspire me. Shahira, a doctor, and Rabia, a teacher, are married. Shahira, hardworking and shy, is the mother of two children, and Rabia, boisterous and an excellent cook, has a daughter. Sattar Agha's youngest daughters still live with their parents; Neela is an art student at Herat University, and Bita is a sophomore in high school. Under the Taliban, the older girls became housewives and the younger ones studied secretly with private home tutors. Now they are all back to working and learning.

Sattar Agha, an administrator at Herat's police headquarters, and his daughters sit quietly while Aunt Masooda, a petite, soft-spoken homemaker, asks about our journey.

"How was the ride from Iran? Not too bothersome, I hope. We hope you will enjoy your stay here enough to move back."

"Maybe I will," my dad replies. "America is a nice place but it will never be my home."

That evening, Sattar Agha takes my father's hand and leads him to their home's greenhouse, a horticulturalist's fantasy, with a cornucopia of blooming plants and flowers. A wicker table and chairs furnish the space. A water pipe and ornate tea cups are placed in the center of the table. Sattar Agha's daughters must prepare fresh tea, but male cousins serve the tea to Sattar's friends, who gather every evening. The men play cards and some smoke cigarettes as they engage in conversation. My dad will enjoy himself here, I think.

After a day of rest with my father and Sattar Agha's family, I make arrangements to travel to Kabul by plane. I'm in a hurry to leave again, this time to cover the Loya Jirga, or grand assembly, an indigenous form of representation in which influential figures from communities, usually men, gather to make important decisions. My father stays behind, eager to rediscover his city. "Go where you need to. I'm going to be fine here with Sattar Agha as my guide. We're going to have a good time."

The post-Taliban changes and gleeful mood of the country are more prevalent in the capital. Women are everywhere in public: shopping, laughing, eating. The deep bass of the drumbeat in Afghan folk music rings in the shops and restaurants. The child beggars who squatted and held their grimy hands out with frowns during the time of the Taliban now chase each other on the street and smile at passersby. They hold out their hands to their new clients, the thousands of foreigners entering the city with bleeding hearts and full pockets.

Inside the Loya Jirga tent set up on the grounds of Polytechnic University, fifteen hundred delegates from the thirty-two provinces—including women, tribal elders, teachers, and, to the dismay of many Afghans, the former mujahideen—gather to choose a transitional president. It feels like a big village party, with delegates sitting on the carpeted floor around pots of tea, perspiring in the ninety-five-degree heat. But the political backroom dealings and old ethnic rivalries linger. The men who helped the United States oust the Taliban—Abdul Rashid Dostum, Karim Khalili, Ismail Khan, and Mohammed Fahim, the man who replaced Massoud as the Jamiat leader—cause controversy inside the tent. Now that their enemy, the Taliban, have been purged, they are no longer united. Human Rights Watch, the New York—based group, accuses them of using coercion and bribery to influence the elections. Lakhdar Brahimi, the UN envoy to Afghanistan, backs up the allegations. "Voting for the Loya Jirga has been plagued by violence and vote-buying. There were attempts at manipulation, violence, unfortunately. Money was used, threats were used," he tells ABC News.

The members of the grand assembly I interview favor the former king Zahir, now eighty-eight years old, or a member of his family.

"Things weren't perfect, but we had peace when King Zahir was in power. If he's too old, I will vote for someone in his family to run Afghanistan," one of the delegates tells me anonymously, echoing the sentiment of dozens of others unaffiliated with militia or political groups. But assembly organizers tell me the former mujahideen threaten to attack the capital if the king is elected. They say the United States is opposed to reinstating Zahir. When Zahir addresses the assembly, the electricity powered by a giant generator suddenly shuts off. It's unclear if this is merely a coincidence—power failures are common in Afghanistan—or deliberate.

The former king's chances of reinstatement as a leader die completely when Zalmay Khalilzad, the U.S. envoy in Afghanistan, holds a press conference to announce the king's disinterest in becoming the country's leader. "The former king is not a candidate for a position in the Transitional Authority. . . . He endorses the candidacy of Chairman Karzai." Khalilzad, an Afghan native who is an American neoconservative, exercises more power than Karzai in Afghanistan. The U.S. government believes Zahir is too old and too soft for the new Afghanistan.

Karzai is predictably reappointed because the delegates do not have other viable options besides the former mujahideen. After Karzai's victory, two of the Loya Jirga delegates, Omar Zakhilwal and Adeena Niazi, write an editorial for the *New York Times*: "While the Bonn agreement and the rules of the Loya Jirga entitled us to choose the next government freely, we delegates were denied anything more than a symbolic role in the selection process. A small group of Northern Alliance chieftains led by the Panjshiris decided everything behind closed doors and then dispatched Mr. Karzai to give us the bad news."

Khalilzad's direct involvement in shoving the king and other monarchists out of the Loya Jirga delegitimizes the democratic process and taints it with American meddling. Even if the king or one of his family members were selected as the Afghan leader, the same problems Afghanistan faces today might have occurred, because the institutions and infrastructure of democracy are absent. However, the choice should have been given to the Afghan delegates, to prove that the assembly elections were free from external influence. In order to succeed, a nascent democracy must be a native-supported process.

Three thousand women gather in a girls' secondary school in the dusty district of Ghoryan, in Herat province. Districts in Afghanistan are akin to counties in the United States. Scattered villages across the desert make up a district, and each district has a governor and a town center.

Today's gathering is in a large tent, with a stage for the speakers and performers. No chairs are brought in for the audience; there's just the ground to stand on. The stage is cluttered with vases of fake flowers, miniature paintings of women, and wrapped gifts. There isn't enough room for everyone, and many people stand outside the tent, anxious for the program to begin. It is perhaps a hundred degrees with the July sun shining on the women's black chadors. The large crowd leaves little room for movement. The open air should provide plenty of room to breathe, but the intensity of the event—such a large gathering of women in a school after they've been banned from education for the last six years—makes the space claustrophobic. The assembly is in honor of Afghanistan's Mother's Day, which is normally celebrated in June.

My friends Angeles Espinosa, Spain's renowned newspaper correspondent, and Heike Schütz, a fearless German photographer, have accompanied me to Ghoryan because they heard that a women's movement is in motion here. I've read that many Afghan women are active in politics and pushing for independent candidates to join Afghanistan's first election process toward democracy. Ghoryan is also Mr. Jawan's home district and the route he used to smuggle opium to Iran.

I expect to hear speeches about the resilience of mothers, their patience and kindness, the same talks I heard as a child in celebration of Mother's Day in Herat. One of the organizers, a teacher, welcomes the audience and introduces the first speaker, the district governor, Jalil Nikyar. A mustachioed bureaucrat with graying hair and a polyester suit steps up to the microphone. "Our community has suffered greatly from this evil drug. We need to fight against the enemies who have polluted Ghoryan. A place known

for producing scholars and doctors is now the center for smugglers, drug addicts, and thieves. You have a responsibility as mothers to advise your sons and husbands to stop using opium and seek
work. We have lost too many sons, too many of our men to this
trade, and now you women are left to bear the scars," he says. "Once
drugs enter your house, you can no longer control it. You lose your
pride and your dignity."

I'm dumbfounded by the speech. Why is he talking about drugs
at a Mother's Day event?

Two girls step onstage, one dressed in boy's clothes, and they
perform a skit. It is like an assembly at my California high school,
where students performed skits to encourage sobriety. In Ghoryan,
the girl plays the role of a mother, and the boy is her son, who has
become an opium addict. The mother begs her son to stop smoking
opium.

I can hear women in the audience crying quietly. I know that
Afghanistan produces 90 percent of the world's illegal opium
supply; I know that opium becomes heroin and is distributed on
the streets of London and New York; I know that agriculture in
Afghanistan has evolved into poppy farming. But I had little idea
of the impact this illicit business was having on communities in
Afghanistan.

At one point I find myself onstage with Angeles and Heike, in
front of the three thousand women. They want their foreign guests
to speak. I am not sure what to say.

Angeles speaks first, and I translate. "We would like to thank you
for having us here," she says, her tone friendly and soothing. "We're
very happy to see you and we want to hear your stories so that the
rest of the world can understand your pain."

The women in the audience push closer to the stage. The lack of
room makes me nervous. The women in the back are stepping on

one another to get a closer look at us. They are so curious. They stare at us without discretion.

"What else? Is that all you have to tell us?" one older woman shouts, her chador covering her mouth.

They want us to say we can change their lives, that the new government and the fall of the Taliban will mean the end of the drug trade and better economic opportunities. But we cannot. The answer is in them, these women who are ready to fight back and re-capture their district from the drug lords. The strength of Ghoryan is in the women's willingness to resist a much more insidious aggres-sor than the Soviets or the Taliban.

We are presented with gifts, beautiful shawls, and we step off the stage and are led to a classroom. The headmistress brings us chairs and soft drinks. The mothers and their daughters who attend the school hover around us, all wanting to tell their stories at the same time.

"We have nothing to live on, no money, no food—we need help," one woman laments.

"I prefer to put on the chador and beg on the street before allow-ing my children to enter into the [drug] business," says another. Her name, I learn, is Fatema Alizai. Her husband, a drug dealer, was shot by the Iranian border police twelve years ago.

"We have to stop the drugs from coming here because it's de-stroying our families," another woman interjects. These women do not have the self-discipline to give each other a chance to speak, but they all seem to be relaying the same message: help us.

Nikyar, the district governor, tells us that this district of fifty-four thousand people includes dozens of villages sprawled across the desert. Men, women, and children survive by working in the opium industry as couriers, dealers, pushers, smugglers, or drug lords. The drug's cultivation and sale have been outlawed in the country, but

Ghoryan became hooked long before Karzai took power. Addicts, who include women, hide in their homes. When they do come outside, they sit on the streets and beg. Some women become prostitutes to feed their habit. No red light districts exist in Ghoryan; men know which houses to go to for sex.

"In our community they circulate heroin, cocaine, hashish, and other colorful substances that I don't even know the names of," Nikyar admits. "Of the thirty-seven hundred addicts we've identified, between a thousand and fifteen hundred are women."

We are all sweating from the heat, and Angeles and Heike are getting restless. The three of us head back toward the city of Herat in a beaten-up taxi. On the unpaved road exiting Ghoryan, we see a woman who allows only one eye to show through her chador. She tries to stop our taxi, stretching a hand into the open window. Before we can give her anything, the driver speeds away. Her hand falls out of the window forcefully. She looks me straight in the eye, as if I have betrayed her. She looks like a monster, with one eye bulging out of blackness.

"She's an addict. She doesn't deserve any handouts," the driver says. I don't know how he knows this, but I take his word for it. I am shaken up. A U.S. dollar might have fed her for a week.

Nikyar pointed out in his speech that Ghoryan was once more than just a port for narcotics. It was a landmark district, one that produced scholars. The district is known for its eight-hundred-year-old fort, located at the end of the main road, in the Ghoryan town center. The citadel, with its several towers, crumbling thirteen-meter-thick walls, and steel gate, is now home to the Ghoryan police station and prison. The native authorities proudly refer to this military maze as a reminder of a glorious era, from the late eleventh to the thirteenth century, when Ghoryan was a strategic base for the Persian Ghurid dynasty, which stretched from Iran to India. The

Ghurids' rich culture focused on the arts, languages, and literature. But Ghoryan was also a place of constant warfare. Local tribes wanting to keep their independence fought against the various empires that wanted to rule them. It was a polarized society, with a tiny educated community facing off against conservative tribes. Ghoryan's contemporary history boasts some highly accomplished individuals who studied in the United States and have written books on physics and Islamic scholarship and served as sterling examples in government posts in Afghanistan. But that history and those individuals are forgotten in the wake of what Ghoryan has come to represent: poverty and smuggling.

Three decades ago, before the Communists seized control of the country, Ghoryan smugglers trafficked tea and fabrics, but only small amounts of opium. Opium was illegal in Afghanistan and Iran, but the other commodities were smuggled to evade tariffs. Villagers would fill some tin cans with green tea, others with opium, then load the cans in cloth bags onto their donkeys and ride across the border. If they got caught, they paid a small bribe to authorities on both sides of the border. The tribes who smuggled passed on the job to the next generation, making it a family tradition, like farming.

Most Tajik villagers depended on agriculture and sheepherding to survive. Pashtun tribes, such as the Soltanzi, the Nurzai, and the Achakzai, became the patron smugglers in Ghoryan. These were the tribes that Abdur Rahman Khan forcibly relocated to the area in the late 1800s, ordering them to fight back if Iran attacked the border. The king did not want Iran to claim Herat, which was predominantly inhabited by Tajiks with roots in Iran. He gave the tribes land but few economic opportunities. They farmed and grazed animals but made their money chiefly through smuggling. Herat province is now home to people of multiple ethnicities.

For Angeles and Heike, Ghoryan is just another story, while I cannot stop thinking about the desperate pleas of the women gathered at the school and the one-eyed woman beggar whom the taxi driver dismissed as an addict.

In Herat city, my father has lost weight and gotten a deep tan from sitting on the orchard lawn drinking tea and watching Sattar Agha water his rosebushes. Today I walk in the house with Angeles and Heike to see my father sitting uncomfortably on a red *toshak* (mat) in the living room, his eyes fixated on the tea leaves in his cup. He wears a white *pirahan tomban,* an outfit he would have worn with disdain during my childhood because he thought Western clothes were more dignified. When he hears my footsteps, he looks up, frowning. "I want to go back," he says, his voice rising. "I have nothing to do here."

We had planned to stay for the entire summer, but he tells me he has had enough of the new Herat. "This place and its people are not what I left behind. There's nothing for me here. No one. Where are the intellectuals, the people who can change this place? People have become greedy and selfish. Sattar Agha's family has been very good to me, but the rest of the city is full of potato vendors and taxi drivers with narrow-minded mentalities."

I sit down next to him, forgetting to remove my sweat-soaked coat and head scarf. Angeles and Heike leave the room, to give us some privacy.

"Agha, it's going to take time to change things," I tell him. "What about our land? Do you want to sell it?" We have seven acres of agricultural land in Abdi, a village an hour away. "If you want to sell it, you'll have to stay longer."

"I visited Abdi and I was happy to see barley and wheat and fields of green," my father says. "The farmer who has manned that land for the last thirty years is dying and his family needs the harvest from that land. No, I don't want to sell it."

"Can't you stay another month and we'll leave together?" I beg.

"No, get me out of here. I don't want to come back here. Don't even bury me here!" he orders.

That night, after dinner, when my father is asleep, I ask Sattar Agha if something happened while I was in Kabul for a month.

"He feels like he doesn't fit in here anymore," Sattar Agha explains. "He listens and doesn't talk much with my friends. The type of people he wants to be around—the older thinkers and writers—are either dead or living elsewhere."

I arrange for one of Sattar Agha's sons-in-law to take my father to Iran; from there he'll fly back to California.

My father's reaction disappoints me. I hoped the trip would bring him out of his twenty-year depression. He returned with the expectation that he could regain what he'd lost, that sense of home and belonging, but he leaves feeling more alone. Perhaps he did not feel welcomed by the Afghans he met. Afghans who did not leave the country are angry, envious of the exiles repatriating. "You left us behind, experienced the good life in the West, and now you're here to make money by working with foreign companies," I overhear a man tell a friend who has also returned to Kabul from California. "Don't come back."

Perhaps it would've been better if I had never encouraged my father to come with me. I've taken away the majestic dream of the Herat he remembered. I worry that his depression might deepen now.

My reaction toward the new Herat has been more positive, perhaps because I have fewer good memories of the past. I compare what I see now to the Herat under the Taliban two years ago. I can hear the hope in the voices of people in my hometown. Once-forbidden sounds echo throughout the city. In the bazaar, women's high-heeled shoes clip rhythmically on the pavement, and songs from Bollywood films resound from the ice-cream shops.

I write about the transformation, but sending the stories to English-language news outlets is problematic; reliable phone and Internet service is rare. Only international organizations such as UN offices, with their large satellite dishes, can support telecommunications. The office closest to Sattar Agha's is the UN High Commissioner for Refugees. I slip on my red Payless sandals and head there with my laptop bag slung over my shoulders.

The summer air is hot and grimy, with the Herat dust covering my clammy palms. My head scarf and long black coat cling to my damp clothes. The UN office will also have air-conditioning; it's a bubble of modernity I can't wait to enter. At UNHCR, I find the director and offer to edit reports in exchange for daily access to Internet service. She says there's no need for my editing but I can spend twenty minutes a day on the guest computer.

She introduces me to an IT technician, Naeem. He has bronze skin and a deer's brown eyes; his brow furrows in a frown. He wears jeans, a striped t-shirt. "You can ask me for any help you need with the computer," he says. He speaks to me in flawless English, mistaking me for a foreigner. I compliment him on his English.

"Why wouldn't I? Why is it that people who come from abroad think we can't be smart like them?" he replies.

"I didn't mean it like that. I just haven't heard Afghans here speak with such a clear accent before," I say. "*Biazoo tarji midaham ka Farsi gap zanim.* [Anyway, I prefer we speak in Farsi.]"

Naeem doesn't smile much; he is a brooding, serious twenty-four-year-old troubled by Afghanistan's tragic fate. His office is in the basement of the building. Instead of my allotted twenty minutes, I spend hours hidden away there writing my stories and chatting with

Naeem and his officemate, Hamid, who is nineteen and enthused to
have a female guest open to conversation. Afghan men and women
are normally too afraid to talk to one another. Ismail Khan discour-
ages contact between people of the opposite sex who are not related
or married. Under the Taliban, women were banned from working
in offices. And even now, under the mujahideen, men and women
cannot speak freely to each other. Ismail Khan believes the only ac-
ceptable professions for women are teaching and child care. Women
who work with foreign organizations are considered improper.

"We heard that if [Ismail Khan's] soldiers see a man and woman
sitting too close and talking and they know they are not related, they
take the woman to the hospital and check her virginity," Naeem tells
me with disgust. "He's doing what the mullahs in Iran do, and it's
making him unpopular with the youth here."

"What do you guys want it to be like here?" I ask. "What kind of
freedoms do you want?"

"The ability to talk to a coworker woman without being afraid
that we will go to jail," Hamid responds quickly.

Naeem takes an interest in my work. He Googles my name and
finds my undergraduate thesis on Afghan couples in the United
States—a study of how changes in gender roles and identity have
transformed the rules of marriage. I'm impressed by his open-
mindedness and flattered that he is engaged by my controversial
writings. We discuss his frustration with the conservatism of the
culture in Herat, how women's options are limited, and how he
wishes they had more freedom. Our conversations take place as we
work—I face my laptop and address him when I'm thinking out
loud, and he responds while entering data on his desktop or fixing
a hardware breakdown. We don't face each other to speak directly
for any extended period of time, and I do not remove my hijab in
the office.

"Did you see on Herat TV how women are burning themselves more because they have such miserable lives?" I ask him. "I just can't understand how this society blames the woman."

"Women tend to be the most critical of each other," he says. "This society doesn't see that misery. They only know how to blame the woman. They don't give women the rights they are given in Islam. Self-immolations are a form of protest."

"Parents need to understand that these women should have a choice and that they are also human beings."

Naeem is fond of literature and photography, and he's a vegetarian—a rarity in Afghanistan. A technology expert and database administrator who knows how to repair most electronic equipment, he opened the first computer store in the city in 1999. Within four years, his family controlled the city's hardware and software business through their Ibn-e-Sina shop. He learned his computer skills by taking courses in Iran and reading thousand-page instruction manuals from Microsoft and other Web sites. Then he taught the men in his family how to fix, buy, and sell technology. He seems to belong more in Silicon Valley than Herat, but I'm glad he lives in Herat, that there are men like him to break the stereotype of the close-minded Muslim male bent on oppressing women.

I tell him about Ghoryan and how I plan to go back there when I return the following summer.

"Why are you so interested in Ghoryan?"

"The drug trade is a war few know about in Afghanistan, and Ghoryan tells the story of what's actually happening inside the war. Maybe you can come and be my guide there. I always have to have a man as a guide to be safe in this country."

"Maybe," he says with a shy smile, visibly pleased but taken aback by my brazen invitation.

FIVE

Meeting Darya

Ghoryan is a district on the edge of destruction. Many of its residents are drug addicts, dealers, or widows. More than half of Ghoryan's men are unemployed but work in the drug trade sporadically. No statistics exist to show exactly how much of the population is benefiting or suffering from the narcotics business. Drug lords rule the district, aided by a weak and corrupt local government. The drug lords hire husbands and sons to carry opium on foot and by donkey through the desert, where they risk coming under fire from Iranian border guards. Those who do make it across the border safely hand the drugs over to Afghan and Iranian dealers, who sell them in Iran, where they are then transported to Turkey, the Gulf, Europe, and, finally, the United States. But many couriers never return, as they are either killed in ambushes or executed in Iranian prisons. These men leave behind thousands of dollars in opium debt, which is inherited by the trade's greatest victims: their wives and children. Drug lords knock on the widows' doors demanding their opium money. Between 2001 and 2003, the number of women dousing themselves with accelerant and setting themselves on fire rose from two burnings a week to three, according to Ghoryan Hospital.

After the Communist regime fell in 1992, many refugees returned to find that the only jobs available were in the drug trade—for all ethnicities, not just Pashtuns. What was once a business for a select few families thus became a source of income for perhaps half of Ghoryan district. Meanwhile, worldwide demand for opium and heroin also rose. With three to six million addicts, Iran became the world's largest consumer of Afghanistan's opium. In Europe, heroin became the drug of choice. As Afghanistan is closer to Europe than Burma or Southeast Asia, where most of the world's suppy of opium was previously grown and exported, Afghan villages, especially those on the borders, began to drown in opium.

Ghoryan is one of hundreds of Afghan villages that are links in the drug chain, and the devastation is visible everywhere there: in the unpaved roads, the dry riverbed, the bullet-riddled walls.

Dr. Gol Ahmed Daanish, head of the hospital in Ghoryan, invokes Ghoryan's history, citing the district as once a place of bravery and scholarship. Now all that has changed. "We're the armpit of Herat province," he says. "We're considered the smugglers and thieves. Unfortunately, smuggling is the only income that has been encouraged during the Taliban years." According to Daanish, Ghoryan's geographical proximity to Iran has made the district a victim of the drug trade.

Daanish, delicate and polished in his Western slacks and shirt, represents the small minority of educated residents fighting to change the district and its reputation. Several of the educated in Ghoryan have formed a council and they gather once a week to talk with the local government. They fight an uphill battle. The trend of trafficking has changed, Daanish says. "It was run by a few locals who are now dead or addicted. Now there are invisible drug mafias and bandits who control the trade, and people here have become the pawns."

Mr. Jawan is a proud member of one of the Pashtun tribes in Ghoryan. I ask his son Kamran, who's visiting from Iran, to accompany me from Herat city to Ghoryan when I return in the summer of 2003.

Painted stones, which mark the sites of land mines on the side of Afghan roads, are a normal traffic hazard in Afghanistan. Many of the stones on the narrow, unpaved road from Herat city to Ghoryan are red, indicating danger, with a few white stones marking areas that have been cleared of mines.

"Are there any mines on the road itself?" I ask the driver, Abdul, an hour into the three-hour drive. "I mean, is it possible that your car could blow up right now?"

Kamran, who sits in the passenger seat, interjects. "Don't worry. The road has been cleared. Although I don't recommend you come here by yourself. This has never been a safe road. Drug dealers are in charge of this road."

Kamran has lived in Iran with his wife, Abida, and son, Khalid, for ten years. He's the only child of Mr. Jawan's still living near Afghanistan. Mr. Jawan's other three children are spread across Europe and the United States. Kamran travels back and forth between Iran and Afghanistan to see relatives or to do business, mainly managing his father's properties. At thirty-six, he is just like his father: a smooth-talking, generous social animal. He loves to talk on the phone and tell stories. He has even inherited his father's thick, dark hair and almond-colored skin. Mr. Jawan's experiences in the drug trade are well known by his children, but Kamran, his father's right hand, shuns that lifestyle now, and he isn't forthcoming with information about his past involvement. His generosity and the fact that we were once neighbors will not allow him to shut me out completely, though. He has joined me on this trip to check on the farmers cultivating barley and cumin on the dozens of acres of land his family owns in Ghoryan district and to introduce me to Zamir Agha's family, who will become my hosts for the next six weeks. Zamir Agha was Mr. Jawan's loyal cook for ten years, and the two families have remained in contact.

"Zamir Agha's family lives a simple, Sufi-like lifestyle," Kamran says. "They are very kind and giving people. His son Saber will take you wherever you need to go. You can trust him, but don't get yourself in trouble. Opium smuggling is not what it used to be like, as my dad has described. People die every day because of it. I know you're brave, but don't be stupid." He says this last part in a brotherly way.

We reach Ghoryan. The central road in town is narrow, with adobe shops on both sides. The main intersection, a roundabout similar to that in other village centers I've visited in Afghanistan, features a rectangular concrete structure. Men lie around the shops in the afternoon, taking naps or watching who passes by. I see some drug addicts crouching lifelessly in alleyways, their hands held out for donations. The few women who appear in public are inside the fabric and jewelry stores. The elder ones wear the blue burqa, and the younger ones wear the black chador.

Zamir Agha and his wife, Amina, and their six sons and three daughters live near the landmark fort in Ghoryan. Their house, which Zamir Agha owns, is a traditional mud-brick square structure

with six large rooms, a kitchen, an outhouse, a small room for bathing, and a cement porch, all connected by a courtyard. The family's
water comes from the deep well in the courtyard, and they use a
mobile gas stove. They have three hours of electricity every night,
as dim as candlelight, powered by large generators operated by the
town. Zamir Agha is in his fifties but still has enough energy to do
construction work. His sons contribute to the family income by digging and reinforcing wells in remote parts of the desert, while he
focuses on remodeling homes.

One of Zamir's middle sons is Saber, my guide in Ghoryan. His
mother tells me that the twenty-year-old is hot-headed and stubborn. He's also a newlywed. His wife, Tarana, has just joined the
family. The couple has inherited the fanciest room in the house,
with red velvet mats and matching curtains, but as soon as I arrive,
the family gives me that room.

My presence in their home and in the town becomes news. I'm
a single girl wearing Western clothes inside the house and interact-
ing openly with men not related to me. Rumors spread that I may
be a spy working for the CIA, which locals call *sazman-e-Siah*, or
"the black organization." For some in town, my presence among
non-kin men is shameful, and I can tell that Saber's mother and
wife are wary of me. They don't say it, but they give me uncomfortable stares. I befriend them by conversing about our different
worlds.

Saber and I chat as we eat sweet watermelon on the porch. His
wife sits nearby listening. He tells me, "When I went outside today,
the shopkeepers couldn't believe that you're staying with us. I think
they're jealous that we have a guest from America. But I'm glad
you're here." He yells to be heard over the muezzin announcing the
call to evening prayer.

"In America, men and women who are not related to each other sit together and eat and chat all the time," I tell him. "It's normal, and no one talks bad about it."

"Really?" Tarana asks. "They don't wear hijab?"

"No, they don't cover their heads, but they also don't wear bikinis when they meet in their homes."

We all laugh.

"Isn't it sinful for uncovered women to meet men like that?" Tarana inquires.

"I don't think so, but that's for you to decide if you live there. You have the choice to wear hijab," I explain.

"It would be nice to see America, but I don't think I want to live there," she decides.

I try teaching Saber and his wife, who are both illiterate, how to speak a few words of English. I suggest that Tarana enroll in the local high school.

"I would love that so much," she says. Tarana's much quicker to learn the words than Saber. She greets me with "hello" and says "good-bye" when I leave the house. But Saber's not pleased by her intelligence. "She can't go to school, because they don't have room for married women. I'm glad, because I don't want my wife to know more than me. That would be shameful," he says in the loud wind blowing against our faces.

A fierce wind cools Herat province in 100-degree summer temperatures. It is known as the 120-day wind because it blows for four consecutive months, hard enough to clear away the dust, freshen the air, and provide power through windmills. It's an antidote to the stifling heat. The wind gusts swifter in Ghoryan than anywhere I've been in Herat, thrusting the dust into the Ghoryan River. Some Ghoryan residents believe that the wind will one day wreck the district. But the victims of the opium business say it is the drug that will wipe out the villages. Their apocalyptic prediction is that men will die trafficking on the border, those who stay behind will become addicts and eventually perish, and the children and women left behind will die of starvation.

While Zamir Agha's family is not involved in the opium trade, they are engulfed by it. Most of their neighbors and relatives have ties to it.

Saber, a lanky, broad man with wild brown eyes, is not stubborn or hot-headed with me. He tells me he's looking for an adventure. One evening as he and I wait for dinner to be served on the *sofra*, the plastic sheet laid on the floor for food to be served, I ask Saber what the worst part of the drug trade is for him. He takes only a second to answer.

"The girls being sold off to pay opium debts. These cowardly smugglers will sell their daughters at young ages to save themselves. It takes away any honor we have," he says, his voice rising.

Families normally ask a bride price for their daughters. It took Saber a few years digging dozens of wells before he could pay the $2,000 dowry Tarana's family requested. But Saber explains that normal bride prices are different from bartered opium brides. In normal arrangements, "you marry the daughter to someone you know and trust. These smugglers are settling a business deal with dangerous criminals."

"Do you know anybody we can talk to?"

"There are a lot of families. Few would talk about it. They're ashamed. But I'll find you one."

The next day, Saber finds a family willing to talk because the father has gone missing. The mother is in charge and financially desperate.

"I told her you might be able to help her," Saber says.

"Don't make such promises," I warn him. "I can only help by telling their story, and other people who read or hear the story can give money if they want."

The drive to the family's home is a ten-minute rattling ride along the dry Ghoryan River. The white station wagon Saber has hired stops next to a tiny alleyway with high walls. Saber knocks on one of the doors, and he and the driver, Jalal, remain outside out of respect for the women. Men are not supposed to enter homes if the male host is not present.

A smiling little girl with a brown bob opens the door. She doesn't say a word. She points to an older woman carrying a toddler. The woman wears a yellowish-brown lace dress with an untied pink floral head scarf. She looks about forty-five years old, but I know she's younger—most rural Afghan women look older than their age. Her laugh lines frame her mouth, and bunched wrinkles hide her tired eyes. The skin on her hands is coarse and cracked. She's thin, so much so that her lace dress hangs limply.

"*Salaam,*" she greets me, looking me over with curiosity and sus- picion. "Please come this way." She leads me up a porch and into a hallway. She points for me to take a seat on a ripped, aging carpet there. A dozen children from the neighborhood crowd around me, including the children who live in this house. The woman shoos away the curious neighborhood children and orders one of her daughters to bring tea.

After a minute of polite greetings, she introduces herself as Basira and points to her six children, four girls and two boys. One of the girls, fair-skinned with light brown locks falling over her forehead through her blue head scarf, brings me green tea. I note her dirt-caked fingernails. "This is Darya," the girl's mother tells me. "She's twelve, but no one believes that, because she's blooming so fast. She doesn't have her period yet."

Darya's dark green eyes dart to the floor. Basira's mention of a period embarrasses her. She is about five feet tall, with a playful gait. Her curves are evident under her long green dress and matching pants. Her head scarf is loosely tied, but she keeps it on skillfully as she serves her guest.

"*Salaam,* Darya Jan. *Ishtani?* [How are you?] Do you go to school?" I ask the girl.

"I'm in the second grade," she answers, smiling through yellowed teeth. At age twelve, she should be in the sixth grade, but since the Taliban forbade girls from attending school for six years, Darya fell behind. She has now joined the 4.8 million children in elementary school, 37 percent of them girls, the highest ratio of girls attending school in the country's history.

"She's a smart girl, a bit rebellious," Basira informs me. "I wish I could keep her, but she'll be leaving to be with her husband."

Darya slams the silver tray with my finished tea glass and looks up at her mother angrily. "He's not my husband and I'm not going anywhere. Why do you keep talking about it?" She storms off to the kitchen.

Basira ignores this outburst. "My oldest child is Saboora; she's fourteen. But she will stay with me. The man her father sold her to has not shown up."

Saboora stands at the corner of the hall, her arms folded against her chest. She resembles her sister but she's taller and has light brown eyes. She has been looking at me with disdain, not smiling, not speaking. I hear her whisper to an older woman next to her, "Why is my mother talking to her? This is our private information."

I change the subject to ease the girl's discomfort. "Is this your house?" I ask Basira.

The house's structure is similar to Zamir Agha's home, but it is much smaller, dirtier, and older. The outhouse does not have a door, a makeshift piece of wood is placed in front of a hole in the wall, and there's a small water well next to a kitchen blackened by soot. Basira and her children occupy two of the rooms.

"It's my cousin's house," Basira says. "He's in Iran, and we can stay here until he comes back. The clay oven and well are shared by the neighbors. We don't own anything," she adds bitterly, "except these rags we're wearing."

Hana, the one-year-old in her lap, a girl with sun-bleached hair and greenish-blue eyes, tugs on her mother's dress. Basira nurses her and lights the water pipe. Between sucks of tobacco and the sound of gurgling bubbles, Basira begins to tell me her story. Her face is slack and nearly all her teeth are gone. She speaks with fatalistic absolutism. "Life and God have cursed me," she says. Her words are sparse, her expressions unreadable. "I lose my temper whenever the children fight or scream. I can't control them," she says. Her oldest son, Yama, refuses to attend school. Darya doesn't do her chores and instead plays in the sand barefoot with the unseemly neighborhood kids. Basira resorts to violence to control them. She hits them with a two-foot-long wooden stick she keeps on a windowsill.

The thirty-year-old Basira is half Pashtun, half Tajik, a mix that is common in this part of the country. Neither she nor her children speak any Pashto. Basira's family members are sheepherders, but her maternal uncle, Ali, is a high school teacher, and the only male figure present in this family. Twenty years ago he taught in Kabul, and when Basira came to visit with her parents, he tried to convince them to let her stay and attend school there. At that point she'd studied up to the fifth grade in Ghoryan and could read and write. But her parents politely refused the invitation and brought her back to Herat, and at age fifteen she was married to Touraj, whose family were also shepherds.

"My life may have been completely different if I had stayed with my uncle," she says.

Basira became pregnant with Saboora a year later, and every two years, she had another child—except for Hana, who came four years after Asifa, now five. Hana was not planned. Darya was born in 1990, near the end of Communist rule. The family stayed on in Ghoryan, enduring the war. Basira and Touraj led a humble but happy life. They lived with his family. She tended to her housework and children while he worked skinning sheep. Their family had no connection to the opium business.

Then, in 1995, the Taliban seized Herat from Ismail Khan. Just when Saboora, then seven, was to enroll in the first grade, the schools for girls were closed. A drought killed livestock and dried up the Ghoryan River, one of the few sources of water in this desert, and farmers began cultivating opium. Before the Taliban, poppy production occurred in southern, eastern, and some northern provinces, while Herat served as the trafficking route. After the rise of the Taliban, the district was transformed from merely a trafficking route into a producer of the drug as well. The Taliban's main income was the illicit narcotics trade—in 1999 they made between $25 million and $75 million just from taxing opium farmers and traffickers.

The Taliban ensured that farmers in Herat learned the skills necessary to farm poppy, sending experienced farmers from Helmand and Kandahar to teach Ghoryan farmers how to convert from traditional crops to poppy. Poppy is a resilient crop that grows in almost any climate and takes little water to ripen. Ghoryan farmers learned fast, especially since, for the first time, the practice was now legal and profits were ten times more than those for wheat, which is the most cultivated crop in Afghanistan.

The Taliban also encouraged unemployed young men in villages on the borders such as Ghoryan to become involved in the labyrinthine trade. The men became couriers, the trade's most dangerous job. Drug lords and smugglers who do not want to cross the border regularly hire couriers. These mules may carry a knife or an

AK-47 for protection, but they're no match for the big traffickers, who are armed with RPGs and machine guns and riding in Toyota trucks whizzing across the desert. Couriers can die in the crossfire between the more powerful competing smugglers or from the bullets of Iranian border guards, who shoot to kill anyone attempting an illegal border crossing. The desert frontier is a battle zone, with no demarcations of alliance and loyalties. When one group of drug bandits feels threatened, they shoot, and the other smugglers on the road fire back. If Iran catches the couriers or smugglers alive, the men languish in Iranian prisons, where some are hanged. According to Afghan Parliament member Gul Ahmad Amini, who went on a fact-finding mission to Iran in 2010, as many as 5,630 Afghans are currently in Iranian prisons, with more than 3,000 sentenced to death. The majority of those on death row are alleged drug traffickers. Iranian officials say the number is much lower, but they refuse to disclose the exact number of Afghan men who will be executed for drug crimes. Iranian law states that if an individual is caught three times with as little as half a kilo to as much as twenty kilos of opiates, he or she may receive the death penalty. But some of the Afghan inmates on death row say they haven't even had trials.

In Ghoryan, the numbers do not matter. The line of graves in Ghoryan cemeteries with an Afghan flag flying over them reveals the truth.

Basira's husband, Touraj, was not familiar with the cruelty of the drug trade when he decided to become a dealer. The drought all but ended work in sheepherding for him and his extended family, and with several children and a wife to feed, he was forced to find a new job to support his family. It didn't take long for Touraj, thirty-five, to become friendly with influential smugglers and the Taliban. He began recruiting couriers. He made a small fortune buying opium and hiring and training couriers to smuggle drugs. Like most successful drug dealers in Afghanistan, Touraj also opened a currency exchange business. He became a *saraf*—the word means "money changer," but in border towns such as Ghoryan, it also implies "drug dealer." It's one way to launder drug money.

Touraj's lifestyle and appearance changed with his burgeoning profits. He wore a Rodo watch, a sign of wealth in Afghanistan, and a gold ring that opened up to sport another smaller watch. In a matter of five years, he built a blue-tile, two-story home on an acre of land that still shines on a street among mud-brick shacks.

Basira and her daughters say little about the marble-floored, ten-room house with the rose garden. They rarely mention the kilos of gold jewelry that hung from Basira's neck and ears. They try not to recall their motorcycle parked in the driveway. But everybody else in Ghoryan remembers them well.

"They were the envy of this town," Saber's mother, Amina, says. "Few here had that kind of wealth."

Basira did not ask many questions when Touraj was making money. She liked being rich for once and did not mind the gold he bought her. She wore makeup and dressed in glitter-embossed velvet dresses, and she made sure the house was clean and the foods Touraj liked were prepared when he arrived for dinner. The trouble came when he decided to marry a second wife.

Basira did not approve of the marriage but had no power to stop it. Touraj wed Azin, a young girl from Herat city, and wanted to make her feel like the world was hers. On their wedding day, he decorated almost every Toyota Land Cruiser in town with fresh flowers. With the couple in front, the procession of motorcycles and cars circled the bombed-out roads of Ghoryan as guests fired rounds of bullets into the sky to celebrate. Azin moved into the blue-tile house with Basira and had two children with Touraj. Basira's attitude toward her husband changed. She no longer made his favorite meals or flirted with him when he came home from work.

Opium wealth for Touraj was as fleeting as the drug's high. He continued to work in the trade, but the four thousand tons of poppy produced in Afghanistan in 1999 oversupplied the market and slowed business. The Taliban's ban on opium production in 2000 raised opium prices again, but it was too late for Touraj. He stopped benefiting from the trade and quickly went into debt when Iran seized six of his drug caravans. He now owed about $10,000 to smugglers from Helmand.

When he traveled to Helmand to settle his debt, the drug barons held a gun to his head and threw him in jail several times, demanding their money. Touraj offered his most prized possessions: his two oldest daughters. Their fair skin and curvaceous figures made the girls worth thousands of dollars. But even with the sale of his daughters, he still owed money.

In 2002 he went into hiding, leaving Basira pregnant with Hana. He was constantly on the run. Siar Agha, one of Basira's neighbors, an elderly man with a white beard and turban, enters the hallway and joins my conversation with Basira.

"One day I was sitting with my wife having tea in our yard and he jumped over the wall," the man tells me. "Touraj looked disheveled and frightened. He asked if we could give him shelter because the drug barons were out to kill him. We didn't know him that well, but we made sure he was taken care of for a few days. Then he took off again, and we don't know where he went."

The drug barons came to the blue-tile house, knocking down the doors. They gave Touraj's wives a few hours to pack up. They took the house and everything in it—the Persian carpets, the gold, the motorcycle, and the generator. Touraj's second wife, Azin, moved with her two children back to the city, where she lives with her parents. Some of their old neighbors say they see Touraj once in a while, in the crowded markets in Herat city skinning sheep, his old job.

Basira and her children became homeless, moving from one relative's house to another. Her uncle Ali told her to abort her sixth child, but she refused. "Instead she tried to kill herself, and we stopped her," Ali says. "We tried to help with the kids, because they're out of her control."

Basira serves others now, making a sporadic daily fifty cents baking bread or washing clothes. The family barely has enough to eat. They have two outfits each, a pair of shoes, and several head scarves.

Darya goes to the kitchen to make more tea. I ask Basira if I can take some photos of Darya, and she shrugs. "It's fine as long as she has her hijab on," Basira answers. Darya holds her baby sister Hana in one hand, opens a can of Chinese green tea, and sprinkles loose leaves into a shiny silver-colored teapot. She picks up one of the large steel kettles boiling on the baked-mud stove lit up with charcoal and pours in the boiling water.

I put the camera away and walk back to where Basira is smoking her water pipe.

Malik, Saboora's husband, has not shown up to claim the girl. Basira is too afraid to wed Saboora to another man, in case Malik appears. But Darya's husband, Haji Sufi, has come from Helmand— several hundred miles from Ghoryan—several times with gifts in the last two years to take her away. Basira says Darya does not want to be married. She is a young girl who is ecstatic that she can go to school after six years at home during the Taliban regime. But when her husband arrives, this carefree girl morphs into a raging, terrified child. Her mother tries to convince her to go with him. Basira is so destitute that she wants the entire family to become the husband's servants. But Darya refuses. He's thirty-four years older than she, does not speak Farsi, and has another wife and eight children. When he arrives, Darya curses him and runs away from him.

"She's lucky he's not forcing her to go. Next time he comes, she's going to have to go, because I'm afraid of what he might do to the rest of us if she doesn't."

Basira stops chugging on the water pipe. She looks me in the eye and tells me life seems cliché to her, from riches to rags. "I only live hour by hour," she says, "wondering when the next meal is coming from, when are the smugglers going to take my daughters, is my husband ever going to come home? We have peace now, but what good is this peace when my family may go hungry tomorrow?"

I thank her and promise to return and speak to her more. At Saber's home, I share Basira's story during a dinner of tasty okra and potatoes. Saber's mother, Amina, blames all of Basira's troubles on the greediness of men, be it with money or wives. "One of the first things men in Ghoryan do when they make some extra money is marry another wife," she says. "If they have two, they'll marry three, and if they have three, then it's four. Some of the bigger smugglers don't respect the four wives allowed in Islam. They'll marry six, seven wives."

"They want a harem," Saber adds.

Girls want the choice to refuse marriage to these men. Darya is in the majority. More than 60 percent of Afghan girls face forced marriages. Most of them comply—they are young girls, after all— but Darya is putting up a significant fight.

SIX

A Smuggling Tradition

I watch the sun set on the porch of Saber's house and think back to Mr. Jawan's days of smuggling. The stories of the past weigh less on the heart—I prefer those to the ones I hear today. Most of my relatives in Herat met our neighbor Mr. Jawan when they came to our Behzad Road home. Mr. Jawan visited my father on the weekends and had dinner with us. He invited the children and adults to sit around him and listen to his stories. My maternal and paternal aunts and uncles were fond of him. The gregarious smuggler was willing to help any of them, anytime, especially if it involved traveling to Iran.

Uncle Rostam was eighteen and wanted to go on vacation to Iran with his cousin Tahir. He did not want to go through the hassle of getting a visa and paying for the trip, so he turned for help to Mr. Jawan, who could easily smuggle out people as well as drugs. But Uncle Rostam wasn't aware that Mr. Jawan also needed his help.

"It was winter 1977 and we were on break from school," Uncle Rostam tells me. "We went to Mr. Jawan's house in Herat city and he said he would make sure we got to Iran safe, as long as we could carry a few sackfuls of potatoes and onions for him to Iran. We agreed. The next morning, we all met up and he gave us these big vests to wear over our *pirahan tombans*, and over our clothes he gave us thick winter coats to wear. The vests felt heavier than anything I'd ever worn. His first wife, Narinji, now deceased, and he sat in front of the American Jeep he owned and we sat in the back on top of the sacks."

A few hours later, they reached Ghoryan town center and Mr. Jawan saw the district governor walking along the main road. Mr. Jawan pointed to the teenagers and said to the district governor, "*Salaam*, these are my cousins." (They were not his cousins.) "They're going to Iran. You need something from there?"

"No, thanks," the district governor answered.

But Mr. Jawan insisted. "They'll bring you some candy."

Uncle Rostam said he didn't understand what the exchange was about then but later realized that the candy was a bribe. Mr. Jawan offered something small such as candy to the man in charge of the government in Ghoryan so that he would not search his vehicle, because the official knew there was opium inside.

Mr. Jawan drove them to his house in Ghoryan town center and they ate *quroti*, a soup made from yogurt curd and fried onions. At two PM they jumped in the Jeep again to head to Tirpul, Mr. Jawan's village. On the way, Mr. Jawan passed another vehicle and stopped and asked, "Is the path clear?"

The other driver was a fellow smuggler, and he confirmed that it was safe to continue. "I'm not sure if he had a weapon with him," Uncle Rostam recalls, "but he had binoculars and he kept looking westward through them."

After two hours, they reached Tirpul. Mr. Jawan's relatives greeted them with warmth. They killed a sheep for their guests and made them rice and meat stew. "Then Mr. Jawan told us to take off our vests. We were shocked to find all the insides and pockets of the vests filled with ten to fifteen plastic opium packets."

"That's opium, isn't it?" Uncle Rostam asked Mr. Jawan.

"Yes, it's opium. Don't worry about it,' he answered as if Uncle Rostam should've known.

"He sat on the sand cross-legged and ordered his relatives to bring a scale, the kind you weigh wheat with. When the scale came, he took the sacks out of the Jeep and began to take out much bigger plastic bags of opium and started weighing them on the scale and dividing them up into smaller packets. He handed four or five packets to each relative. He didn't say anything to them. They knew what to do with them."

At around six PM, Mr. Jawan told one of his relatives, a demure man named Kaftar, to get ready to leave for Iran. Kaftar took the packets of opium and placed them clandestinely in tea cans, then wrapped the cans in packages and threw the packages into cloth sacks, which Kaftar had to carry. Kaftar hoisted the sacks over his shoulder. "We just carried bags full of our clothes," Uncle Rostam says. "We were a bit scared, but we knew Mr. Jawan knew his business well. He didn't even give us the sacks of onions and potatoes we had promised to take.

"Kaftar told us to lie on the ground if he dropped to the ground. We agreed, not asking any questions. We started walking and walking and walking. We had no donkeys, nothing except our feet. Apparently that was the safest way to get across. We also didn't have any food or water. As we walked in pitch dark, a group of stray dogs ran toward us barking. That was the biggest danger then, a stray dog mauling you. But Kaftar threw something at one of the dogs, and they all got scared and left. Nobody would get killed by the police in those days. The fear was being jailed by the Iranians. They didn't hang many people, though."

At two AM, after walking for eight hours, they crossed the border—there was no marker except electrical poles and wires. They reached a house similar to the one they had had lunch at in Tirpul. Kaftar dropped off his sack at the house and told the boys to rest and that he would take them to Mashad, the closest and largest city to them in Iran. The next day, Uncle Rostam wrote a letter as Mr. Jawan had requested, reassuring him that Kaftar had helped them get to Iran safely. Mr. Jawan stayed in Tirpul until Kaftar delivered the letter, then drove back to Herat city with his wife. Uncle Rostam and Tahir enjoyed their winter holiday in Iran.

Mr. Jawan's days of safe trafficking and candy bribes ended with the 1978 coup. Many of Ghoryan's men joined the resistance, and hundreds of its families fled to Iran. Ghoryan fell to the mujahideen. Farmers in the country turned their wheat fields to poppy fields to make money. The mujahideen cleared the paths to trafficking wherever they had control. The traditional traffickers began to carry more dangerous weapons, supplied by the mujahideen, and many became leaders of the resistance movement. Mr. Jawan's relatives died by the dozens fighting the Soviets, and those who survived moved to Torbat-e-Jam, the Iranian border town where his son Kamran lives.

My daily routine in Ghoryan begins at sunrise in Saber's home. I'm awoken by the crowing of roosters from a nearby yard. The weather is becoming too hot for us to stay inside—all of us sleep on the porch, on thick mats inside mosquito nets. Saber's wife, Tarana, a stout, square-faced woman with coarse hands, pumps a pail of cold water from the well, transfers it into a plastic water can, and summons me to the garden in the courtyard. She hands me a bar of cheap soap and pours the water on my hands as I lather them. I cup my hands to hold the water and splash my face. Then I brush my teeth. The dirty water from my hands and face wets the drying plants and sunflowers in the garden. No one wastes water here.

Saber's sister Tina calls us to breakfast. The dozen of us sit around a white tablecloth on the floor, drink green tea, and devour Afghan bread, a flat, elongated, chewy wheat staple that tastes sweet and salty at the same time. At six thirty, Saber and I head out to the desert with a driver. The drivers keep changing, depending on who's available on a given day. We endure the endless miles to more than two dozen speckled villages, which can be spotted from a distance. Ghoryan's dozens of villages make up the sixteen-thousand-square-kilometer district. The villages all look similar: wells for water, outhouses for bathrooms, hurricane lamps for light, children playing outside, shepherds tending flocks, tents or mud-brick homes, a cemetery. About a hundred families live in each village. As I meet more people and hear their stories, their various plights begin to echo one another.

We have few men left in this village because our men died in the wars or transporting opium on the border. The women are in debt. The men left behind are too old to work, and the boys are too young to make money or they are addicted to drugs. The women are left in charge to take care of their household.

One tribe, which has long been part of Ghoryan's opium smuggling tradition, personifies the transformation of the drug trade. The Soltanzi traveled the hills and deserts of Ghoryan for seven generations, and no one—not other smugglers or Iranian border guards—dared to stop them. But as Iran toughened its anti-drug laws and various mafias took control of the opium market during the Soviet invasion, the clan lost its authority and income.

In Gandomi Soltanzi's three-room mud house a few miles from Saber's on a corner street, one room is locked. It has no windows. When the door creaks open, the light shines on a row of photographs nailed high on the wall. There is no carpet on the floor, and dust blows about, fogging the view of the pictures. Gandomi introduces the people in the photographs.

"On the left is my husband, Shayan, and my son Baitullah, both executed in prison in Iran eleven years ago. My oldest son, Tanai, died in a battle against the Soviets. My son Noman was captured by the Iranians and has left me with a huge opium debt. My other son, Wais, is a drug addict on the streets of Iran," she says nonchalantly, as if reciting her grocery list.

Gandomi is in her fifties with a large black mole on the side of her mouth; long curly hair down to her waist, jet black with no gray strands, tied together by a rubber band; and small sunbaked brown hands with well-defined veins. Around her neck is a silver talisman case that normally holds a Quranic verse, to cast away the evil eye, but now the case is empty; Gandomi took out the folded paper one day to clean the silver and doesn't remember where she put it. She wears a faded red dress with black loose pants, her chador draped over her head even at home. When she tells her story, she wavers between the past and present, forgetting the details that connect events. Yet, with a patient listener, she becomes a lucid thinker and poignant storyteller.

Gandomi and Shayan were paternal cousins when they married. They made a living from sheepherding, farming, and smuggling. During the Soviet invasion, Shayan and their first-born son, Tanai, joined the mujahideen. The rest of the family—Gandomi, the three younger sons, and two daughters—moved to the Khaf Mountains in Iran, where the government initially donated coupons for food and fuel. Shayan and Tanai spent half the year fighting in Afghanistan and the other six months living with the family in Iran. Then the first tragedy struck.

Tanai died on the battlefield fighting the Soviets.

I ask Gandomi how it felt to lose her oldest son.

"Like my heart was cut in half," she responds. "But with every child I lose, the pieces of my broken heart turn more numb."

Shayan minimized his time on the battlefield but he continued to travel between his country and Iran to traffic opium. He recruited his youngest son, Baitullah, to join him.

"As long as I can remember, my family transported opium," Gandomi says as she spins yarn with her fingers. "We didn't make much money in the old days. For a kilo the men took across the border, they got a sack of flour. Now the stakes are higher, and so is the cost to your life."

One day in the early 1990s, the father and son were riding a motorcycle in a bazaar in Torbat-e-Jam in Iran when the Iranian police arrested them for smuggling. They were in the Torbat prison for three years.

"Informants in our own tribe turned them in. The police came to search our home and found nothing. I went to visit them once in the prison. They were crying for me to find three million *toman* [$3,750] to bail them out. They knew they would die. I didn't have the money. Ten days later, they were executed and the Iranian government sent us a letter that both of them had been hanged. We asked for the bodies, but we never got them."

After fourteen years as refugees in Iran, the family repatriated to Afghanistan in 1993, during Ismail Khan's first term as the governor of Herat province. Gandomi still had two sons and two daughters left. She had become one of the million war widows in the country.

When the Taliban arrived in 1995, her son Noman, twenty-four, became a well-known drug dealer recognized for his ruthless behavior. Like Darya's father, Noman sent the younger shepherds to cross the border, and many of them died on the way.

"I wanted him to stop and convinced him to get engaged," Gandomi says. "The bride's family demanded a four-thousand-dollar bride price. Noman wasn't making much money; in fact, he was in debt at the time. He decided to make the dangerous trip to Iran to earn the bride price and pay off his debts. That was it. Then he disappeared." Her stoicism falters and she begins to cry.

Noman was gone for three years when Gandomi received news that the Iranians had caught him alive with three dead cohorts and three Kalashnikovs. A relative brought an Iranian newspaper clipping and read it to her. "[Noman] told the reporter that he was in Iran to avenge his father's death," Gandomi says. "He talked to them from jail, I guess." She believes her son is dead, executed by Iran like his father and brother.

For Gandomi, Noman's loss was not just another tragedy—it was a calamity. He had borrowed $6,000 from drug smugglers in Helmand and from a local drug lord in Ghoryan named Haji Sardar, to buy narcotics in the hope that he could triple the money once he sold the drugs in Iran.

Now the debt fell on his mother, but she had nothing to give his lenders.

"They were Taliban and they came and took the carpets, the motorcycle, the prayer rugs, and the land. Haji Sardar sent his cronies and left me with nothing. And they're still coming," she says, weeping.

In the room where her family photos hang on the wall, two of her children's pictures are missing. She did not put up pictures of her daughters, Tooti and Aabi, because it's not proper to display women's photos in Ghoryan. But she brings her younger daughter, Tooti's, photo in a clear plastic bag with a death certificate from the local hospital. Tooti was pronounced dead two years ago, from severe burns on her body. She poured cooking gas on herself and lit a match. The seventeen-year-old lived for two months, moaning from the pain, before she died, joining the increasing number of women who self-immolate to death in Herat.

"Tooti's husband was killed carting opium on the border," Gandomi explains. "Her two brothers-in-law both wanted to marry her, according to tradition, but she refused. The in-laws accused her of wanting to remarry for a bride price. The in-laws beat her until they tore her eardrum, and locked her up in the house. They would not let her family see her. She kept a knife under her pillow when she slept, afraid that her brothers-in-law would rape her. One day Tooti lost hope."

Tooti's mother—left with only her other daughter, Aabi, also a widow and with two small sons—is losing her mind. As she sits on the floor weaving wool into yarn, she is not able to articulate a thought without changing subjects and time spans. I prod her to focus on one story at a time, and she tries.

Despite her mental state, she is physically active and able to support the entire family. As she talks, Aabi plays with her sons in their front yard, which consists of dry earth with no greenery. The boys, Hatam and Maqsud, laugh and stick their hands in the dirt. When they get bored of the game, they throw their arms around their mother in a bear hug, then run over and kiss their grandmother. Gandomi pushes them away but cracks a faint smile, the first I've seen since we met.

For work, Gandomi and Aabi spend a dollar to buy four kilos of wool, then weave it into yarn used for carpets. It takes them ten days to finish the job. They sell the yarn for two dollars. They spend a dollar a day on expenses, which include their daily diet of onions, bread, and dried yogurt curds. They have egg soup if their hens lay eggs. Gandomi, in her chador and tattered pair of shoes, searches for thorns and hay in the desert every morning. She makes a few cents selling them to the shepherds to use for fuel and animal food. She also owns a small plot of her father's land, which the drug lords are trying to seize from her to settle Noman's debt.

In 2002, Ismail Khan, then the governor of Herat, announced that all opium debts for widows of martyred mujahideen were forgiven, yet Gandomi's lenders keep coming—some of them are members of the police, she says.

Gandomi and her daughter are illiterate. (Only 12 percent of females fifteen and older can read and write in Afghanistan.) They have no clock or calendar in the house and do not keep track of time. Neighbors tell them when it's Friday, the Islamic holy day, and Gandomi grabs her chador to go to the cemetery. A ten-minute walk from her house are several grave sites, mounds of stones with no identification. She squats in front of two of them—the graves of her dead children Tooti and Tanai the freedom fighter—and howls for fifteen minutes. She wipes her tears on her dust-covered clothes and walks swiftly into the desert in search of thorns.

Back at Saber's home, I watch the shooting stars through my white mosquito net and think about Gandomi. How does she cope? How can she still sit there and work? Has she ever attempted suicide? These questions trouble me. Her story is one of hundreds I've heard, but her tragedy is greater than most. I find hope in her spirit, her resolve to live. Gandomi's resilience is not uncommon among Af-

ghans who have endured decades of war. The average life span in
Afghanistan is forty-five years, but Gandomi has managed to survive beyond that. It consoles me to know that she has her daughter
Aabi and Aabi's two young sons living with her. She's not alone. But
then I think of Darya, the bartered bride, and my anger and frustration build up. I can feel my eyes welling with tears. Darya's only
twelve and has no future ahead of her. Once her husband takes her
away she will become a slave. But then, maybe not. Maybe he's a nice
man who will take good care of her, who will encourage her to go
to school and buy her shoes and books and let her be free-spirited.
"Wishful thinking," I say out loud in English.

"What did you say, Fariba Jan? Did you need something?" says
Tina, Saber's sister, who sleeps next to me. Amina has assigned Tina
to meet my every need. I smile at her and shake my head. She is
observant, kind, and beautiful. Her large black eyes mirror those of
the women in Persian miniatures. She rarely ever sits down to relax.
She and Tarana take turns with the housework. They are in charge
of cleaning, cooking, doing the laundry, ironing, and answering the
calls of the elders and the males in the family. The sisters-in-law
work graciously, joking and laughing with each other throughout
the day. If one is feeling tired, the other takes over her chores. I never
hear them complain.

"Why do you look so sad?" Tina asks.

"I was just thinking of Darya, the opium bride. It's sad that she
will be taken away to a place where she doesn't speak the language
and knows no one. She's a child still."

"Fariba Jan, my mom married at nine, and my father will probably do an exchange with me [giving her to a family who will offer
a daughter to one of her brothers] next year, and I'm only fifteen.
That's the destiny of girls here. I wish I were a boy," she adds, sighing.
"*Dokhtar mala mardoma* [a girl belongs to strangers]."

"I know that's a famous Farsi saying, but do you really believe that?"

"Does it matter what I believe? I don't really have a choice," she says, sighing again. "I like that star. It's the brightest."

I look up into the night sky. "That is called Sirius. I don't know what it's called in Farsi. But it's beautiful, just like you," I tell her.

SEVEN
The Opium Bride

The next morning, I wake up a little later than dawn. Saber has gone out. As I wash my face in the garden with Tarana, he rushes through the door toward me.

"Darya's husband is in town. He's at their house right now and he might take her with him. You want to meet him?" he asks me, panting.

"Let me put on my hijab." I run with soap still on my face. I put on the long black coat over my pajamas and the white polka-dotted head scarf I wear every day and race to the street.

The door to Darya's house is closed and no children play nearby. It's unusually quiet, except for the howl of the wind. I hold the head scarf over my eyes to keep the dust away.

Saber knocks loudly. Darya's eight-year-old brother, Nemat, answers the door and smiles when he sees me. "It's the city lady!" he turns around and yells to his mother. He opens the door, and I enter. Saber and the driver stand outside.

Basira nods her head in a cold greeting and walks up the porch to the hallway. "I heard Darya's husband is here," I say, following her.

"*Bale*, but she's giving him a hard time again. He wants to take her this time. He's tired of coming all this way."

Darya stands in the hallway in the green outfit and head scarf I saw her wearing last time. Her arms are folded across her chest. Her mesmerizing green eyes flash. Her twelve-year-old body shivers. She takes two steps back toward the mud wall in the hallway. It is a dead end.

"I'm not going! I'm not going!" she shouts at her mother.

The husband, Haji Sufi, waits for her inside the room where the family sleeps, sitting cross-legged on a thin mat drinking black tea with cardamom. He can hear her shouting.

Darya looks at me for support, but her mother scowls at her daughter and shoots me a warning look not to interfere. "It's your forsaken father's fault that has put us in this hell. What's done is done!"

Darya turns her head toward the wall and says nothing. Basira motions me toward the room where her guest is sitting with her uncle Ali. Darya's husband looks up at me but doesn't get up. Typically in Afghan culture, men and women stand when new guests arrive. A look of curiosity crosses this man's wide, wrinkled forehead. He resembles the Taliban members I saw in 2000—an unruly long black beard, a white-striped black turban curled on his head with his right ear exposed, khaki-colored *pirahan tomban* with the pants rolled up to show his ankles. He sits between Ali and another elderly man, a neighbor of Basira's. The other men sit cross-legged like him but they fold their feet neatly under their legs. He exposes his dark brown feet, a sign of uncouthness. He wears a watch, but I can't make out what brand. I wonder if it's a Rodo, like Touraj used to wear.

I sit across the room on another mat, my back against a window.

Haji is a title for men who have made the pilgrimage to Mecca, and *Sufi* is a Muslim mystic. In Haji Sufi, I had expected an overpowering, loud Pashtun man—my image of a southern smuggler—but Sufi is soft-spoken and passive.

He says he's between forty and forty-five years old, but Ali, translating, says he's closer to forty-six. "He's illiterate and doesn't know how to count from the year he was born," Ali adds. Haji Sufi owns five acres of his family's fifteen acres of land. He denies growing opium on his farm, but, again, Ali adds the truth to his translation. "He farms opium but he's too scared to tell you."

Still, maybe because I'm a woman, or because I'm a foreigner, Sufi feels comfortable talking fairly openly with me. "I used to grow opium but now I plant wheat, watermelons, and have pine nut trees in the orchard," he says. "I have no cars, no motorcycles, just donkeys and tractors. Everything's expensive and hard without opium, but the government has forbid its planting now."

Ali translates with skepticism in his voice.

I move to a safer topic. "Tell me about your family in Helmand. How many children and grandchildren do you have?"

He says he has four daughters and four sons; the youngest is eighteen. His first wife's name is Khwaga; she's thirty years old and his first cousin, but she's ill. "She's bloated and she gets shots to feel better."

"Did she give you permission to marry another girl?"

"Yes, she did, because she cannot meet my needs anymore. She can't even do housework. But she complains that I married a young girl who won't be good for anything."

"Why did you?"

"My relatives had imprisoned Touraj in Helmand and he needed help," Haji Sufi explains, avoiding my gaze. "He owed ten thousand dollars to my relatives. I gave him forty-six hundred, and in return, he gave me his daughter's hand. He told me she was twenty years old. I never saw her but I agreed to it. If I had known she was so young, I would've given her to my son instead. But we did the *nikah* in Helmand, with Touraj. It's too late to give her to my son now."

The *nikah* is the Islamic ceremony that weds a man and woman. In some regions the woman does not need to agree to the marriage if she's underage. In more enlightened interpretations of the *nikah*, the woman must agree to the marriage during the ceremony. The ceremony, presided over by a cleric, consists of a gathering of men, including the groom and close family of both the groom and the bride. The bride chooses two witnesses and a representative, usually the father or older family member, to present her answer to the cleric when he asks if the bride is in agreement to the marriage. When the question is asked during the ceremony, the witnesses come to the bride, who's normally in a green dress among women in a separate room, and ask her three times if she wants to marry the groom. Often Afghan brides keep silent to show that they are modest, but silence is interpreted as assent. The witnesses then return to the cleric and deliver the bride's response. Later, if the groom divorces her, his family must give a *mahr*, or financial restitution, to the bride personally. Such economic agreements are documented on paper, with the signatures of those present, including those of the bride and groom.

But for Darya, her father's approval was enough to marry her to Haji Sufi.

"But she is not happy with this marriage," I tell Haji Sufi carefully, trying not to offend him. "She is scared to go with you."

"I do not want to force Darya to come with me, but eventually she will have to agree. In our traditions, girls do not have the right to decide whom they marry. It's the father's right, and her father promised her to me. I will be patient, but I am her husband. I have come here six or seven times now in the last two years, and her father's not here each time I come. I gave this family two years until she's old enough to separate from her mother, and now those two years are up." His voice rises and his brow forms a frown. He answers my questions, but his anger is directed at Ali, the man currently responsible for Darya.

I sip my tea. Darya walks in with her baby sister, Hana, in her arms. She hunches next to me and tugs on my coat. Her fingers tremble. "Please don't let him take me," she whispers to me.

Her words echo in my ear and I turn toward her. I look at her as if I'm seeing her for the first time. She's not crying but she's imploring me, a complete stranger. Her plea and desperation slowly sink in. Our eyes meet and I look away from her. Am I her last hope?

But what can I do? I'm in a male-controlled society that blames women for their unfortunate fate. The laws may protect women, but the majority of the citizens will not. In the eyes of the men and women I meet in the villages, girls who set themselves on fire out of desperation are selfish, women who fight back are shameless, and women who run away are prostitutes.

Darya's family and neighbors want her to go to Helmand in order to keep the family's name respectful. It's shameful enough that she was sold to an opium smuggler, but it will be more of a dishonor if she runs away or divorces her husband.

The three men in the room notice Darya's entrance and closeness to me, but they do not acknowledge her. Sufi does not look at her. He stares at his glass of tea. "I want her to become my wife's friend, like her sister. I will treat them with justice, but I will give them separate quarters. My wife is ill and needs help around the house. I expect this girl to help her, but she is too unruly and rebellious right now. She needs to be trained, and we hope, in time, she will change."

"He wants me to become his slave," she whispers.

Ali pauses in his translation and turns to me to comment. "He has been here only three times, not five or six like he says. He's getting restless, but I think she's still too young to go."

"Why does she have to go if she doesn't want to?" I ask Ali, fully knowing the answer.

"Because it's not a choice for any of us," he says.

Darya's marriage is not a union between man and woman but an opium deal that has to be fulfilled to save her family. She is the sacrifice for the greater good. I realize that her marriage is not about honor but about lives. Haji Sufi may have the power to kill her entire family if he's jilted. He can simply unleash his relatives, the ones who jailed Darya's father, to attack them in Ghoryan. What Darya wants is irrelevant.

Ali tells Sufi that Darya's still too young to go. Sufi objects, "She must be thirteen. She looks like a woman already." Then he softens his tone. "But I will be patient and then we will talk. I come here and bring gifts and food each time. I don't want to force her, so maybe when she's fourteen, fifteen, she will know what's good for her. I want her to like me."

"You're a good man, we know," Ali tells him. "She just needs time."

I sit in silence for a few minutes as they talk in Pashto together. Haji Sufi may be a good man compared with other ruthless drug dealers, but everyone in the room is treating Darya like property. Her family is accepting her loss too easily. I feel my anger directed at her mother and uncle. They can help her if they go to the government and ask for protection, can't they?

Saboora and Basira enter the room. Saboora grabs Darya's hand, ordering her to come to the kitchen. It's close to lunchtime, and I should not overstay my welcome. I finish my cup of tea and excuse myself. I walk toward the kitchen to talk to Darya, but Saboora stops me. "She has to cook lunch now," she says. "She's busy."

My head's spinning from the charged emotions of the last few hours. Saboora's rudeness irks me, but I know I should not push her to let me see Darya. Saboora seems to be more of a mother to their family than Basira. She wants to protect the family and their privacy. I hope I can come back. Darya has become a part of my life, not just a character in a story. I leave Ghoryan for Herat city to rest.

Over the next few days at Sattar Agha's, I sit in the garden surrounded by grapevines and purple petunias and consider what I could do to help Darya. I swirl my glass of green tea like it's wine and ponder my last few weeks in Ghoryan.

"You can't do anything," my cousin Neela insists. She sits across the table from me in the garden, her legs crossed. "You can report it to the government, but they won't do anything. That might harm her more. You can tell the Americans, but I don't think they care. Besides, do you want to be responsible for risking the rest of the family's lives? I think you should just report your story so that people can become aware of it." Neela has just summarized in one breath the options I have been ruminating on for hours.

"Yes, I know, but this is different," I say. "She's not going to be a normal bride. God knows what will happen to her when he takes her to Helmand. I know that she's not alone. There are thousands like her, but when she reached out to me, she became a part of me. I can't explain it. Maybe I see myself in her. Maybe I see the fate of this country in her struggle."

Neela is a twenty-four-year-old student of fine arts. She draws miniatures on hand-blown blue glass and expresses her frustrations and feelings with paint on canvas. One of her paintings hangs on her family's living room wall. It depicts a somber woman behind steel bars. Above the bars is a realistic version of the Kaaba, the house of God, in Mecca. Under the Kaaba is an eye with tears dripping down. "That's how I felt under the Taliban," Neela explains. "I had to stay home and study in secret." She's devout and committed. She fasts once a week, even when it's not Ramadan, and prays five times a day. Her head scarf stays on in the house, sometimes even covering her serious brown eyes. However, contrary to the common stereotypes of devout women, Neela is not submissive. She takes advantage of any rights she was given after the fall of the Taliban. "We have to take back the religion they tried to take away from us," she tells me during one of our soul-searching conversations. She plans to choose her own husband, finish university, work outside the house, and be financially independent.

"I would run away if I were Darya," I say. "I couldn't become a slave. What would you do?" I ask Neela.

"The same, but what happens to girls who run away here?" she asks rhetorically.

"The female prisons are full of runaways," I say, nodding. "It's a crime to run away from becoming a slave. How can I ever accept this element of life in Afghanistan? It disgusts me. It's a part of who we are, it's our dark side, and Afghan men and women will sit here and tell me that Darya's to blame for rebelling against becoming property. Even educated people believe this, not just illiterate women like her mother. How can I ever accept that? How can you?" I say to Neela.

"You have the luxury of an American passport. You can leave

when it gets hard. We find ways around it. I'm lucky I come from an open-minded family." Then she says with her usual candor, "If it disgusts you, why do you keep returning here? I don't think it's just for work."

"Because I can't stay away."

It's July 2003 and my third time back in Afghanistan. The traveling back and forth from Afghanistan to the United States is a physical manifestation of how my identity wavers, how often I can change nationalities, hiding one and bringing forth the other. I can both wear a head scarf without much trouble and walk around in a bathing suit by a pool full of men. For my female cousins in Herat, swimming half naked in front of men is an unthinkable sin. For some of my American female friends, wearing a head scarf would be a blatant offense to their freedom.

The incoherence in this actually gives me comfort. But it also takes away any sense of rootedness. When people talk about feeling grounded, I wonder what they mean. I don't feel grounded or have a sense of home. I had an imaginary home, Herat, until I returned in 2000 and saw the changes there. I am envious of those who call one place home and enjoy a sense of belonging, of ownership of that place. In the Afghanistan of my childhood, I remember feeling that sense of belonging during the war. My world was simple, intact, innocent like Darya's green eyes. Afghanistan was falling apart, but I felt whole.

In Darya, I see the Afghanistan both of my childhood and of my adulthood. I see a connection to my homeland in this frightened girl. I barely know her, but I feel like I've known her all my life. She is Afghanistan—her beauty and innocence, her resistance to control, her yearning for independence, her desperation, her plea for help to an outsider. Throughout its history, Afghanistan has been trying to form an identity outside of foreign interference while seeking help from those same foreigners. Now it is no different. The United States and its allies say they are here to save Afghanistan, but they are destroying it at the same time. I hope I won't do the same to Darya.

EIGHT
Traveling on the Border of Death

A few days after meeting Haji Sufi, Saber and I go to Darya's house again. But when we arrive, no one opens the door. I can hear voices inside, but our knocks are ignored. A young boy with unwashed hair comes out of the house across the street.

"They don't want you coming over anymore. They are afraid that their father might find out they're talking to you and he might beat them," he informs me.

"Where's Darya? Did she go with her husband?" I ask.

"I saw her playing outside yesterday, even though she should be inside helping her mother," the boy says. Even this boy, who is about eight or nine years old, is judgmental of bold Darya.

"We should leave," Saber admonishes. "Maybe they're afraid

she's turning to you for help and you might take her from them."

I feel rejected but relieved that Haji Sufi has not yet taken Darya. I decide to return another day. Saber and I drive toward the home of Gandomi Soltanzi, the widow who lost her husband and four of her children and who owes a large opium debt. She opens the door and flashes me a toothless smile. She begins complaining right away.

"The damn smuggler won't leave me alone—that godforsaken Haji Sardar wants the little land I have left. Can you ask the Americans to shoot him?" she pleads. "It would be a favor to mankind."

I offer to speak to this notorious smuggler.

The most feared drug lords in Ghoryan are cousins, Sardar and Paiman, who live on the dirt road running between Herat city and Ghoryan town. Their twin two-story houses, with manicured gardens and locked brass gates, tower over the rows of walled-in, dilapidated mud homes. The cousins hail from a smaller village in the desert called Haft Chah (Seven Wells), which breeds drug dealers with important connections in Iran. Their village is the only one where I've seen four-by-four trucks and $1,000 satellite phones.

Sardar and Paiman are illiterate hajis. They made the obligatory trip to Mecca three years ago. Many Ghoryan residents respect them for that title and their rise to affluence. They were shepherds, then refugees working construction jobs in Iran, and now they have carte blanche in the district as the leading drug lords. They're part of the new mafia in Afghanistan. Their cronies terrorize women and families with opium debts.

Yet even they have lost men to the drug business. Sardar, thirty-five, supports his sister's and brother's families since their men died smuggling narcotics. Sardar has an untrimmed beard and small, round hands. Puffy circles under his eyes and a pudgy nose stand out on his deep brown face. He agrees to an interview under the condition that we not talk about his smuggling activities, but he says he will give his opinion on the issue.

"This route [Ghoryan to Iran] has belonged to smugglers since Afghanistan's history," he tells me. "It's not a shame or a crime. People here do it because they are hungry."

Inside his spotless seven-bedroom house, the whispers of his wives and extended family echo from behind closed doors. Jasmine incense burns in the large living room. Sardar sits cross-legged spitting tobacco juice into a decorated container on the gleaming Persian carpet, next to his adopted daughter, Sepida, ten, who sports sunglasses. Behind them are half a dozen vases with colorful artificial flowers. In the middle of the vases is a fourteen-inch framed photograph of Sardar in his younger years, without the beard, turban, or wrinkles he has now.

Sardar says he has everything in life he could want, except for children. He has three young wives and, under Afghan law, which is based on Islam, is allowed to marry one more, but instead he has decided to travel to Pakistan for fertility treatments. He says his family made their money from sheepherding and money changing. They have a currency trade in the town's main market, which serves as a front for their drug business, according to locals. Sardar says his fortune amounts to only $20,000. He has not had any problems with any change of government—he was friends with the Taliban and now he's friends with the new coalition-backed government. "I'm illiterate and do not interfere in politics," he says. "My family's able to adapt to government changes."

I snap a few photos of Haji Sardar and his adopted daughter, Sepida, his slain brother's child. She and Sardar sit next to each other, both with legs crossed, their hands on their laps. Sepida leaves on her purple sunglasses while Sardar tilts his head to the side. They both look at the camera with straight faces. Sepida wears a hint of a smile. Then I ask politely if I can meet Sardar's wives. He dithers but agrees. A confident second-grader, Sepida waltzes over to the marble-floored kitchen and introduces me to the women of the house. A dozen women huddle behind the tiled kitchen counters, eyeing me. The three wives come forward; they are light skinned with light eyes, all from his Badorzi tribe. Their faces are made up like China dolls: the foundation is lighter than their skin, their green and blue eye shadow is applied beyond the boundaries of their eyes, and their lipstick is glossy and thick. They wear *tomban,* the loose white hand-embroidered pants afforded only by wealthy city women. The fine silk embroidery of the pants is done best by the women of Herat and Kandahar. I wear the two white *tombans* I own under dresses on special occasions. These women seem to wear them on a routine day. I smile at them, and they return the gesture.

"You have a beautiful house," I tell them. "You're very lucky, because most people here cannot live in homes like this."

"Thank you. *Chishma shama maqboola* [your eyes are beautiful]," one of the women responds. "Your eyes are beautiful" is a Farsi response to a compliment from a woman.

"How can you afford all this?" I ask.

I do not know that Sardar has been standing behind the doorway listening. As soon as I ask this question, he appears and interrupts the conversation.

"It's getting late, and they have guests coming. They have to get ready for them," he tells me. "Go away!" he commands them.

Later that day, Saber and I are talking to a shopkeeper on the main road when a large, shiny motorcycle races toward us and suddenly brakes. It's Sardar, wearing sunglasses and a leather jacket, his black turban wrapped tightly. He resembles the villains in Bollywood films. He climbs off the vehicle and commands Saber, "Where's the camera she took pictures with in my house? I want her to erase the pictures of us. Now!"

He ignores me, but before Saber can respond, I take out the camera from my purse and give it to him. It's a thirty-five-millimeter Canon, but Sardar thinks it's a digital and looks for the screen to view the images.

"There's film in there," I say.

"Take it out! I want to see it," he hollers.

"Haji Sahib, why are you so upset?" Saber says, trying to calm him. "She's not going to do anything bad with the pictures."

"I don't want my photos in any newspapers in America or Europe," Sardar explains.

"But I have many other photos and if you take out the film, it will destroy everything. Do you want to be responsible for destroying all my photos?" I ask. "I'll make you copies of your photos when I develop the film."

Sardar hands me back the camera. He's not happy, but he appears reluctant to push me further. He turns to Saber again. "If my photos are published, somebody will pay for it."

I choose not to mention the widow Gandomi to Sardar, because it might hurt her more if he is aware that I know he is intimidating her. I have no power in Ghoryan, despite the impression the residents seem to have of me. They think I can help them merely because I come from the United States.

Across the street, a retired smuggler named Zikria is watching the incident with Sardar with keen interest. As Sardar speeds away, Zikria walks over to us to inquire. "I can tell you all about drug smuggling, if you'd like," he offers. "It was my occupation not too long ago. Come over to my house when you'd like."

Later, at home, Saber tells me about Zikria. "He was one of the biggest smugglers in all of Afghanistan not too long ago."

"Why did he quit?" I ask.

"I guess he was losing money like the others. Now his family's into robbing jewelry stores and currency exchanges. But he's easy to talk to," he says reassuringly, "so let's pay him a visit."

When we visit Zikria's large, untidy house, his ten-year-old son, Cyrus, greets us and takes us over to his father, relaxing on a large carpet-covered cushion. Zikria is a jovial businessman, cracking jokes and smoking a cigarette. A mass of black curls frames his expressive face. He's about six feet tall and thirty-two years old.

In the 1990s, Zikria loaded up ten men, each armed with a Ka-lashnikov, in his Nissan truck and headed for the Iranian mountains carrying hundreds of kilos of opium. Of the twenty-one of his closest trafficking allies in Ghoryan, he is the only who is still free and alive.

Zikria's foray into the drug business began with his desire for a woman. The maverick wanted to marry a second wife. The father of the girl he chose asked for a $14,000 bride price, and the opium trade was the fastest way for Zikria to get it.

"I borrowed fifteen hundred kilos of opium from farmers in the south and took it to Iran. In two instances other traffickers shot at us from afar, and I turned onto unmarked trails to lose the gunmen. Many traffickers die in battles with other smugglers wanting to steal their dope, arms, or money. Our crew reached the mountain where the opium was to be unloaded, buried it underground, and hid our vehicle behind trees. It took thirty days before our Iranian contact appeared at the bottom of the mountain.

"Iranian shepherds deliver messages between Afghan vendors and Iranian buyers, and, in return, take a cut of opium from both sides. The same shepherds serve as informants to the Iranian government."

Zikria considers himself lucky. He made it back to present the $14,000 to the girl's father and married her. His son, Cyrus, is the offspring of that marriage—he sits next to his father, proudly listening.

"How do you survive now?" I ask Zikria.

"We sell legal things," he answers, bored with the question. "I've learned my lesson."

While Sardar's active dealing as a drug lord caused him to be distant and distrustful toward me, Zikria's retirement from drugs allows him to open up and divulge information. While Sardar is nouveau riche, with flashy taste in home decoration, Zikria shows a more urban flavor in clothes and décor. He doesn't flaunt his wealth. But both men display the typical lifestyle of an Afghan smuggler: the multiple wives, the large homes. They're both criminals who should be prosecuted, but instead they punish the innocent with their crimes.

With a 40 percent unemployment rate, drug smuggling is the best paying and most available job in Afghanistan. An American DEA agent who has worked in Afghanistan puts the chain of the narcotics link in this order: farmers—broker—trafficker—transporter, (courier/smuggler)—processor—broker—transporter, (courier/smuggler)—distributor—dealer. "The drug business model is very fluid, and any one of these functions may be skipped or combined, with a trafficker operating as his own broker or a transporter also being a distributor. Interestingly, marijuana dispensaries in California combine all of these functions into one-stop shopping," he says.

There are few codes to communicate with or rules to engage in—it's not a corporation—but it is managed by money. The currency exchanged between drug vendors is U.S. dollars, and they deal in crisp $100 bills. Drug trafficking is mixed with weapons smuggling: drugs are exported, and arms made with drug money are imported on all sides of the Afghan border. American troops have seized Iranian-made weapons used by the Taliban several times. NATO officials tell me that the Taliban exchange drugs for weapons with corrupt Revolutionary Guard soldiers, an elite branch of Iran's military. In a bazaar in Tajikistan bordering the Badakhshan region of Afghanistan, merchants trade heroin for guns. The weapons are disassembled and smuggled into Afghanistan on donkeys. "We trade a kilogram of heroin for ten Kalakovs or fifteen [old-model] Kalashnikovs," a trader told a journalist from the Institute for War and Peace Reporting in 2008. "After that, we sell them to smugglers from Helmand and Kandahar either for cash or for more heroin." But the Taliban are not the only ones who buy the weapons. Aminullah Amarkhil, the former head of security at Kabul Airport, told an Australian journalist that he had caught American private contractors smuggling weapons parts in their luggage.

Tribes with ties to the Taliban tend to be in charge of border control in the east and south. Traffickers pay the Taliban to protect their drug convoys, and in some cases the Taliban are the traffickers. But in the north, it's a free-for-all—drugs are simply a business that Taliban sympathizers, government officials, the police, and merchants all take part in, and control rests with the particular mafia ruling the area. About 65 percent of opium is processed into a morphine base or heroin inside Afghanistan; the rest may be raw opium. Iran is the quickest route to Europe, with 50 percent of the drug smuggled through Iran, but large quantities leave also through the northern and Pakistan borders. Morphine base and raw opium may also be transported to Turkey, where established illegal laboratories refine them into injectable heroin.

Russian authorities report that 175 drug syndicates, or mafias, operate from Afghanistan, including Russian mafias. Internationally, the Pakistani-based Quetta Alliance, which involves the Pakistani truckers who smuggle all types of goods across borders, is closest to the Taliban. Firms owned and operated by the Pakistani military are linked to the Quetta Alliance. The DEA says the Quetta Alliance is responsible for large shipments of heroin and morphine base to Europe and the United States. Nigerian drug trafficking organizations also move Afghan drugs to West African syndicates inside the United States, who then team up with African-American gangs to supply consumers. Experienced Turkish organized crime groups include the Uzan group, led by Turkish businessman/politician Cem Uzan, and the Britain-based Arifs, who run Afghan opiates to Europe. Albanian mafias are also connected to the Afghan heroin trail. And as India has become a more popular transit route for drugs, Dawood Ibrahim, the Indian crime boss, has dabbled in Afghan heroin deals. Domestically, Afghan mafia groups include the Afridis and Shinwaris, working in eastern Afghanistan and the Khyber Pass in Pakistan. The United States and Great Britain have had success in removing several Afghan kingpins, including Haji Bashir Noorzai, Haji Juma Khan, Haji Bagcho, and Haji Baz Mohammad, but their networks still operate.

During the Taliban years and in the beginning of Karzai's rule, narcotics were exported from Kabul Airport to the Arab Gulf on commercial flights. Gulf Arabs are prominent investors in Afghan drugs, and wealthy Afghan and Pakistani drug dealers maintain lavish homes in the United Arab Emirates. According to the *New York Times*, $1 billion to $2.5 billion a year is transferred from Afghanistan to the UAE. Before U.S. intervention, investors flew in on Afghan Ariana Airlines to meet with the Taliban and flew out on the same planes with boxes stashed with narcotics. The planes landed in UAE airports with impunity. After Amarkhil was hired in 2005, better technology and police work allowed him to capture more than one hundred heroin traffickers en route to Dubai. The arrests prompted smugglers to begin ingesting the drugs in protected capsules and to change their destination to Urumqi, China. Amarkhil says he did not have an X-ray machine but could recognize drug mules by their dry lips and dehydrated state. Mules often look drugged, managing as they do up to one hundred white capsules the size of a hot dog and filled with fifty to a hundred grams of narcotics. They carry exactly $1,000 with them and have dozens of visas stamped on their passports. Once Amarkhil detained the mules, he either got a confession from them or sent them to a clinic that was equipped with an X-ray machine. One Pakistani man Amarkhil caught at the airport admitted to carrying 111 capsules in his bowel. The man also carried hair oil, to help him excrete the contents when he reached China.

Unfortunately, Amarkhil was too good at his job. After nabbing a powerful woman smuggler with connections to the government, the Afghan attorney general fired him.

Large and organized drug cartels like those in Latin America and Southeast Asia are not common in Afghanistan. The country is still ruled by community links, which protect ordinary people. No one drug baron controls more than a three-hundred-kilometer stretch of road. There aren't death squads roaming the country—not yet anyway. But with its combination of a weak and corrupt central government, a shattered economy, and an insurgency that benefits from narcotics trafficking, Afghanistan is an incubator for drug cartels.

The wealthy drug merchants launder opium cash inside and outside the country in a variety of businesses, including real estate, construction projects, car dealerships, and currency exchanges. If the opium business suddenly closed down—an unlikely scenario—Afghanistan would suffer immeasurable economic consequences.

Zikria and Sardar are the experienced smugglers in the chain, but I want to meet the younger generation of drug dealers, to see how a young man or woman becomes involved in such a deadly job. When

I ask Saber to find an amateur dealer, he points to our driver that day, Jalal. Limber and lanky, Jalal is a small-time dealer new to the business. He's eighteen, with cropped hair, a straight nose, and a clean-shaven face. Eager to show his fearlessness, he explains how he's just benefited from his first year of opium harvest. He learned from the Taliban how to turn his wheat and watermelon fields into poppy blossoms. His family's harvest in Ghoryan yielded twenty kilos of raw opium.

"My father asked me if I wanted a wife and a car," Jalal says on one of our long drives. "I said I want two cars. I now transport passengers for twenty dollars round trip from Ghoryan to Herat city. I had nothing, not even a bicycle last year. Now I feel rich and I have a job."

His long, thin fingers tap on the steering wheel while we listen to Iranian pop. He leaves all the windows of his station wagon open and frequently sticks out his arm to wave at people we pass by. Jalal says his best friend also began dealing drugs recently. On the way to his best friend's house, Jalal stops to salute a group of men on the street. One offers him eight kilos of opium for his car. Jalal eyes the station wagon's steering wheel like a five-year-old boy with a new toy. "I just got this and I can't give it up for less than ten kilos. Let's talk later," he says, accelerating.

Jalal's best friend is Tarek, a chubby mustachioed twenty-three-year-old who manages dozens of acres of land belonging to families living outside the country. A year ago he planted opium on that land and now has enough money for his wedding. He bought a brand-new Honda motorcycle and painted his concrete house white.

Chatting inside his newly painted house, Tarek brings out his fresh batch of black opium, a bitter, gooey liquid. "If you sell, you don't use it. We have people test to see if it's pure or not. They're addicts," Tarek says, tying the plastic bag filled with half a kilo of the treasure and hiding it away.

Jalal and Tarek say they are taking part in a Ghoryan tradition, but unless they are desperate, they will not cross the border with drugs. "We deal here and hire the shepherds as our fall guys. This is the only way to stay alive and become rich," Jalal says, his smile turning smug.

We exit the house. Saber and I decide to walk the several blocks to his house. Jalal leaves the station wagon parked inside Tarek's yard and says he'll meet us later if we need him. Like two eagles taking off from a mountaintop, the best friends ride off on Tarek's motorcycle, leaving a trail of dust.

These two young men like the new government, since they have the contacts in it that others do not. Jalal says the district government sends a six-member commission in the fall to view the cultivated land and asks for a kilo per half an acre. In exchange, the government does not destroy the crops. One hazy morning, Saber, Jalal, and I visit the police intelligence unit in Ghoryan. The assistant intelligence director gets up to welcome us and then directs his attention toward Jalal. "I'm upset with your father," the bearded official says. "He didn't give me my share. I expect that share."

"I think my father gave enough this year," Jalal replies under his breath. It's obvious they're talking about the official's share of the opium profits. The conversation comes to a halt when Mohammad Sobhan, the intelligence chief of Ghoryan, arrives. He offers to show me videos of the government destroying opium crops. I politely decline.

"I'd actually like to know how you capture smugglers and how many smugglers are jailed right now?"

"Very few," Sobhan says.

"How many are in the local jail right now?"

He shifts his legs and fidgets with the papers on his desk. "I'm not sure there are any, and if there are, they usually are released within a week."

"Why is that?" I insist.

"We can't be very hard on these guys, because we don't have the manpower to fight them, or the weapons. They are much stronger than the government. We do not have a unified government in Herat. If we capture them, they get out with a bribe and then run to Zir Koh," he admits. Zir Koh is a nearby district run by Ismail Khan's rival, mujahideen commander Amanullah Khan. He is notorious for alleged drug running.

Jalal is concerned about his father. After we've left the official's office, he says, "When families don't want to give a cut, the government eliminates their crop."

"Do you think that man will hurt your father?" I ask, referring to the official.

"No, he doesn't have the power, but he might destroy our crops next year. I'll tell my father," he replies with fake confidence.

Ghoryan residents do not trust the government officials or the police. On a cool, star-filled night, a crowd gathers around a pyre of burning hashish at the Ghoryan fort. The stench is like skunk spray, mixed with the aroma of burning wood. The police chief has just weeded out some hashish plants from a local farm and is burning them in public to scare residents off from farming drugs. It is show and tell, and everyone seems to know it. One of the bystanders whispers to Saber, "They probably kept most of it hidden in the fort to sell later."

In Herat province in the summer of 2003, Ismail Khan was the warlord and self-proclaimed emir. He had an army of twenty thousand soldiers backed by Iran. Publicly, he condemned the drug trade and supported a treatment clinic for the booming number of addicts in western Afghanistan. But Khan prohibited the central Afghan antinarcotics office from opening a branch in his fiefdom, saying there was already a bureau operating under his control. Still, if he was reaping the benefits of opium trafficking, the evidence was hard to find.

The question was how could he be so powerful without the support of drug traffickers? He may have been ignoring the men and mafia that could threaten his fiefdom, allowing them to do their business while he controlled most of the province. Despite the tight security in the region—Herat at this time was one of the most peaceful provinces in Afghanistan—big traffickers continued to cross from the Afghan side of the border into Iran.

In 2004, Karzai forced Ismail Khan to give up his control of Herat with the help of American bombers. An aim of the Afghan central government was to exercise control over Herat and have access to the customs revenues Ismail Khan had spent developing the province. Karzai gave Ismail Khan the job of running the Ministry of Energy in Kabul, and Khan accepted. But after his departure, drug trafficking remained in place, if it didn't increase, and the peace Heratis once enjoyed ended as robberies, kidnappings, and corruption skyrocketed. The violence slowed the pace of reconstruction. Khan's absence from Herat allowed lower-ranking commanders to solidify their place in the drug trade and magnified the crimes associated with the business.

Meanwhile, Iran tackled the low-level border war with a vengeance. It had lost more than 3,700 troops on the border fighting traffickers since 1979. With a growing addict population, the Iranian government was desperate to keep drugs out of the country. But it wasn't just Afghans who were smuggling drugs. Double agents inside Iran's intelligence agencies dabbled in drug dealing and betrayed their own comrades in the battle zone. After spending billions fighting the trade over the previous thirty years, Iran requested monetary aid from the United Nations, estimating that it would need another $3 billion to continue its battle in the next few years. With more than 100,000 troops stationed on the border, Iran also installed six hundred miles of barbed-wire fence, trench systems, canals, and cement barriers to stop the traffickers. Its border with Afghanistan stretched 575 miles, but the barbed-wire fence and canals extended into the Pakistan border. Iran also now used remote security surveillance and control systems to prevent the flow of narcotics. The results were impressive: in 2009, Iran seized a thousand tons of opium, 85 percent of the globe's opium seizures. But the seizures, the executions of drug traffickers, and the billions spent did not stop the other tons of narcotic that crossed the border.

In 2000, when I travel to Iran on my way to Herat, I have a guide in Tehran, Shahram, who helps me navigate the metropolis. His arrow-like eyebrows frame large brown eyes and he wears the same brown shirt and black slacks every time I see him. Shahram is a twenty-five-year-old civil servant who wants to get married but doesn't have the money for a wedding. One day, we have a lunch of sandwiches with bologna and pickles on a bench in a quiet, pristine park in the upscale neighborhood of Vali Asr. After lunch, he lights up a hashish joint after making sure no police are on site and begins to lament about life in Tehran, a city of ten million.

"I smoke because I'm bored and unhappy," he says. "There are no jobs in this city to move one forward in life. I'm from the south of this city and we are middle class among the poor there. I'm lucky I have a government job, but I make seventy dollars a month." He takes a slow drag of hashish, looks at the pink roses in front of us, and sighs.

"What do you want to do that you can't do?" I ask.

"Be somebody—a doctor, an engineer, a musician—but I didn't get accepted to university because my test scores were low and I don't have any artistic skills. I have to help support my family, so I'm stuck in a dead-end job. The only job I can do to make more money is be a drug dealer."

"Do you know any other men your age who are doing that?"

"Too many of the boys in my neighborhood do it, too many."

Later, in the basement of Shahram's sparsely furnished home in southern Tehran, I meet two of his friends who are drug dealers. They tell me what happens to the Afghan drugs once they reach Iran.

Mehdi, twenty-four, and Hassan, twenty, were both schooled in minor drug dealing on Tehran's streets, though they both have other day jobs. They each have around twenty regular customers, ranging from laborers to doctors. They make about $100 to $200 a month—not much, considering the risks they take to avoid the police, but the job pays for their daily expenses. Like Shahram, they are both single and live with their parents. Both of them are high school graduates but cannot find steady work that makes more than drug dealing. Their illicit merchandise includes not only opium and heroin, but also vodka, cognac, hashish, and, for the wealthier customers, cocaine. Alcohol is prohibited in Iran and Afghanistan.

Mehdi, a soft-spoken, thoughtful truck driver, plays with his mustache while he speaks. He says when he first started dealing several years ago, he would go to Mashad, the most populated Iranian city close to the Afghan border, load up his truck with bricks—the bricks were filled with opium and heroin—and then come to Tehran, distribute to smaller dealers, and keep some of the product for himself, to sell on the streets.

"Where did you get the drugs?" I ask him.

"There were the wholesale dealers who risk their lives to cross the border. They're almost all Afghans. We bought from them, but our profit margin is nothing like it is when it goes to the West. People can't afford that here."

He takes a piece of opium the size of a pill out of plastic wrap, saying, "This is the amount I normally sell now. It sells for about fifteen hundred *toman* [two dollars]. The profits are less, but so are the risks. We don't have a set price. Profit depends on friendship—if the man is close to you, you give him a cheaper price."

A few years prior to our meeting, the Tehran police captured Mehdi for transporting large amounts of drugs. He spent three nights in jail and received forty lashes before being released. He was frightened enough to revert to small-time dealing inside Tehran.

"I heard they hang Afghans. Are they easier on Iranian dealers?" I ask.

"They hang Afghan smugglers. It all depends on how much you're caught with and how many times. They'll hang Iranians, too, but Afghans have it much worse," he admits.

Hassan, a soldier, plays with the cast on his foot. He broke his foot jumping a fence. He says he has young boys, not even teenagers, who come up to him to buy but that he refuses to sell to children. He confesses that he smokes hashish three times a day because he has nothing to look forward to. "This life is it," he says, sighing just like Shahram did.

Mehdi and Hassan both explain why Iran has the biggest drug addiction problem in the world: a lack of jobs and freedom.

"I think there's too much freedom in America," Mehdi says. "That's why there's a drug problem. And I think there is no freedom in Iran, and that's why there's a drug problem here."

"Are you ashamed of what you're doing?" I ask both of them.

Mehdi answers: "In this part of Tehran, in every family, there's an addict and a dealer. In my family, my father's the addict and I'm the dealer. Opium smoking is like cigarette smoking here."

"If we could find a job that pays more and lets us be our own bosses, we would give this up," Hassan says.

Mehdi, who at first defended his actions, looks down at the floor and scratches his mustache. "In a country where dignity is everything, we give up our dignity every day."

This cycle of poverty and unemployment leads to smuggling and drug use across the globe. Men and women in Afghanistan become smugglers because they cannot find alternative work, and the drugs they carry to Iran are sold and consumed by the unemployed and disillusioned. What is the difference between Jalal, the teenage Afghan smuggler, and the Iranian Hassan? Jalal lives in a village in one of the the world's poorest countries consumed by drugs, and Hassan is a resident of a much wealthier and educated nation that is also consumed by drugs. Jalal is not an addict yet, but I wonder how long he will remain just a dealer.

The frontier of Iran and Afghanistan is a two-hour drive from Ghoryan town, through minefields and over dirt roads. The length of the border where Ghoryan is situated cannot be crossed legally, because there are no customs officials or a border patrol. Saber knows a family in Gorgabad, a village right on the border. We hire a van with a young driver, Fawad, willing to risk his life with us across the wild desert. We depart at dawn headed against the sunrise; Iran is westward. Despite the thuds and thumps under the tires, I fall asleep.

"Wake up, Fariba Jan. We're here," Saber says, cheerful.

We've reached Gorgabad, an enclave with several dozen families. We knock at the wooden door of a house Saber knows. The women come out smiling. They hug me when they hear I'm a guest of Saber's. They make a feast, rice with *shorwa*, lamb soup with potatoes and garbanzo beans. The meal includes okra, eggplant, salad, and fresh watermelon for dessert. The family is poor, but as is typical in Afghanistan, they're generous. After Saber and I eat, we walk to the border.

Signs of modernization make it clear which nation dominates here. On the Afghan side, three sleepy-eyed guards come out of a bombed-out barrack. They eat bread and drink tea all day and sleep by the glow of a lantern as night falls. Each has a rifle in hand, but they say they have no communication devices, no vehicle or binoculars. They have little power to fight armed traffickers.

The guards deny working with smugglers and say that Iranians watch this place carefully for traffickers passing through. In the last two years, they have caught only five men, carrying ten kilos in sacks on their backs.

"They're probably too high to catch a fish, let alone traffickers," Saber says to me of the three guards.

Two hundred yards away is the Iranian border post, a two-story building with armed guards standing on all four sides scouting the vast desert with binoculars. Beyond a large, bullet-holed black stone and bushes of thorns is Iran, with its paved roads and electrical poles. Trenches and barbed wire divide parts of this border. The wild wind wails, blowing debris from Iran to Afghanistan.

The Afghan guards say they had a row with the Iranian guards recently because the latter shot some sheep one night for crossing the black stone—the border mark. The guards' orders are to shoot anything that moves past the foot-long rock. "We told them that sheep don't understand borders, and they are people's livelihoods," says Khan Mohammed, one of the Afghan soldiers. "They say they have to follow orders. They stick to the law and are scared to do anything without their superiors' orders."

I stand next to the black stone facing Iran, remembering my family's escape from Afghanistan. In 1982, after six hours on a donkey in the desert heat, I found that the sight of Iran literally quenched my thirst. I had refused to drink the salty well water from the desert during the journey and endured a dry mouth until we crossed the border to Iran and Mr. Jawan's relatives brought a bucket of cold water. I stuck my head in the red pail and drank like a dog. We walked through the battle zone of the mujahideen and the Soviets. The Iran border symbolized freedom and life for my family then. Iran had just experienced its Islamic Revolution and was in the throes of war with Iraq, while Afghanistan's Islamists fought communism. Both countries were in the grip of change, revolutions that would destroy the lives of millions. Nearly three decades later, I return to the border craving the peace that could justify the bloodshed of these revolutions. But the wind blows hard, and all I can see is dust.

Two weeks later Saber comes to Herat city, where I'm back at Sattar Agha's enjoying the greenery of the orchard and the company of my cousins. I had asked Saber to check on Darya through her neighbors and relatives. We converse outside Sattar Agha's on the street.

"Did Haji Sufi take her?" I ask him.

"The next morning, after we talked to him, the Ghoryan police questioned Haji Sufi on smuggling charges, but they let him go after a two-hour interrogation. I didn't have to go to Darya. She came to our house looking for you a week after you left."

My heart begins to pound. "What did she say?"

"She said, 'He has left but he swore to come back and take me. Can Fariba Jan make him go away? Please tell her to make him leave me alone.'"

I'm in a daze as I board the flight to Dubai en route to New York. My mind is swirling with unsettled issues. My thoughts shift to Darya. I'm not sure what I'm going to do for her, but I know I will be back to see her. The angry and desperate tone she used to tell her mother she did not want to be married to Haji Sufi still rings in my ears. The shine in her penetrating eyes revealed her fiery spirit to fight a future that threatened to enclose her behind mud-brick walls.

NINE

Where the Poppies Bloom

Spread out against an emerald-green mountain is a field of thin stalks five to ten inches high. The wind carries the leaves off the ground, but the stalks don't move. The sun shines on the dead plants. Every morning, Parween stands on the edge of the field, her scarf wrapped tightly around her head. Her wheat-shaped eyes gaze at her land; tears drop on her wrinkled olive skin.

"Why did they come to my field? Why did I become a target, why?" she thinks as she walks from her house to her field. "Who were the enemies who turned me in, or did they just find my land? My little acre is hidden away from the street, behind the mountain, visible to no outsiders."

Parween, a poppy farmer and mother of nine, lives in northeast Afghanistan, in the remote province of Badakhshan. The rain-fed earth her husband inherited is her family's livelihood. In June 2004, when I meet her near the capital, Faizabad, she is a victim of the Afghan government's haphazard poppy eradication campaign.

The Afghan government and its international backers have decided that the best way to rid Afghanistan of the opium trade is to tackle it at its root—by eliminating poppy farms. But the Kabul government has little to no control in this remote province. In 2004, Badakhshan, a magical, verdant landscape bordering Tajikistan, China, and Pakistan and snuggled in the Pamir Mountains, is the third largest poppy-producing province in Afghanistan. After the Communist government fell in 1992, mujahideen leader Ahmad Shah Massoud managed to keep the Taliban out of Badakhshan; since then the former mujahideen, now warlords and drug dealers, have ruled the area, which is part of the 10 percent of the country the Taliban were unable to seize during their seven-year reign.

Poppy farming has been a tradition here for centuries, but the level at which it's grown now, on thousands of acres of land, is unprecedented. During my time here, I uncover tales of triumph, alongside the countless tragedies, resulting from the drug trade in Badakhshan. The conventional wisdom that opium farming is a crime and hurts people is cast in doubt by experiences such as Parween's, which show both the tragedy and the triumph.

Parween is one of hundreds of women in Badakhshan who have bettered their lives through the opium business. These women are often landowners, and with the money they make they are able to purchase cars, clothes, and more land, and to build homes. The women landowners work side by side with the men, usually their sons, as their husbands may be too old and fragile. A 2000 UN report on the role of women in the cultivation of the drug trade, conducted before the poppy ban, confirms that the Taliban allowed women to work in poppy fields, which led to both an increased physical burden for women and financial gain. Women used the cash to improve nutrition for their families. It also gave them leverage and status in their villages. Even after the Taliban, some women profited, as in the case of Bibi Deendaray of Kandahar. She told UN surveyors in 2004, "In fact, I should say that it is not an illicit crop but rather a blessing. . . . It is the only means of survival for thousands of women-headed households, women and children in our village whose men are either jobless or were killed during the war."

Yet other women mentioned in the 2000 UN report complained that their families used them as unpaid labor, and that poppy farming had increased their workload. In addition to farming, they also had to perform housework, supervise livestock, engage in dairy production, and cook for migrant laborers. These overworked women lamented that they suffered from leg and back pain. They also said they had no time to teach moneymaking skills, such as embroidery, carpet weaving, and sewing, to their daughters, so that they could one day have a legitimate income. The report concludes that although women had more access to cash, decision making remained with the men in the family. Parween's case is an exception to the UN findings.

Men in Afghanistan, as in many other parts of the world, can marry women decades younger—Parween is forty-four, and her husband, Kemal, is sixty. He used to make a living from loading his donkey with sacks of bricks for delivery to construction sites. Now his back hurts and he needs to rest every hour. His wife is in charge of the household. When I meet her on a breezy, sunny day, she is grieving the loss of what could've been thousands of dollars in poppy profits.

I arrive at Parween's colorful home unannounced. Her daughter Samarkand answers the door and takes me to the field, where Parween is hunched over a wooden frame weaving a *gilim*, a flat hand-woven fabric that can be used as carpet or tapestry. Samarkand's daughter, Shakila, plays with her grandmother's waist-length black braids, which peek out of her burgundy scarf. The wooden frame is spread out on the field where they plant their poppy.

Parween is unlike the women I've met in Herat. She's physically stronger and more confident. She walks with flair and isn't shy about sharing her opinions. She does not waste time on lengthy Afghan greetings.

"The government came and destroyed my crops and gave me nothing in return. Go tell them that they need to give me something back," she orders me as she weaves. She does not look up to speak. The *gilim* she is creating is striped with earth colors—red, mustard, olive green.

A month before, in May, the poppy flowers bloomed, a breathtaking violet color. When the petals fell, Parween stayed in the field from sunrise to sunset lancing the bulb-size capsules. Planting and weeding the poppy had taken four months. Parween owns another half acre on top of the mountain, and there she planted potatoes, but the seeds failed to yield anything. Poppy's reward is ten times greater. A kilo of opium extracted from poppy plants can bring a profit of $30 to $400.

In 2003 she sold twenty kilos of dry opium for $8,000, more than any of her relatives or neighbors could imagine making with wheat or potato farming. "I sold the opium to the Pashtuns who come to the villages. Men in motorcycles come to small farms like mine and buy the opium we package in plastic bags. We don't have to go to them," she explains.

With the money she made, she bought one of her sons a car,

which he's using as a taxi to support his family. She bought clothes for the entire family and a new frame for carpet weaving. But most important, she bought food, including rice and meat, to feed her family three times a day, a luxury she does not remember having in her lifetime.

Samarkand says when she was younger her family went to sleep hungry three nights a week. Then her father, Kemal, moved them close to the city of Faizabad, and since then, her mother and father have been working tirelessly to provide for their six sons and three daughters. Samarkand, the eldest, is twenty-six; the youngest, Shaima, is six years old. "My father would carry the bricks and my mother laid them wherever they went to do construction work. My mother is like a man but with a kinder heart," says Samarkand, a thin, smiling woman with sleek black hair and chiseled cheekbones. "My mother is illiterate, but most of us have finished high school. My father was a firm believer in education."

Yet most of Parween's children still depend on their parents financially. Parween is getting old and tired. Her kidneys give her pain, and she has headaches in the morning. Despite the ailments, her energy level is still high, and she hopes she can help her children become self-sufficient. When drought dries up her farmland, she sews, weaves, and runs her household. She is a member of the women's weaving organization in Badakhshan—the group gives small loans for women with skills to open businesses. Parween and Samarkand have received $150 from the organization to weave carpets, tablecloths, and towels to sell. But the income from the weaving business pays for only one meal a day.

Parween is a workaholic. She cannot sit still at home or in the field. Drinking a glass of tea, she feels, takes too much time and impedes her productivity. "I did all the work on the land myself. I bought the poppy seeds from"—she pauses—"people." The pause is an attempt to preserve the identity of the creditors who loan farmers seeds. Once the harvest comes in, the creditors take a cut of the opium or demand cash. "I learned poppy farming by watching other poppy farmers. Nobody had to teach me," she insists.

"I have God, and God says we have to be hopeful, but on the day *they* came, I never felt more hopeless. I cried perhaps three times in my life in front of others. Once at my mother's funeral, the second time because my daughter was ill with the measles and I thought she would die, and the third was at my father's funeral. But since they came with their swords, my tears will not stop flowing."

Parween puts down the knife she cuts the yarn with and looks at the mountains. "The view calms me," she explains. The uncut grass sprawls from the field through the hills; the sky is spotless blue as the sun shines on a kaleidoscope of wildflowers at the bottom of the hills.

"It was four in the afternoon when my field was raped," she begins. "I had scored the bulbs the day before, to ooze out the opium gum. Samarkand and I went out after our afternoon prayers to the field to collect the opium dried on the outer part of the bulb. I had heard that the government was trying to show that it was fighting opium farming. Planting opium was officially illegal, but every influential family in Faizabad had an opium farm."

The government fights the planting after the fact, when it is time to harvest. Soldiers are paid six dollars a day to thrash the poppies, while farmers watch with anxiety. The reality is that the crops of landowners and farmers who have power and contacts in the government are spared, while those of people such as Parween, poor and disconnected from the higher ranks, are destroyed. Parween had been so afraid of the poppy killers that, on some nights, she slept next to her field on a mat under a mosquito net. And when they came, she knew her efforts, her hours of labor, and her main income for the entire year would be gone.

"There were ten of them, in four cars. They wore camouflage uniforms and carried Kalashnikovs and long blades. The men burst out, pointing their guns fearfully. I took a kitchen knife I kept in my dress pocket and held it to my throat. I told them, 'You come near this field and I'll kill myself. Stay away because this is all I have.' They told me, 'Khala, we have to do this. This is the law. We don't want you to hurt yourself, and we don't want to hurt you. But if you attack us, we will shoot,' a tall man with light skin firmly said. But there was a man who looked like their boss—he was wearing pants and a shirt—and he told them to leave my land alone. But no one listened to him. They listened to the light-skinned man, and the soldiers pushed passed me."

Parween dropped the knife in defeat and grabbed her daughter. What if they raped us, too? she worried. "I ran inside the house to call my sons." The entire neighborhood soon descended on Parween's land to witness the pillage. The soldiers swung at the juicy, ripe bulbs, severing each head from the body. They left only the stalks. Their police caps hiding their faces, they sweated and panted under the blue sky heat until every single capsule was on the ground.

Samarkand held her mother, burying her face in her chest. Parween made no sound. Her eyes were wet and her face stung, but she felt nothing. Her sons made a fuss. They cursed the soldiers. They ran to the field to stop the destruction. But the commander raised his gun and fired a warning shot. So the sons could only watch like caged, hungry tigers whose last morsel of food was being trashed in front of them.

After their task was complete, the soldiers demanded water. Parween called her sons to get them a pail from the water storage tank—water her sons had walked an hour to collect from the mountain spring. Then the men jumped back in their cars and drove away quickly.

"I bet we're the only ones in town they did this to," Samarkand whispered in her mother's ear. "If we had bribed the mujahideen groups in charge of the police, maybe they wouldn't have done this."

"It doesn't matter now," Parween retorted, pushing her fragile daughter away. She took the edge of her scarf and dried her eyes. Walking like an old haggard woman toward the mud-brick house, she paced herself. Once inside her darkened room, she dropped to her knees and howled.

When the U.S.-led coalition defeated the Taliban in late 2001, poppy cultivation was at its lowest due to the Taliban's successful ban on opium farming the previous year. Cultivation in Afghanistan had been reduced from two hundred thousand acres to about nineteen thousand, a 91 percent decline. The only places where production rose were provinces under mujahideen control, such as Badakhshan, where it increased nearly three times, from six thousand to sixteen thousand acres. This rise would spread throughout the country over the next year. The power vacuum that followed the Taliban defeat and the skyrocketing price of opium, at $500 a kilo, encouraged farmers to plant again. Soon mujahideen warlords regained control of their turf, and they had no objections to opium farming—they would find ways to benefit from it.

The return to mass opium farming worried the international community, but a cohesive counternarcotics strategy eluded Afghan and foreign authorities, in part because the American military did not want to confront illicit narcotics. Foreign troops were in Afghanistan to fight terrorism, and many Afghan informants bankrolled by the U.S.-led coalition were drug dealers. The Pentagon considered the drug trade a low priority and left it to the British to develop an antidrug strategy. The experienced officials in the State Department, however, warned that the money the insurgency made from opium grown in Afghanistan would go toward buying arms to be used against coalition soldiers.

In the Bonn agreement, the British were assigned the lead on the counternarcotics front. The United Kingdom initially considered buying the entire Afghanistan poppy crop for $50 million to $150 million from all the farmers who'd planted, but that plan was abandoned for fear it would be an incentive for more farmers to plant poppy. It might have worked better than what occurred: a series of grave errors that led to record poppy output.

From April to June 2002, the British compensated farmers $350 for less than half an acre for eliminating their crops. Boxes of cash to the tune of $3.5 million were flown in to opium-cultivated areas and distributed to local authorities to hand out to farmers. Soldiers then ripped out the crop from the soil with their tools and tractors or slashed the stalks just before harvest. About 11,120 acres of poppy harvest were destroyed.

But many of the officials who received the cash from the British, former mujahideen, pocketed the money or took a cut, instead of giving it all to the farmers. In order to collect more cash, farmers claimed that more acres than they actually possessed had been destroyed. The British had not counted on the corruption of the Afghan government and, as in the case of many other development projects, did not have enough international monitors to ensure that the funds reached the farmers.

A UN report published in 2003 states that farmers in Faizabad received the cash, but their crops were not destroyed. In the same report, a farmer in Helmand province admitted that he paid an Afghan official $180 to tell the British that he had eradicated double the amount of poppy he actually had, so that he could get double the compensation. Instead, the Afghan official did not pay him anything, and the farmer was left with a large debt he'd accrued on the crops destroyed. He said he had to sell his seven-year-old daughter into marriage to pay his lender.

Poorer farmers and sharecroppers under the Salaam (peace) system take a cash advance from lenders, who are normally traffickers, on their opium harvest. That money is used to pay for poppy seeds and to support their daily survival. The opium crops are sold at half the price of their value at least two years before the actual harvest. If a drought or other event, such as government eradication, prevents the harvest, the farmers fall deeper into debt. The 2003 UN report says that more than 70 percent of the farmers whose crops were destroyed said their debt had increased.

In the spring of 2004, in the southern provinces of Kandahar and Helmand, the American company DynCorp paid five dollars a day to dozens of Afghan troops to eradicate poppy fields. A year later, the soldiers plunged into one of the most dangerous areas: the poppy fields in the district of Maiwand in Kandahar province. As DynCorp supervisors watched, the Afghan troops, armed with bush hogs, knives, and tractors, slashed the ripe poppy stalks. A group of three hundred villagers gathered at the site shouting in protest, but the crowd dispersed after the police fired warning shots. Meanwhile, about twenty-five miles from where DynCorp was monitoring the poppy slashers, some six hundred demonstrators descended on Kandahar city to protest the eradication. The farmers shouted that their livelihoods were being destroyed, without any compensation. The protest degenerated into violence and ended in tragedy. Local police—who DynCorp points out had not yet been trained—fired into the crowd, killing twelve people.

This failed attempt at eradication propelled a shift in strategy. Other options were considered: providing poppy farmers with alternative employment and lucrative crops, such as saffron, that could offer higher returns compared to wheat. But opium profits were too enticing. Not only that, but the plant has other benefits. The stalks and pods make soap, fuel, and animal fodder. The seeds of the crop can be used to make oil: ten kilograms of poppy seeds provide five kilograms of edible oil.

Afghan farmers are open to alternatives, says Tom Brown, a consultant with the nonprofit Central Asia Development Group, which works with drug farmers. "The idea is to find new markets for new crops, like okra, and sell it," he tells me. "The benefits may be less than opium in the short term, but in the long term, farmers understand that it's for the best."

Brown's group as well as other aid organizations are working on promoting alternative livelihoods, which require a multifaceted solution, including providing the jobless in poppy districts with employment in digging irrigation canals and building roads so that it will be easier to transport food crops. The strategy also includes training the local police and authorities to provide security for farmers so that they will not be forced to grow poppy or to hand over their profits to corrupt officials.

Donor countries have provided the staff and money for such alternative livelihood programs, with the United States giving the largest amount of aid: hundreds of millions of dollars. But initial programs failed, for several reasons: The large sums allocated for cash-for-work programs, and the seed and fertilizer handouts, provided a perverse incentive for farmers to take the handouts and continue planting poppy when the aid ran out. Agencies such as USAID used the programs, normally implemented in emergency conditions, as a strategy for long-term agricultural change, with unrealistic deadlines and expectations. As a result, some NGOs (nongovernmental organizations) assigned to execute the programs were forced to return donor money.

The Taliban also contributed to the program's failure: In Hel-

mand, the Taliban and their friendly drug traffickers sabotaged
projects quickly. In spring 2005 they killed eleven Afghan aid workers taking part in the attempt to draw farmers away from poppy.
By 2004 the United States had curtailed its funding for the program
and promoted a "fast-and-furious" approach to eradication. The
U.S. strategy snubbed the soft British approach and encouraged a
"random, certain and universal—with no areas exempt" eradication
of fields, to instill fear in farmers. This method also failed, as poppy
production rose each subsequent year.

In some provinces, however, alternative livelihoods have shown
some signs of progress. In Nangarhar, and even Ghoryan in Herat,
profitable substitute crops, such as saffron, have produced small-scale
successes and have convinced farmers to stop growing poppy—for the
time being. Yet the fact remains that no crop is as profitable as poppy.

The long-term goal should not be to reduce acres of poppy, as alternative livelihood experts David Mansfield and Adam Pain wrote
in a briefing for a Kabul think tank, but the "establishment of those
institutions for formal governance, promotion of strong civil society, and strengthening of social protection mechanisms."

In Badakhshan, no one offered Parween any other alternatives.

The *gilim* is half done and Parween orders her daughter to bring
tea for me. She seems emotionally drained after recounting how her
land was eradicated.

"Was it the worst day of your life?" I ask her.

She pauses, looks at her field again, and replies, "It seemed like it
at the time, but now I know it was just another day of life. We can
plant again, but we won't if we find a way to irrigate the field without dependence on rain."

The Kokcha River, a major tributary in the north of the country, cuts through Badakhshan, but getting the water to the fields is

a challenge the aid community is grappling with, and farmers such as Parween say they can sustain themselves if they have the water to grow food.

"My sons tell me I should stop working and they'll give me food. They can drive taxis, work construction jobs, and farm, but it would be better to stop living if I stop working."

"Would you work as a drug dealer? You can make more money that way," I joke.

She takes me seriously. "Never!"

"Where are the drug dealers in Badakhshan?" I ask.

"I don't know where they are, but I'm sure you'll find some in Argu district. There they're all drug dealers. They haven't destroyed their farms there because they pay the *oshor* [tax] and bribes to officials. You'll find an entire market of opium and heroin vendors."

I leave Parween, perplexed—is the drug trade really a detrimental business when so many poor families are profiting, especially women? In my mind, the moral clarity that drugs are evil and have destroyed families in Ghoryan is complicated by the various ways in which they have affected lives in different parts of the country. While widows fall into debt and must give up their land to drug lords in Herat, women with land in Badakhshan turn their poppy profits into sustainable income. Pierre-Arnaud Chouvy, a French expert on the international drug trade, summed up the paradox of Afghanistan's opium economy in an article for *Jane's Intelligence Review*: "On the one hand, the war economy has favored the growth of the drug economy and opium trafficking has given warlords the means to perpetuate conflict. But, on the other hand, the opium economy has made survival possible for many farmers and contributed a great deal to the overall country's economy. Hence, to some extent, the opium economy has helped stabilize a country coming out of over two decades of war and facing a derelict economy." The industry has provided jobs, stimulated the rural economy, helped reconstruct villages, and, in some cases, when the opium harvest was plentiful, helped lower farmers' debt burdens.

The root of Parween's success is that she used poppy profits to invest outside the poppy business, such as in transportation (her son's taxi) and carpet weaving. The end result of opium—the abyss of addiction—has no justifications, but until other options provide them with an income, farmers must be weaned from poppy farming slowly; for now, planting drugs is their only livelihood.

"Are you sure you want to do this?" my driver, Abdul Adeeb, asks. "These people are dangerous. If you're not concerned about yourself, I'm concerned about me."

It is too late for this conversation. We are already heading toward Argu district.

In the van with Adeeb, I feel like I am hang gliding as we drive upward along jagged cliffs, so close to the edge against a forceful wind that if Adeeb turned the steering wheel of his Tunis van a little too much to the left, we would actually fly.

"Frankly, I'm more afraid of this road right now," I say, smiling with fake confidence.

"*Khwarak* [sister], I know these roads like the back of my hand. Don't worry, but when we get there and drug lords want to take you hostage and beat me up, my hands are tied," he continues his lecture on my imprudence.

Adeeb has been my driver for a week in this hideaway engulfed by mountains and raw beauty. A venture capitalist might come here and see the potential for another Switzerland—with waterfalls, wildflowers, emerald-green hills, mountain springs, and the Kokcha River crashing and foaming against Gibralter-like rocks—and build ski resorts and tourist attractions. The place's ruby and emerald mines are fabled in all of Central Asia. What makes Badakhshan such a pleasure to explore is that it remains somewhat uncharted territory—that coupled with the largest variety of dust. I never thought dust had flavors, but this dust does. The dust from the roads would satisfy a cigarette smoker's palate; it's ashy. The dust in my room at the NGO house where I'm staying is sour; it must be from my own perspiration, which is not surprising in the ninety-degree heat with no fans or air-conditioning. The dust from the poppies is a little bitter, like the Australian spread Vegemite.

The purple and white poppy flowers have become part of the area's natural beauty. Adeeb and I pass countless poppy farms. Laborers, including many women, work in the fields scoring the poppy bulbs. The petals have fallen under the searing sun. There are no workers where there are poppy flowers, because opium is harvested once the petals fall.

"Look at those white flowers. They will maybe make up to a kilo of opium and then become heroin and be used by some addicted teenager who will defame his family. I'm so ashamed of my *watan* [homeland]," he says.

"We can't be moralistic about all this," I reply. "It's basic economics here. People farm it because it brings them the most money." I used to think like Adeeb, but after meeting numerous women such as Parween, who've improved their lives through poppy farming, my mind is not on the crop's inevitable use.

"Aren't you the American capitalist!" Adeeb retorts.

Adeeb is perhaps the most articulate driver I have had in Afghanistan. He's small of stature and thin, but his smallness belies his outsize gregariousness. He seems to voice all his thoughts. Adeeb, who has studied up to the seventh grade, asks me a lot of questions about my life, but unlike other drivers, he isn't judgmental about my choices. Most Afghans want to know why I'm not married with

children or living at home with my parents. They give me disap-
proving glares when they find out I'm traveling without my family
for work. It's not ladylike for an Afghan girl, they tell me. But Adeeb
is simply excited to be working, and in the company of a young
woman he can protect. I am instantly comfortable with him.

"Why did you come back to Afghanistan for work?" he asks.

"Because there's a lot to write about," I tell him.

"Is that all? I mean is there something about Afghanistan that
made you want to return?"

"Yes, look around," I say. "Its beauty, for one."

"You haven't seen the ugliness, have you?"

"Yes, I have. When I was a child during the Soviet invasion, I saw
the ugliness of war. But that's what makes it fascinating, that combination of beautiful and ugly."

I do not share with him the cruelty I have seen traveling around
the country over the past few years. The ugliness of Afghanistan
was clear in the Pakistani soldier who whipped an Afghan porter on
the border; in the plight of the women I have come to know, such as
Darya, the bartered bride, and Gandomi, the widow whose daughter self-immolated because she feared her brothers-in-law would
rape her; in the destitute men who beg on Herat's streets to support
their drug addiction; and in the drug lords such as Haji Sardar, who
prey on women like Gandomi. I don't mention these stories because
Adeeb already knows a version of them, having lived through the
years of war in the country. I'd rather focus on the exquisiteness of
Afghanistan.

"You seem to be a smart girl," he tells me, "so I don't understand
why you want to go to Argu." He wants to be my protector, but on
this trip he isn't feeling like a savior. He is Tajik, and the residents of
Argu are Uzbeks. He is small, and they are bulky and lanky. He's a
driver, and many of them are drug dealers and smugglers.

We stop at one of the farms, probably about an acre in size. The laborers all look up with a little fear and a lot of curiosity. I have on a long tunic, loose pants, and a large scarf wrapped around my hair and bosom. What always gives me away as an outsider are my sunglasses. I remove them immediately and walk over to one of the men in the field.

Twenty-two-year-old Mohammed Sharif says he and the several other men in the field have been working on this farm for over four months. This is not their land, but they perform the labor and then divide the profits with the landowner, splitting the harvest fifty-fifty.

"We might just get ten kilos from this field. That means we the workers keep five kilos and the owner, who does nothing, keeps the other five."

The men labor from six AM to six PM, seven days a week. The cycle for poppy cultivation is six to seven months. Sharif and the other farmworkers first have to pluck any unwanted grass, so that it doesn't destroy the crop. They plant in the fall three times a week, digging holes in the ground with shovels and throwing fertilizer on the soil. Then they throw in the poppy seeds and wait for them to germinate. The seedlings take fourteen to twenty-one days to sprout, and the stalk can grow from one to two feet. It takes about six weeks for the bulb to form in the shape of a small cabbage. Then it blossoms into a four-petal flower. After three months, the petals fall, and in the final stages, sap develops inside the pod. Poppy needs only a little water and can be cultivated in various types of soil. If the prices decrease, farmers can stockpile their harvest and store it in a cool, dry place for up to five years. Farmers in Helmand and Kandahar have larger plots of poppy; those in the rest of the country, such as in Badakhshan, have smaller plots, one-third of which they plant with poppy, leaving one-third fallow for rejuvenation and cultivating the last third with wheat or some other subsistence crop for their family's consumption.

"The workers and the landowner each have to pay half a kilo of their harvest to the government as tax, or risk the threat of poppy eradication the following year, and harassment that same year," Sharif concedes.

His feet bare, pants ripped, and shirt stained with opium juice, Sharif takes a piece of wood the size of a lipstick, with nails attached to it, and uses it to slice the first layer of the poppy bulb. A black, gooey liquid spurts out. The workers leave the liquid on the bulb for the night, and in the morning, when it has turned gummy, they collect it in plastic bags. This is raw opium. What remains are the seeds inside the bulb and the stalks.

"How come the government didn't destroy these crops?" I ask Sharif.

"No one's bothered us since we've been here."

"Do you care that it's *haram* [forbidden by religion] to plant this and sell it?"

He stops his work and looks distressed. "I've been working on opium fields for twelve years, and this is how my family of eleven eats. I don't know if that's *halal* [sanctioned by Islamic law] or *haram*," he responds.

His family has been eating well for the last two years, but Sharif is still in debt. "I don't know how long it will take before I can pay off my loan. Maybe when my back breaks and my son can do this."

If Mohammed Sharif could see the addicted woman in Ghoryan whose glazed eye gazed hopelessly through her chador as she reached out to me through a taxi window, would he continue farming opium? Is it even a fair question to ask him when he has so few other options? The discussion of whether opium farming is ethical is a luxury for this farmer, who would rather leave the debate to the government officials who make the laws. When the international community and Mohammed Sharif's own Afghan leaders fail to come up with alternatives, farmers must continue to score bulbs and collect the black gum from the field.

Of the $4 billion generated from illicit drugs in Afghanistan, farmers receive only 20 percent, while traffickers, drug kingpins, and their political connections inside the country snatch the other 80 percent. The United Nations estimates that 245,000 farming households in the country—that's about 1.6 million Afghans—remain dependent on opium production. But sending armed soldiers and tractors to pull out the fruit of their labor is no solution to an intricate issue that will take decades to resolve. The farmers are part of the problem in the rise of drug addiction, but the solution needs to address them within the broader questions of poverty and security, not demonize them.

I wrap up my conversation with the farm workers and climb into the van to head to Argu's opium bazaar.

TEN

The Smiles of Badakhshan

It's a three-minute drive from the poppy fields to the opium bazaar in Argu. Adeeb drives through the rows of two dozen or so shops, mud huts with rotting wooden doors. The huts are built three feet above the ground. The unpaved road is topped with gravel mixed with fresh mud. Men mill around the shops in turbans and their *pirahan tomban*. There are no women in sight. When Adeeb reaches the end of the strip, he does a U-turn, whizzing past the bazaar.

"What are you doing?" I ask.

"You saw the bazaar once, and I'll do a U-turn and you can see it again, and then we can return to Faizabad," he responds.

"Stop the van. I'm getting out," I order him firmly. It's the first time I've used a bossy tone with him.

"What do you think you're going to achieve at this place? These men are armed and will have no qualms about hurting you," he insists.

"Observation is my goal, and I'll take my chances," I persist.

He grunts and shifts gears. "Let me just go back to the exit of this road so that we can make a quick getaway if something bad happens."

"You're paranoid. But that's fine," I agree.

He drives back to the beginning of the strip, near the road to Faizabad, and finally parks the van. "I'm not getting out," he says. "They see you as a threat."

"Okay. Then you stay in the car," I reply coldly. I'm annoyed that he no longer wants to protect me. But I understand that he lives in this province and that his life will be in danger after I leave. The chances I take are mitigated by the protection my American passport offers—a protection that my guides do not enjoy in this country. They could be ostracized, harassed, or killed for working with me.

I wave away my concern for Adeeb and confidently step out of the van. It's hard to see inside the small shops, even though it's eleven in the morning. There are no windows, or visible electricity, but a small generator roars in the background, giving light to a few of them. All transactions seem to occur at the shops' entrances; shopkeepers stay inside while the customers stand outside. The owners sit on the edge of their stores. Some of them spit tobacco; others drink tea. The merchandise for sale includes kilo-size clear plastic bags with black and white substances inside. I assume the white powder is heroin and the black goo is opium. Underneath the plastic packets is grayish opium, shaped like cow dung.

Some of the shopkeepers, who normally work as money chang-
ers when the opium season is finished, are plopped cross-legged
on small carpets behind their old-fashioned scales. They use small
rocks to balance the rusty silver scales. One vendor, with long arms
and dirt under his fingernails, has five bags of heroin on one side
of the scale and several rocks on the other. The buyer urges him to
throw another bag on the scale.

"It's not enough. Another *podar*, brother. I'll give you a good
price," says the buyer, a stocky fast-talker.

"Of course you're going to give me a good price. Otherwise, you
won't get any of it," the store owner answers with a smirk.

Next to his scale are stacks of dollar bills, held tight by rubber
bands, each bundle two inches thick. There are no other products
visible in these shops besides money and drugs.

The shops have no signs, no awnings, no paint—they're stark
mud-brick huts with two-piece wooden doors closed with padded
locks. In front of one shop, a bearded man tastes the white powder
inside a bag. Several others gather around him and raise their arms,
waving dollars. They bid and bargain with the shopkeeper.

"I'll give you three hundred for that whole package," one voice
shouts.

"Here's five hundred. Take it!" another voice screams louder.

An impatient customer slaps his dollars on the scale. "Let's settle
this. Decide already!"

A big drug deal seems to be going down, but before I can capture
any other details, the men in the bazaar suddenly seem to notice
that a foreign woman is among them. For a minute, all transactions
stop and a silence falls over the bazaar. This is my cue. I walk toward
the shop where the men are waving their dollar bills.

"*Salaam. Chitorastid?* [Hi, how are you?]" I greet them.

I tell the dozen bewildered men that I am a journalist from

Kabul. The shopkeeper, a broad-shouldered man in a big turban, steps out.

"What do you want?" he asks, uncharacteristically impolite for an Afghan.

"No Afghan politeness and hospitality at the opium market? No invitations for *shorchai* [tea with milk and salt]? I am hurt. I heard people here were very hospitable," I joke.

No one laughs. They aren't buying into my innocent intentions. Just then I realize the danger of the situation and wonder if Adeeb was being realistic, not paranoid.

I sputter out an explanation: "I just wanted to know what the price of opium was. Just wanted to get some harmless information. I'm coming from Kabul."

"It has gone down from three hundred dollars [a kilo] last year to thirty-five dollars this year. It's destroying us," the shopkeeper says abruptly. Then he shuts his shop door.

I'm surprised that he has even offered to share the price. It's not clear if he's upset with my presence or with the falling price of opium. But shutting the door is a clear sign that no more questions are welcome.

I look around to see that three dozen men have encircled me and are inching closer. I can feel myself panicking, the back of my neck sweating. I'm a talker, I tell myself. I've talked myself out of hairy situations in conflict zones in the past and I can do it now. Just talk.

"If you do not feel comfortable telling me anything, I can leave," I spit out. "I'm not here to snitch on anyone. I'm not the police and I have no involvement in the government. I have no weapons, no video cameras. You can search my purse if you want."

A chorus of voices respond. I can make out a few of the comments.

"Why should we believe anything you say?" one lanky man asks.

"Let her be. She's harmless," another voice echoes.

The same shopkeeper who revealed the price of opium steps forward again.

"Everybody in the town is a drug dealer. From the start of this bazaar to the end, we all sell and deal opium and heroin. It's how we live," he shouts, righteously pointing his index finger at the bazaar.

His indignant candidness is a confession of power and a refusal to bow down to the official ban on the growth and sale of drugs. It's a refreshing change from the usual self-victimizing martyrdom of farmers and smugglers in the drug trade.

I wait for any other comments, any other information about their business, but there's a petrifying pause.

Then I see Adeeb, obviously frightened, slowly walking toward me. He enters the circle. "We should get back before dark," he almost whispers.

All eyes turn on him, a thin driver surrounded by towering, beefy drug dealers. I'm relieved that he has come to rescue me and at the same time terrified that the drug dealers will hurt him for trying to save me. His welfare is more important than mine because he has children; he's come here because of me.

I want to apologize to Adeeb right there for my impudent bravado. I hope he's aware of the guilt I feel for putting him in this position. But I don't say a word.

No matter how equal I consider myself to men, this moment confirms that my belief in egalitarianism is irrelevant in this country. I already knew this, but this is the first time I'm tasting that imbalance, the sheer powerlessness of being a woman in a mob of men. Still, even though Adeeb is an unarmed man, he can still be my savior, for the mere fact that he is a man. A lone woman walking through an opium bazaar is not honorable, but with a man by her side she can be forgiven. The other men immediately notice that I have a protector and the circle around me breaks.

I find my voice again. "Well, thank you all very much. I hope to see you again." I pretend to be courageous as I walk toward Adeeb. The men continue to stare, mumbling words I cannot decipher, perhaps in the Uzbeki language, but they let me through the circle. Adeeb and I walk back to the van, looking over our shoulders occasionally as we walk.

Once we're inside the van, Adeeb reverses it all the way to the main road and drives faster than the rocky road can handle.

"I'm sorry," I say, looking him in the eye. "I should've listened to you."

"We're alive, and that's all that matters. God was with us," he says in a calm tone. He avoids my eyes, perhaps because it can be considered flirtatious to look a woman in the eye or perhaps because he's too upset.

"I just hope you got what you wanted," he says pointedly.

"Some of it," I reply, admiring the magenta poppy flowers that grow as far as the eye can see.

We arrive in Faizabad in a much shorter time than it took us to get to Argu.

Badakhshan was an important path on the Silk Road, and poppy and opium have been part of its history for centuries. Alexander the Great and Marco Polo both traveled through this enchanting landscape, and the armies of Alexander the Great tried to conquer Badakhshan in 250 BC. In their temporary reign over the region, the Greeks, with the aid of local natives, built many forts and towns here, some of which are still standing. Some of Alexander's soldiers settled here, and Afghans in the Wakhan and Pyanj valleys in this province are Greek descendants. In the thirteenth century, Italian explorer Marco Polo found gemstones such as lapis, rubies, and emeralds, still some of the province's hidden resources. The Pamir and Hindu Kush mountain ranges contribute to the area's natural splendor; the melting snow from the ranges in the spring and summer flows into the Kokcha and Amu rivers, the latter formerly known as the Oxus. Hawaiian waterfalls pale next to the cascades I've seen traveling through the province. The population here is sparse in relation to the province's size—823,000 people spread over 44,000 square kilometers—partly because arable land is scarce and weather conditions are harsh. The majority of the population is composed of Farsi-speaking Tajiks, but there are several smaller groups with their own languages, including Uzbeks and Ismailis, a Shia sect active in reconstruction efforts. The mass production of opium here began during the 1980s, when the province was on the front line in the war against the Soviet Union.

Burhanuddin Rabbani, one of the influential leaders of the mujahideen, came from Badakhshan and helped encourage poppy farming to bankroll the insurgency against the Soviets. Rabbani served as president in the 1990s, during the mujahideen's rule in Kabul, when civil war raged and the country's capital was destroyed. Badakhshan's primary border is with Tajikistan, a former Soviet republic; the mountain hideouts there made it a convenient location for the Soviet military. Its capital, Faizabad, became a Soviet garrison town until the Red Army pulled out in 1989. Rabbani kept his base in Badakhshan and, along with other mujahideen, looted the mineral and gem mines and sold his treasure to smugglers in Pakistan and abroad.

Once the Taliban gained control, the mujahideen were pushed farther north, and many of them took refuge in Panjshir and Badakhshan. Rabbani returned to his province, but he has few supporters left. "He didn't do anything, except build one bridge connecting the old Faizabad to the new part of town," one of the town's nurses tells me. Rabbani's wooden bridge is now falling apart.

From 1992 to 2001, when the mujahideen commanders exercised absolute control, poppy cultivation rose by 43 percent. The Taliban did not occupy any part of this province at any point, and when they banned poppy in 2000, Badakhshan produced the entire 185 tons accounted for in all of Afghanistan. The people here, as in most of the country, rejoiced when the U.S. bombing campaign began in October 2001.

"They abandoned us and now they were coming back to save us," a teacher with blue eyes and a white turban says. Afghans felt this sense of abandonment after the United States pulled its resources and allowed the mujahideen to terrorize the country with their American stockpile of weapons. The Cold War propaganda spread by the United States was etched in Afghan hearts and minds—the Soviets were evil infidels and the Americans were kind Christians who helped Muslims—until the civil war in 1992. Then a sense of betrayal prevailed, as Afghanistan became the United States' jilted lover.

Afghans chose to forgive and forget their pains after 2001, but they unrealistically expected rapid change and reform. When the mujahideen reclaimed their positions of power, Afghans once again realized that no one was coming to their rescue.

In the summer of 2004, during my visit to Badakhshan, that sense of hope for change is still prevalent, despite the small skirmishes between the mujahideen factions and drug dealers that are the de-stabilizing threats against security. I travel day and night on the precarious roads, and the people there—with the exception of those at the opium bazaar—welcome me with warmth.

The faces of Badakhshan's residents mirror the natural wonders of the place. Green and blue eyes with coal black hair and
honey-colored skin are typical. Badakhshi smiles are not jaded,
like the smiles flashed in the big cities; no hidden intentions con-
ceal the friendliness. People show what they are inside—poor but
kind. The ongoing wars have not hardened these people's hearts or
compromised their humanity. Here, I come across coeducational
elementary schools for the first time: boys and girls huddled in
tents studying intensely. I meet some of the most inspiring Afghans: a fifteen-year-old girl who lives in a small *khishlaq,* a village
constructed on the edge of mountains, who walks downhill in a
burqa two hours every day to reach her school. Then she walks
uphill for three hours to get home and prepare lunch. After lunch,
she gathers her mother and a group of illiterate village women
to teach them what she has learned in class. I meet a family of
four young women, nurses and students, who lost their parents
and who now live without any men to protect them. They spend
their days caring for the sick in the town hospital. The most controversial person I get to know is a man, Haji Barat, revered by
residents in Faizabad. Although he is, of all things, a drug smuggler, he spends some of his profits from smuggling to provide basic
services such as health care to Badakhshis.

Yet Badakhshan's economic dependence on an illegal crop offers
a dismal future. The only other income people have is remittances
from relatives working in Pakistan, Iran, or Tajikistan. Opium has
temporarily improved the lives of some families, but the majority
suffer from its side effects, mainly debilitating addiction. Furthermore, people in Faizabad tell me that opium is actually a currency
in some districts of the province. Newspaper reports, such as an
Associated Press article from the Shahran district, corroborate this:
"When children felt like buying candy, they ran into their father's

fields and returned with a few grams of opium folded inside a leaf. Their mothers collected it in plastic bags, trading 18 grams for a meter of fabric or two liters of cooking oil. Even a visit to the barbershop could be settled in opium."

Badakhshan, similar to Nangarhar in the east and Helmand in the south, is a factory for opium—here the drug is grown, consumed, sold, and refined into heroin and other opiate-based drugs. The province has the largest share of opium addicts in the country, twenty thousand, or 2.5 percent of the population. The addicted include a large number of women and children. Mothers smoke the opium in pipes, then blow the smoke into their children's mouths. They say it relieves their pain. Badakhshan also houses the second largest number of heroin laboratories in the country, anywhere from fourteen to eighty, according to the United Nations. But Russian authorities say there may be as many as four hundred makeshift labs across its Tajikistan border. Labs can be mobile, depending on how much opium they're capable of refining. They are situated in mountain caves or on any compound with a couple of rooms, close to border crossings or in isolated locations. The instruments chemists use to refine opium include metal drums, wood-fired stoves, and iron levers such as car jacks. In the past, the majority of opium was smuggled to Iran, Pakistan, and especially Turkey for refinement, but the United Nations reports that two-thirds of Afghan opium is now processed domestically. Experienced foreign chemists come to Afghanistan to help Afghans refine large quantities of the drug.

The moral question of opium being forbidden by any authority, be it a religious cleric or the government, seems to be extraneous to the people here. Despite its negative effects, opium guarantees their survival, however short-lived. Few judge the farmers or smugglers who engage in the trade. Some of them, such as Haji Barat, have become role models who have done more to aid Faizabad's residents than any NGO or government agency. "I read about this man named Pablo Escobar from Colombia and how he helped poor people in his city with drug money," one of the NGO workers I talk to says. "Haji Barat is our Pablo Escobar."

I hear of Haji Barat the first day I arrive in Badakhshan. People speak of him with admiration. He is a rare Good Samaritan who has built a health clinic with fifty beds; he plans to open a factory, too. Barat is one of the richest men in this province, and it's known around town that his fortune was made from opium money. Yet people are quick to point out that he has a number of fronts, including his currency trade and a business that imports cooking gas from Uzbekistan.

Adeeb happily drives me to Barat's house. "I'm glad to hear you want to visit this man. He's a good man, not like the thugs in the opium market," Adeeb explains.

"But he's also dealing drugs," I argue. "So what if he uses it for a good cause? It's dirty money."

"I thought you told me not to be moralistic about opium. You're confusing me," he complains.

I laugh. "I'm just presenting the other side. It's good to practice debating with yourself. Have you tried it?"

"Only with personal decisions, not these things," Adeeb replies. "I think you don't know what you think. Why do you make yourself so dizzy with such matters? You are not fully Afghan and not fully American. So you're always confused. You should just accept that," he philosophizes.

He has stepped over his brotherly boundaries. I'm deeply hurt and taken aback. Adeeb has touched a sensitive nerve in me, pointing out my fragile Afghan identity. I become defensive and irritable.

"I'm not confused all the time. I love this country probably more than you do and am just as Afghan as you are—but in a different way. Being Afghan is not one thing, you know. You can't tell people what their identity is. They should decide for themselves." I say these words quietly, though, without much confidence.

"I didn't mean to offend you. I'm sorry, *khwarak*."

We reach Barat's house, which is situated on a tree-lined street in the new city of Faizabad. It's the biggest house on the block, with marble floors, Persian carpets, and an SUV parked in the garage. Barat greets us himself—considering he is wealthy, I had expected servants at the door. He is a striking man of thirty-seven years with icy blue eyes, a neatly trimmed beard, and a firm handshake.

He is willing to talk, but there is an implicit understanding that he will not divulge the secrets of the drug trade or his involvement in it, just like Haji Sardar in Herat.

"I wanted to discuss the condition of Badakhshan and its issues because you're a leader in this community, and a merchant who has money to spend," I tell him with a big grin.

"Of course. I'd be honored to speak with you." He smiles back and gestures to us to enter his home. Haji Barat has other male guests sitting across the room from us, but he tries to stay focused on my questions, answering in educated Farsi, a badge of his formal schooling.

"I was a mujahid and fought against the Soviet invasion for four-teen years," he begins. "I finished high school, then enlisted with the guerrilla faction of Ahmad Shah Massoud, the commander who al Qaeda and the Taliban killed two days before September eleventh. I was considered a hero not too long ago, but now the Americans call me a warlord. The Americans used us then for their proxy war and they're doing the same now, but we've caught on. We want our freedom and we no longer want to be anybody's servants." This long-winded answer to "Tell me about yourself" reveals his deep anger at the mujahideen's loss of public prestige.

"But the people do not call you a warlord," I say. "They call you a hero still." It is easy to be charmed by his good looks and Robin Hood reputation.

"You've been speaking to friends. I have more enemies than friends," he explains.

He tells me he has a wife and five children.

"Rich men normally indulge in more than one wife," I say, goading him.

"I think one wife is enough trouble." He furrows his brow, then smiles. "I want to be a role model for my children. I want them to do good and be servants to their country."

When I finally broach the topic of opium, he looks at his guests again. He's not comfortable talking about this issue in front of them, but we continue the conversation anyway. "People hate opium here. Poppy will disappear if there are alternatives. They accuse me of being a smuggler because I've made money through other means and my rivals have not. People turned to poppy here because an international mafia, including Russians, Tajikis, and Pakistanis found a footing here. And now all those in power are in bed with the mafia," he says condemningly.

"Aren't you one of those in power?"

"If you're accusing me of smuggling, I don't need to. I did when the Taliban were in power, out of desperation. But now I trade and travel. I sell sugar and buy cars to resell and am doing well, *Mashallah.*"

"What made you build a clinic and help people here?"

"God. He is in my conscience, and I'm on this earth to serve Him and make His wishes come true. People in Badakhshan are in dire need of health care and food, basic services you take for granted. A better question is how could I not help them if I have the money?"

Conscientious smugglers such as Barat are precious gems among drug traffickers and kingpins. He is far from the notorious Pablo Escobar, who aided poor people in his native Medellin but also killed and terrorized thousands of others before he was assassinated. It's impossible to know how many people Barat has abused, killed, or terrorized, if any, but the people I talk to in Faizabad see this drug lord as their only hero.

From the 1990s to 2004, the opium economy changed the lives of thousands in Badakhshan for the better. The locals call the period the Opium Festival. Adam Pain writes about the province in the report "Afghanistan Livelihood Trajectories" for the think tank Afghanistan Research and Evaluation Unit:

> For most households, this expansion was a time of unparalleled prosperity.... It brought income either directly from cultivation on owned or sharecropped land or indirectly by providing new employment opportunities. It was a time of food security, investment and debt relief, and many households were able to recover from debts incurred during the drought.

After my visit to Badakhshan, profits from the opium economy drop rapidly. The "festival" ends with bad weather conditions, successful government eradication programs in some districts, and rising wheat prices. Some of the farmers believe mistakenly that the government will compensate them for their eradicated crops, as the British did. They voluntarily destroy their crops to receive cash but are disappointed when the government informs them that the previous strategy of cash for eradication has been abolished. Farmers abandon poppy and again grow traditional crops such as wheat. The decline in opium profits causes a drop in farm labor, wages, and purchasing power. The quality of life for those who depended on poppy money deteriorates so much that some Badakhshis do not have enough to eat. I hope that innovative farmers such as Parween, who used poppy cash to find other work, no longer need poppy profits to live well.

ELEVEN

My Mother's Kabul

Sayed Begum Nawa—better known as Nafasgul to family and friends, and Madar to me—slowly steps off the Ariana Afghan Airlines plane at Kabul International Airport, clasping the railing of the stairway so she will not fall. Her two-inch beige heels click on the tarmac. She clutches her matching gold-rimmed beige purse and wipes off imaginary dust from her beige-and-brown skirt. Then she fidgets with her matching embroidered *gaach* (silk) head scarf. One side is draped over her shoulder; the other falls over her bosom. Her appearance to her liking, she stops to notice the sight before her.

It's a hot, dry, dust-filled day. The August sun stings her eyes and blocks her view. She holds her free hand over her eyes to filter out the sun and see as far as she can the country she has missed for twenty-two years. Jagged mountains loom over the capital, a valley home to nearly four million people. But the mountains are the only familiar sight. Kabul has changed, is barely recognizable to my mother, who lived here with my father and his siblings in the 1960s.

Her heart sinks as she looks around, and she begins to cry quietly. The airport is in shambles. Kabul, which was home to only half a million residents when she lived here, now houses so many people, all strangers. They look disheveled and poor, with greasy hair and tattered shoes. Furthermore, when they speak they do not sound like native Kabulis, as they're from the provinces, with village accents in Farsi and Pashto.

The last time my mother visited Kabul before we left the country was in 1982, when my family was planning our escape. She traveled from Herat to the capital to get an Indian visa, but then we decided to leave through Iran and Pakistan. Twenty-three years ago, Kabul was clean; the buildings were intact; there was electricity, greenery, water; and the people were *lux* (classy). There were few *pirahan tombans* and turbans. Most people wore suits, dresses, and other styles of Western clothes.

My mother's barometer for people's status has often been appearance, which is common among Afghans of all generations. Snazzy Western clothes, such as miniskirts and flared jeans, as opposed to traditional dress, were an indication of the freedoms men and women had before the mujahideen takeover in 1992.

She exits the airport terminal elegantly and smiles when she sees me. She holds out her arms, and I throw myself into them. Her eyes are tearful. I hand her a tissue. She pays the porter carrying her bags ten dollars, three times more than he usually receives. The driver who's brought me to the airport to meet her loads my mother's suitcases into the van and we head to the Karte Parwan house I share with a British man and American woman. I've taken a job working as an international consultant for an Afghan news agency called Pajhwok; my roommates also work for the agency. Our task is to provide on-the-job training to local journalists in the basics of reporting and writing a story. I moved to Kabul two months before my mother's visit, to join the thousands of repatriating exiles from Western countries aiding in the reconstruction of Afghanistan. I am no longer a visitor or a guest in my homeland. But I'm delighted that my mother is my guest for a few nights.

We haven't seen each other for three months and I miss her warmth and her cooking. She has come to Kabul en route to Herat to see her relatives. Unlike my father, whose relatives fled, my mother still has many cousins and uncles living in Herat. My father did not want to return again after his 2002 trip.

"You look happy," my mother says.

"I am," I agree, holding her hand. "I like living in Kabul. It's more liberal than Herat." We're sitting in the back of the car taking in the city.

"Am I really in Kabul?" my mother asks. "It's so crowded, so many cars, so much smog. Are these big posters for the elections?"

"People are very excited about the first presidential elections. Twenty-three candidates are running, even a woman," I tell her.

"God punish the Soviets for coming here and ruining our lives. I hope whoever gets elected can do something for this city."

My mother has arrived in Kabul at the height of hope in post-Taliban Afghanistan. The Bush administration has declared the war in Afghanistan a success and American resources and military power are being sent to volatile Iraq. The country is relatively peaceful, aside from small skirmishes among the Taliban and coalition troops. The biggest problem is the former mujahideen, who, with American support, are enjoying a comeback. Many of them have returned to extortion, drug dealing, and kidnapping. They kidnap foreign aid workers and Afghans who work for foreign organizations, demanding ransoms. Several of the cabinet members are mujahids, and many of the presidential candidates made a name for themselves fighting the Soviets. Reconstruction is in full gear—bulldozers, freshly poured cement, and construction workers fill the capital's streets—creating deafening but welcome noise. The Kabul-to-Kandahar highway was rapidly built to demonstrate nation building just in time for this year's Afghan and U.S. presidential elections. The corruption in the government, the burgeoning opium trade, and a potential Taliban comeback are topics few Afghans want to focus on. The general attitude is that things are going to be better than they have been since 1978. The uplifting mood does not infect my mother; she has yet to accept postwar Kabul. Everywhere we go she tells me how it was in the 1960s and '70s, the golden era of peace.

"Women who wore burqas were known to be pickpockets in Kabul then," she says as we stroll uphill on a Kabul street. "One of them stole four thousand *rupia* [forty dollars] from my purse in a shop when I went to visit at that time. I wore a burqa in Herat, but in Kabul, I could show my face and be fashionable. But most important, it was safe. We could go anywhere and stay out late and walk alone in the streets, take the bus. I never felt in danger."

Her heels fall in the cracks of the road as we walk to the nearby shops one afternoon. "*Wee Khoda* [Oh God], you can't even walk in this town anymore without being injured," she complains, holding the tail of her head scarf over her mouth to block the pollution.

I'm as annoyed as I was with my father's criticism. I saw Kabul during the reign of the Taliban, in 2000, and the city was like a graveyard. People did not speak out of fear, there was no construction being done, and the only women I saw on the streets were beggars. The Kabul I'm living in now is a city waking from the dead, on the brink of change.

"Madar, why don't you wear more comfortable shoes."

My father gave my mother the name Nafasgul, meaning "the breath of a flower," as was tradition in their generation—husbands often gave their wives endearing nicknames when they first married. But my mother doesn't like Nafasgul or her birth name, Sayed Begum. She's a member of an Afghan elderly women's group in Fremont, California, and the women there began calling her Saida, which in Arabic means the female descendant of the Prophet Mohammed. "I think it's my right to change my name if I don't like it," she tells me. "Saida is much more meaningful than my other names." Perhaps she's right. After all, she does come from a Said family who traces their ancestry to the Prophet Mohammed. It's one of my mother's only attempts at asserting her independence.

Saida has spent her seventy-three years of life being a mother and wife, with a short stint teaching elementary school. The first time she saw my father was on their wedding night, when she was fifteen; their families arranged the marriage. She is a social butterfly who hates to miss a party, and her list of telephone numbers, all of which she has etched in her memory, is longer than my list of six hundred contacts. Saida is kind to a fault, putting others before herself, even when she shops; she keeps a chest full of gifts ready to hand out to friends and family for weddings, housewarmings, and birthdays. She tailors the gifts of clothing with her Singer sewing machine. Ever since I can remember, Saida has been ill, first with an incurable stomach ulcer, then with numerous sicknesses, including a slipped disc, which occurred when she immigrated to the United States. But her ailments have not dampened her desire to connect with others and to enjoy life. No matter how sick she is, Saida will dress up and put on a light coat of lipstick and foundation. She owns a small sterling silver container filled with black kohl, *sorma*, and a silver stick that she dips in the container and uses to draw a narrow line of black on the bottom lid of her cocoa-colored, doelike eyes. Her expensive head scarves are her signature fashion statement, to declare her piety and modesty. I have rarely seen my mother's hair, except the gray bangs that neatly peek out. "My head becomes cold if I take off my scarf," she admits to my father, giving him a gleaming white smile. She even sleeps with two layers of scarves on her head.

My clumsiness and disregard for fashion stand out when I'm with my mother. "Your mother is so beautiful and elegant," people say, politely leaving out "What happened to you?"

Life in the United States has had its perks for Saida. She receives proper health care and has learned some words of English, which allowed her to pass her citizenship test. The clean water and food soothe her excessive need for cleanliness, and she no longer has to wear a burqa, as she did in her last years in Herat. But the loss involved in leaving Afghanistan has been immeasurable. The social fabric of her life unraveled. She was no longer able to hop in a taxi and see her parents, and she could not easily communicate with her friends and neighbors. "I feel mute when I go out," she says.

She tried to become fluent in English, taking several courses, but she was forty-seven when she arrived in the United States, and it was a daunting challenge for her to learn a second language. She has not learned how to drive either, which has left her stuck at home, waiting for calls from the various parts of the world where her brothers and sisters are scattered. By returning to Afghanistan now, can she regain what she has lost, if only for a couple of months?

In my room at the house in Karte Parwan, I lie on the queen-size bed while my mother insists on sleeping on the red *toshak* (mat) on the floor. The electricity is gone for the night and the streets are silent. The only sound comes from the small radio I own. Kabul's media is exploding with dozens of radio and television stations and newspapers with unprecedented freedom of the press. The most popular station is Arman Radio, and tonight they're broadcasting a two-hour special dedicated to the dramatic life and mysterious death of Afghanistan's most renowned singer, Ahmed Zahir, the artist who revolutionized Afghan pop music, fusing Western instruments with Persian poetry. Girls screamed at his concerts, and he became a pop icon. In 1979, Zahir's friends took him for a drive toward the Salang Tunnel on his birthday, and he was shot dead. No one was convicted. Only one man, who lives in the San Francisco Bay Area now, was with him in that final minute on that day and knows the details, but he refuses to divulge any information.

Saida and I listen to the program. Zahir's widow is begging for the man to come forward and speak. Zahir's songs play in the background.

"Life was so different back then," my mom reminisces. I focus on her soft voice in the dark, closing my eyes and letting her take me back to her Kabul.

"The last time your father and I lived in Kabul was in the mid 1960s. Zahir Shah was in power. Hadi was in the third grade, and Faiza was just born in Kabul. We lived in Karte Mamureen, a decent neighborhood, renting the guesthouse of a family. There was a shrine in the middle of the courtyard. We had two rooms, a kitchen, a squat bathroom, and twenty-four-hour power. We had an electric heater in the winter; it was enough to warm us. Your dad was a translator for the Russians at *inhasarat* [Afghanistan Bureau of State Monopolies]. The Russians were here providing aid. Back then he could speak English, Arabic, and Russian. Now he barely mumbles Farsi.

"We were there for three years. We ate meat and rice, and had every seasonal food available to us. We were comfortable and never bored. I went to see our relatives by bus or taxis, or they would pick us up in their cars. Rich folks had cars back then. The men talked politics and I remember it was often centered on Iran. Most women my age were homemakers. We wore head scarves and fairly modest clothing, but the young women wore miniskirts and had beehive hairstyles. I wore bell-bottoms and coats in the winter.

"Hadi was enrolled in Aisha Durani School and it was coed. He came home with sewing assignments. I took care of the house and the kids in Kabul. We did not have servants like we did in Herat, but I didn't mind because we had our own place. We didn't have to live with the extended family.

"Your father and I went to the cinema and watched Indian movies. We used to go shopping; most of the merchandise was made in the Soviet Union. There was no security issue back then. People's biggest fear was pickpockets.

"I entered the continuing education school at the women's center and studied up to the seventh grade. I wanted to finish high school so I could get my teaching degree and be a teacher in Kabul. But my school was transferred to Paghman; it was too far for me to travel."

Her voice trails off as she begins to snore lightly. I turn off the radio and try to sleep, wishing I could've seen my mother's Kabul.

The next morning, Saida excitedly wakes up and gets ready for another flight. She is going home to Herat, to see relatives she has longed to unite with for two decades.

After I drop my mother off at the airport, I face the Kabul that my mother has been anxious to exit.

From 2005 to 2010 the number of opium addicts in Afghanistan increased 53 percent and the number of heroin users doubled. The rise in addiction is a reflection of the drug industry's boom. Women and children account for a quarter of the addicted. Four out of ten Afghan police recruits test positive for drugs. Some of the women addicts are farmers who plant opium; others include carpet weavers who numb the pain in their fingers by smoking opium after working inhumane hours. Children become addicted inhaling the secondhand smoke from their parents, and some parents give opium to calm their children. In some districts, especially in Badakhshan, entire families are addicted. Men who are addicted suffer from joblessness and poverty. Afghanistan traditionally had a minute number of addicts, mostly among the Turkmen ethnicity and the sick, who used the drug to dull their pain. But the neighboring countries dictate the culture of addiction—Afghan refugees who work as laborers in Iran, Pakistan, and the Central Asian states become addicted, and when they repatriate to Afghanistan, they import their addiction. The country has a growing market of opium to supply its own people. Drug pushers encourage addiction because they recruit addicts to become couriers. All the addicts normally get in return is a gram of heroin.

Nejat Center is one of forty-three addiction treatment centers for the estimated one million addicts in Afghanistan. The treatment centers have the capacity to treat ten thousand addicts at a time. Established in 2003, Nejat is one of the country's first treatment centers. In 2010 the Interior Ministry opened a one-hundred-bed center for policemen, and many more centers are needed to treat the rising number of addicts. The increasing number of AIDS cases—confirmed at two thousand, but health experts estimate the figure to be much higher—has prompted centers such as Nejat to hand out clean hypodermic needles to intravenous drug users. The Afghan counselors and doctors at Nejat have formed a rehabilitation pro-

gram for men and women, most of whom are repatriating refugees
from Pakistan and Iran. They treat about twenty patients a month
but have a 70 percent relapse rate. There are ten beds for the resident
addicts, but much of the group's work is outpatient. The men sit in
a circle on a mat and sing, exercise, and talk about their addiction
problem. When they leave, Nejat counselors, many of them volun-
teers, follow up with the patients after a year to monitor how they
are recuperating. The center also offers them job training and loans
for small businesses, which may be shining shoes or selling fruit
from a cart.

Down a muddy road in Kabul, Nejat Center is located behind
the gates of a large house. Inside, photos of the men the center has
treated hang on a wall. One is particularly disturbing: a homeless
man with worms in the back of his head. Next to it is a photograph
of the same man looking healthy and cured. It's an effective visual.
Three thousand addicts are on Nejat's waiting list.

Riaz, a smiling charmer in his twenties, is a recovering addict
at Nejat Center. He says he was a construction worker in Iran and
that he began smoking opium at first to fit in with the rest of the
laborers.

"Opium didn't give me enough of a high so I switched to shooting up heroin," he says nonchalantly. He raises his sleeve to show me
the track marks on his arm. "We realized that if we're high, we can
work more hours and make more money that way. But it got to the
point where I spent all my money buying drugs."

Riaz's tale is all too common in Afghanistan.

Nejat also treats women, as the number of female addicts in the
country has continued to rise. In Kabul's old city, on the hills of
Deh Afghanan, every other household, including men, women, and
children, abuses opium, Nejat counselors say.

Bibigul is plopped in her usual spot near the window looking down on old Kabul, a neighborhood called Mystics and Lovers. The alleyways contain mud-brick homes built a century ago that are falling to pieces. She can see the sewage running through the open canal; its stench overpowers her nostrils. Even though it's eighty-two degrees in the small room where she drinks green tea, she shuts the window. She alternates between the heat and the odor, depending on how long she can tolerate either of them, opening and shutting the green-paneled window.

"Why can't you just leave it open?" her daughter-in-law Parizad asks.

"It stinks," she shoots back.

Sarah and Farah, her two green-eyed grandchildren, chase each other around the room laughing.

"Bibi, open the window, it's hot in here!" they both chime.

Defeated, Bibigul opens the window a crack. She has to change positions, the biggest challenge of the day for her.

"Stop being naughty and help me get up," she affectionately shouts at the girls.

They both run to her and hand over her cane. Sarah, six years old, holds her right arm, and Farah, eight years old, takes her left, and they both lift the 170-pound woman. Bibigul, who is in her fifties, pants and heaves. She takes one step forward and the other foot stays still.

"Come on, Bibi, you can do this. You've done this before," Farah encourages.

The support helps Bibigul walk and breathe with less discomfort. It is her achievement for the day. She has to go to the bathroom five times a day, and each time, the walk feels like a hike through the Hindu Kush. Her knees ache, her back twinges, her legs quiver. She knows what it would take to make it less painful, but today she doesn't have any of her pain relief.

"Last night the forty-step walk was a breeze. But last night I got to suck on that lentil-size piece of opium and feel the soothing calmness and absolute peace. I don't have the fifty *rupia* [one dollar] to buy it today," she says. "I'll have to ask Mirza, my son, for the money. He got up at the crack of dawn to dig a grave. The family of the deceased will probably call me soon to wash the body."

They are a team, mother and son, body washer and gravedigger. That's how the family makes a living.

"I wonder if the family of the deceased has the money to pay my fee [four dollars]. Then I can send Hassan, the boy next door, to fetch me my medicine." Her "medicine" is a dime-size bit of opium wrapped in a small plastic bag.

"I need my medicine," she mumbles to me under her breath. "Can you get me some?"

I shake my head.

"Which one—the one the doctor gave you or the one Hassan brings?" Parizad asks.

"What good have the doctor's pills done for me!" Bibigul shouts. "I need my real pain reliever. People say it's bad for you, but nothing has ever made me feel better."

"It has made you nice and fat, and the whole neighborhood thinks you're becoming a rich woman," Parizad responds with equal fervor. "It made me a skinny woman who can't have children anymore. Do you know I haven't had my period for a year now, and I'm only thirty-five?"

"Damn this fatness. I wish I had your girly figure," Bibigul jokes with her daughter-in-law. "And who needs more kids? The girls make enough noise around here. Besides, who said you were thirty-five? You're probably forty-five and should be reaching menopause anyway. Don't blame opium on your troubles. The only bad thing

it has done to you is make your breasts smaller. My poor son would
appreciate bigger breasts." Bibigul laughs heartily.

I sit on their red-colored mats quietly as they joke with each
other.

Bibigul finally turns to me. "I became addicted when my husband died three years ago in Pakistan. We didn't have enough to eat.
We opened our fast during Ramadan with water. But opium was the
only cure for my aches. It's cheaper than medicine. I didn't know it
could be addictive, but now I know and I want to quit but I can't.
It's like being hungry and you need to eat. My stomach doesn't just
growl, my entire body growls. So I eat it."

At a 2010 Moscow conference about the drug trade in Afghanistan,
Russia reported that it had surpassed Iran as the highest consumer
of Afghan opiates: 549 tons. Iran came in second with 547 tons. However, Iran still holds the highest ratio of addiction per capita. Pakistan
has an estimated four million addicts. The Central Asian countries
bordering northern Afghanistan are seeing a rise in their addiction
population, too, as instability and poverty grow at the same rate as
opium output in Afghanistan. Europe consumes 711 tons. In Britain, the aristocracy used heroin in the first half of the twentieth
century, but the drug has swiftly made its way into the lower classes
in rural and urban areas. Addicts report that the amount of heroin
that cost $100 in the 1970s now costs $20 on London streets, and 90
percent of the heroin in Britain is from Afghanistan. In the United
States and Europe, the addiction rate is steady, but counternarcotics experts are predicting a surge even there, as heroin is becoming
more available, more potent, and more affordable.

The United States leads the world in the number of drug addicts. According to the National Survey on Drug Use and Health, in
2008, 20.1 million Americans aged twelve and older abused drugs—

that's 8 percent of the entire U.S. population. The most popular illicit drug is marijuana (15.2 million). The least used, but the most deadly, is heroin (0.2 million). According to the DEA, 18 percent of the heroin, 212 tons, entering the United States and Canada originates from Afghanistan. Afghan heroin is so pure it can be smoked or snorted; it doesn't have to be injected. In December 2006, the *Los Angeles Times* reported that for Americans who procure Afghan heroin, the number of overdoses is rising, because addicts have not adapted to the drug's potency.

In Afghanistan, American soldiers and contractors face the same risk of addiction that Soviet troops did during war. In March 2009, a DynCorp company team leader died from an overdose and four of his team leaders tested positive for drug abuse. Six months later, a Dyncorp medic was found dead of a possible drug overdose in Kabul. Australian soldiers are also suffering overdoses. In October 2009, the Web site *The Daily Beast* reported that the Taliban were employing a common tactic of war by supplying drugs to foreign troops. The insurgency has found local pipelines to provide drugs to Americans at Bagram Airfield. American soldiers who'd become addicted told *The Daily Beast* that the local bazaar in Bagram sells heroin, and soldiers trade knives, helmets, and flak jackets for the drug. Drug abuse among U.S. troops may have doubled since the Iraq and Afghanistan wars began. The American government randomly tests soldiers and, if they are addicted, flies them home for treatment.

The addicts with the fewest resources for treatment are Afghans. For Riaz, Bibigul, and Parizad, the possibility of a drug-free future is dim, despite their efforts to seek treatment. The overflow of cheap opium and heroin, the dearth of health care, and the high unemployment rate in Kabul will continue to make it that much more difficult for them to surrender the narcotic that temporarily soothes the pain that has lasted three decades.

———————

On her way back to the United States, my mother has to stop off in Kabul again because it has the only international airport in the country. She's beaming with enthusiasm when she arrives from Herat after twenty-two days. She can't stop talking.

"I attended two weddings in one day, my nephew's and my cousin's daughter's wedding. There were so many people I saw and everyone was so kind. We ate sumptuous food and I watched the young girls do these new Iranian dances at the weddings.

"I did get sick from eating salad one day. I was vomiting and my *bacha mama* [maternal cousin] had to bring in a nurse to give me an IV. There was no Prilosec for my stomach problems.

"I wore the burqa just to keep the dust off me, but I am so clumsy at wearing it now.

"I was so impressed with Herat. It is so much better off than Kabul. My relatives are wealthier now than when I left them. They advanced despite the wars. Their kids are more educated, in pharmacy school; one is head of a department at Herat University.

"But I have to say my favorite part were the public bathhouses. They're so clean and nice now. Before women used to dip themselves and jump in the water storage tank, and the bath water was so dirty. But now there's normal plumbing and faucets with sparkling clean water, hot and cold water, and each person can have their own little room to wash in. What was the same as twenty years ago? The women wore gold still, gossiped, and enjoyed each other in the bathhouse."

My mother has one more day and night at my house in Kabul before her flight to the United States. "Madar, would you come back to live here?" I ask the question that has been nagging me since she left for Herat. Somehow, in the back of my mind, I think if my mother returns to live here, I can have my family and homeland together again.

She pauses. "Maybe."

That day, I walk her up to the roof of the Karte Parwan house. A comfortable breeze cools my face. I look at the scene: the kite flyers, the women washing clothes in their courtyards, the children playing hopscotch in the street. It feels good to be part of a Kabul returning to normal life. But my mother has the opposite reaction.

"The houses are so small and ugly. They all look the same, like Pakistan. The courtyards are tiny. They used to have large gardens in Kabul courtyards. Look over there. There used to be so many trees and a little creek there. It's dry with thorns now. And the debris—look at that building; those holes in it must be the places where the bullets entered. And that building over there is missing its roof. Look at the piles of garbage and all the flies. These children on the street"—she takes a deep breath—"they look so thin and hungry."

Then she stops talking. She buries her face in her hands and cries, loudly this time, for half an hour. I just hold her and let her grieve. Only four years ago I stood at the edge of the roof of my grandfather's orchard home in Herat and felt a surge of powerful emotions. The Kabul view is the most my mother has seen of the capital. Driving on the streets and shopping have not revealed the stark nakedness of the city's destruction. The *manzara* (view) is a bittersweet reminder of unwanted changes; the physical picture of the ugly remains of what was once a beautiful city with beautiful people. Her Kabul is dead.

I make cups of green tea for us in the kitchen. "Fariba, I don't think I could live here again," my mother says. "There's no proper health care and I'm sick. It's not safe, and my grandchildren are in the United States. You know I can't live without them. I'm used to it there."

"It's okay, Madar. I understand. You don't have to come back. I'll always come and see you."

TWELVE

Women on Both Sides of the Law

Inside the newly built counternarcotics compound in Kabul, Farzana and Nazaneen stand in the back row with the rest of the women in the National Interdiction Unit—behind the men. They do not want their male colleagues to gawk at their behinds when they bend down for exercises.

"Push-ups!" shouts Jane, their Blackwater-employed American trainer.

The two dozen men and women drop to the ground and pant through their push-ups. Farzana and Nazaneen, at eighteen and nineteen, are the youngest members of the team. The NIU consists of 225 members in 10 groups. They are training to become Afghanistan's elite drug enforcement agents. Men and women are both held to the same physical and intelligence standards. The fifteen women have to pass the same tests of strength and coordination. The women like going to the shooting range in helicopters, but they wish they could skip the workouts. Just a few years ago, under the Taliban, these women weren't allowed to leave their homes unattended. Now they're preparing to fight brutal drug dealers alongside male colleagues. They walk around the compound in police fatigues, caps, and boots. They carry Glock 17 pistols, Kalashnikovs, or machine guns on stakeouts. Few of them have been tested in actual drug busts or other operations, but Farzana and Nazaneen have already proven their might on a city bus. The team calls them the Ninja Ladies.

Farzana, a lively teenager, drinks her cup of green tea in the women's locker room, where there are beds and a dining table for overnight shifts inside the compound. Nazaneen is absent today due to an illness.

"I feel alone without her," Farzana says. "She's my partner in everything."

Farzana is petite, with high cheekbones and a thick braid of smooth, straight black hair. Both of the girls come from the Hazara ethnic group, descendants of Genghis Khan. The Hazaras have been persecuted throughout Afghanistan's contemporary history and are considered the poorest and hardest working people in the region. They are Shiites with East Asian features that physically set them apart from Tajiks and Pashtuns. But decades of refugee life—tens of thousands of them fled to Iran during the wars—gave Hazaras the education and opportunities to mobilize upward when they repatriated to Afghanistan. Hazaras are running for president and seats in Parliament; the only female governor is Hazara; and many of the winning performers on *Afghan Star*, Afghanistan's version of *American Idol*, have been Hazaras. Farzana and Nazaneen exude the confidence of a people freed from apartheid.

"I will do what is necessary to defend myself and my colleagues," Farzana says, beaming. "My parents raised me to be confident and feel equal to men. I'm anticipating going on an operation and fighting criminals. I'm proud to serve my country."

"I heard you've already been tested on a Kabul bus," I say.

Farzana laughs, clearly embarrassed. "Before the unit had their own bus to take them home we had to take public buses," she begins. The buses in Kabul are supposed to be gender segregated, but the crowds prevent any kind of order. Men and women end up sitting together, an act that would've cost several lashes under the Taliban.

"We were both dressed in our usual long coat and head scarf heading home on the *milli* [national] bus. We leave our fatigues at work. Men and women were stacked against each other, with little room for mobility. We clutched our handbags tightly and held on to each other for support. A clean-shaven man with beady eyes and long fingers was making kissing sounds at us. I warned him with a harsh stare. Yet he was turned on by the defiance. He lightly caressed my shoulder.

"Nazaneen watched, livid. She kept a calm face but she actually has a temper worse than any man I know, especially when her friends are being offended. Nazaneen is actually the one who speaks up when comments are made against women. She lost her patience with this man. She grabbed his hand away from my shoulder and cursed him. The man ignored her and touched my other shoulder with his other hand and stroked the back of my leg with his knee. Nazaneen jerked and stuck her elbow into his stomach," Farzana recalls, picking up the thermos to pour another cup of tea.

The harasser wasn't expecting these women to fight so hard. Usually women move away from harassers, because that is considered the polite and proper thing for them to do. If they do fight back, they usually do it verbally. But these women couldn't have cared less about being proper, and they had the confidence to over-power the man.

"His temper flared, and he bent forward and brandished a small knife to strike Nazaneen. The passengers noticed the harassment but apparently not the knife, because they just watched. I saw the weapon and quickly held out my hand to prevent the blow. As the man raised the knife and struck forward, the blade seared my hand, between my thumb and forefinger, and I felt a cold sting and then pouring blood."

Nazeneen didn't stand still. Both girls had been given a weapon—a Ka-Bar knife with a sharp blade and round green handle with a metal cover—the same one U.S. Marines carry. She rapidly reached into her bag to grab her knife and then stabbed the man in his leg with all her strength. He screamed and spouted a string of pejora-tives.

"Stop the damn bus!" he shouted at the bus driver. "These women are whores and killers. Get them!" The clueless driver pressed the brakes suddenly and many of the passengers fell on top of one an-other.

Amid the chaos, Farzana wrapped her hand in a cloth she'd found in her purse, to minimize the bleeding. The back door of the bus slid open and the passengers cleared the way. The man ran off holding his leg, while the girls jumped out and yelled for help. Na-zaneen held her friend's bleeding hand tightly. Farzana's head was pounding, and all she could hear was the rapid beating of her heart. Nazaneen hailed a yellow-and-white Kabul cab.

"When we reached the hospital, the doctor said, 'Who the hell gave you the right to carry a knife?' We didn't tell him that we worked for the government as police. We usually keep our job a secret. We just told him that our knives were for self-defense, and this was such a case. I got several stitches," she says, showing me the wound between her thumb and forefinger. It's her scar of glory.

"You seem to like your job. Why?" I ask.

"Because I can do it well, and as women, we have to prove ourselves."

Adiba, Farzana's oldest female colleague, who is sitting near us, eyes the teenager patronizingly. "It's not as fun as you think, *qandem* [sweetie]," she says.

Adiba has taken part in several drug raids. Forty-one years old, she was a police general for six years and had extensive police training under the Communist regime. She seems jaded and tired. I learn she has three children and is working to support them; agents receive about $150 a month. The adventure of raids doesn't entice her.

"I'm happy to be a part of this team, but these operations are the same. We're just told to search the women perpetrators for now; and the rest the men take care of. They don't really expect us to do any shooting and fighting. The last operation I went on was uneventful. My superiors called me in the middle of the night and told me to be ready. They don't announce the busts sooner because of double agents.

"We went through the mountains in Logar province [near Kabul]. The road was so dark and scary that I considered that the most dangerous part," Adiba shares as she freshens her makeup and takes down her hair from a bun. She's getting ready to go home. Her burqa hangs in her locker.

"Once we got to the location, there were sixty men in a caravan of cars and me, the only woman. We spent two nights there. We raided a house and I was called in to search the women. I was dressed in my police uniform. They didn't believe I was a woman. They asked me to show my private body parts to prove it, so I did," Adiba says as the other girls giggle.

Adiba is extremely feminine, with red painted nails and three-inch heels. She has more makeup on than the other women combined, and her voluptuous figure makes it hard for me to believe she could ever have been mistaken for a man. Perhaps in her uniform she looks more masculine.

"The women resisted, calling me names, but I found nothing on their bodies. I found several firearms in suitcases. My male colleagues confiscated dozens of containers of hashish in the same house. It was a well-off family."

"Was anyone arrested?" I ask.

"No. The man of the house, whom we wanted to arrest, had already escaped."

"Have you gone on any operations that became violent?"

"Yes, in one operation four men were killed and two were injured. I was told to stay put in the car," Adiba says. She doesn't embellish or provide too much detail, like many other law enforcement personnel I interview. She's politely taciturn, well trained in discretion.

Farzana and her other younger colleagues listen to Adiba wide-eyed.

"I can't wait to join you," Farzana says.

"You'll get over it," Adiba responds. She grabs her purse and burqa and drapes the garment over her arm, then shuts her locker. It's three thirty PM, time for her to go home, make dinner for her children, and do the laundry.

During the Bush-Blair years, the four pillars of the counternarcotics strategy in Afghanistan include forced eradication, bolstered law enforcement, interdiction, and alternative development. One key component missing from this strategy, which would have involved the nations that receive Afghan drugs, was reduction in demand. The most effective way to reduce illicit drug consumption is to find ways to prevent addiction, counternarcotics agents from various nations tell me. But Afghan counternarcotics agents know little about this concept. They know only that poppy farms must be eradicated, and that law enforcement must have the tools and skills to interdict and capture the kingpins and traffickers who control the drug trade. Implementing the strategy has been a slow process, as those involved are unable to keep up with the growing number of poppy farms, addicts, and traffickers.

Two Afghan ministries are dedicated to counternarcotics. The Ministry of the Interior handles the policing and interdiction, and the new Ministry of Counternarcotics is supposed to create policy and strategy. But nearly every Afghan ministry must deal with the impact of drugs: the Ministry of Justice is responsible for prosecuting corrupt officials and drug lords; the Ministry of Agriculture has to work with farmers when their crops are eradicated, to provide seeds and fertilizer for alternative crops; the Ministry of Health must help treat the burgeoning number of drug addicts; and the Ministry of Defense is directly involved in fighting the trade as the Afghan National Army, NATO, and U.S. troops battle traffickers in bed with the insurgency. The problem is that in every echelon of the government, corrupt officials receive bribes to look the other way or take cuts from the trade. Some of the officials are traffickers themselves.

The insurgency is using drug money to bankroll its fight against Western troops and the Afghan government. The numbers vary on how much drug money is being used each year to fund the insurgency—from $23 million to $250 million—but now the foreign countries with troops on the front line in Afghanistan no longer separate drugs and terrorism as they did from 2001 to 2007. The Taliban mainly tax the farmers and give protection to traffickers, who in turn give them a percentage of their drug profits. NATO and U.S. soldiers arrest traffickers while capturing militants and work with poppy farmers to help them find other means of survival.

The intensified focus on the drug trade in recent years has made the National Interdiction Unit a critical force, and the women members have become crucial elements as more women become mules and traffickers. Women can smuggle drugs much more easily, hiding a stash in their clothes or suitcases. Some of these women are more powerful than law enforcement officials realize. General Aminullah Amarkhil, the former chief of security at Kabul Airport, once dared to arrest two women and a male member of the Ariana Airlines technical team who were trying to smuggle heroin. The three were headed to India when one of the women was caught with five kilos of the drug. Amarkhil video-taped the arrests. One of the women told Amarkhil, "Do not touch me and do not touch the drugs. If I make one phone call, I can fire you from your position."

Amarkhil asked the woman whom she would call.

"They are powerful people. They are higher than you in the government," the woman replied. She swore she would get back her heroin.

The woman was taken to jail. That night Amarkhil received a call from an angry man, an apparent trafficker, who told him that he should not have apprehended the woman and that she would be released. The general found out later that the woman was freed and fled to Pakistan. Amarkhil told the press that the woman's release was ordered by officials in the government. Shortly after, Amarkhil was charged with a minor offense and fired from his job. The number of drug arrests and seizures at the airport fell after his dismissal. The general fought back, running for Parliament in the September 2010 elections—he lost. Instead, the government appointed him head of border patrol in the north of the country, a job that entails battling drugs.

The woman who cost the security chief his job was well connected to a major trafficking ring, but most of the Afghan women who transport drugs are victims of poverty and war for whom trafficking is a last resort.

There are four official gates through which to enter and leave the capital, on paved roads that go north, south, southeast, and west. Each gate is manned by the Rapid Reaction Force police, who stop buses and suspicious vehicles to search for contraband and criminals. Fifty policemen and one policewoman monitor the cars in shifts. Zainab is one of three policewomen at the northern gate, which is known as Kotal Khair Khana. She searches the hundreds of vehicles from eleven provinces that pass through the gate from six AM to six PM, seven days a week. Cars drive at one hundred miles per hour and halt to a sudden stop at the gate. The gate is not an actual gate but consists of a mere rope blocking the wide road and a booth manned by police. The search police live in a small compound on the side of the road surrounded by the Kabul hills, a mosque, a gas station, and a small grocery. They spend their free time in three rooms where they eat, sleep, and watch the traffic go by. The men's bathroom is a squat toilet inside the compound, and the women's bathroom is a walk uphill through rocks and bushes of thorns to a ditch. Inside the ditch are human waste and cheap Chinese-made pink toilet paper. The heat intensifies the stench of urine and feces.

Zainab usually sits with the men, chatting throughout the day. She doesn't have Farzana's youthful enthusiasm or Adiba's apathetic pragmatism toward her job as a drug buster. She has an ambivalent attitude about being part of law enforcement. "I'm happy when I catch a criminal, but I feel sorry for the women. I feel pity for them, but it's the law." Zainab is not a member of the NIU but a simple policewoman who finished the requisite three months of police academy training. She has a sixth-grade education but a keen sense of smell to sniff out opium. The NIU women have the satisfaction of thinking that they are capturing evil mafia members and big drug lords, but Zainab's job, with an income of fifty dollars a month, puts her in contact with ordinary Afghan women smugglers who eke out a living. Most of them are widows.

At twenty-seven, Zainab is also a widow, and the mother of four children. She rents a room in a house in Kabul without a phone. Her husband, whom she was married to at age thirteen, was killed in the war between the mujahideen and the Taliban, in Takhar province. "He was a mujahid fighting against the Taliban. He could not stand the way they looked at Islam and how they made the religion seem so bad in the eyes of the world," Zainab says in her soft-spoken voice. "If he were alive, I would've preferred not to work, but he would've been proud that I got this job."

Zainab is one of the best among all the officers at sniffing out hidden drugs. "She can smell the opium from a long distance," says her commander, Lal Mohammed. "I'm very happy with her because she's also kind to the people she catches. Having a woman on the team makes us more humane."

We're sitting inside one of the rooms in the compound looking out the window for large passenger buses to arrive. Zainab wears a long coat and over it a jersey jacket with the word *Police* written in English and Farsi on the back. Her head scarf is wrapped tightly, with no hair visible. Her nails are polished red, and her eyebrows are unnaturally black, penciled unevenly to form an exaggerated arch around her eyes.

Zainab has caught more than fifty women with contraband tucked away, mostly in their handbags, including a small bomb, firearms, hashish, and of course opium and heroin. She rattles off a list of her conquests for me.

"It was a Monday, about ten AM. A woman in a van coming from a nearby village had several kilos of opium neatly packed in her vest. I always get suspicious when women wear vests, because they're out of style these days. In another case, it was a rich woman dressed in an expensive pantsuit. I smelled her large video camera. We found sixteen kilos hidden in the camera and its tapes. She was the owner of a poppy farm and was taking the harvest to sell in Kabul.

"Another time, I caught seven kilos in a blanket. Most of the smugglers coming on this route are from Mazar city. They hide it in every place they can think of: thermoses, tapes, inside jewelry. They spray their belongings with a perfume that is usually sprayed on dead people before they are buried, to cover the smell, but that's always a giveaway for me. One woman resisted the search. When I insisted, she slapped me twice and scratched my hands. 'What do you want? I have nothing,' she said. My commander had to calm her down, and when I finally searched her, I found a small amount of opium in a soap dish. She was an addict." Zainab pauses, her voice quivering. "She really had nothing on her, she was so poor. We let her go."

"You weren't upset that she slapped you?" I ask. "You could've arrested her for assault."

"It wasn't worth it," she explains, regaining the composure in her voice.

Zainab's compassion toward the smugglers is uncommon among police, who are known to beat and sometimes torture criminals. She empathizes with the smugglers' desperation; their life stories echo hers. The difference is Zainab had options and chose the law; the women smugglers turned to illicit means for survival. This choice seems to weigh her down with guilt, but she pushes it away.

"It's almost time for the next bus to arrive," she says, eyeing her watch. "We should go stand outside."

A few minutes later a bus the size of a Greyhound stops, and Zainab boards it with confidence. I follow her with the policemen. While the policemen search all the men, Zainab makes eye contact with every woman but doesn't pat down all of them. The passengers look sleepy after a ten-hour ride from Takhar. Zainab picks five or six women. She asks them to stand politely, then digs her hands through all the crevices of their clothes and bodies. Afterward, she picks up their belongings and looks through every item. She finds nothing illegal. "You can sit down now. Thank you." The policemen do not step off the bus until Zainab is done. They have to protect her.

"Let us go. This is a waste of time," one woman shouts. "If you wanted to catch the real criminals, you would have stopped the Benzes with tinted windows!"

The policemen and Zainab do not respond. After the suitcases in the baggage compartment are searched, the police commander motions the driver to pull away. The search team heads back to the compound as a black SUV with tinted windows zooms by.

"Why aren't you going to search that car?" I ask. "How do you decide which vehicles to search?"

"Sometimes informants from the northern provinces will call us and tell us if there are private cars that need to be searched. We usually stick to the public vehicles and search private cars we deem suspicious," Lal Mohammed, the commander explains.

"But aren't the big shipments of drugs transported in private cars?" I ask. "The public vehicles are usually the poor people who smuggle small amounts."

Lal Mohammed gives me a knowing look. "We do what we're told from the top," he answers.

"Don't you feel like your job is futile when the drugs are passing right by you?" I insist.

"We can't stop the real perpetrators," he admits halfheartedly. "If it's a minister or some general, we can't stop them. We have to show respect for them." If his team intercepted these vehicles, an official from the top echelons of the government would make sure the smugglers were freed. Lal Mohammed might lose his job, as the Kabul airport security chief did. Isolated and vulnerable to insurgent attacks, the search team plays it safe and focuses on finding a few kilos of opium on the poorest. When I ask Zainab how she feels about the injustice of this, she takes her time responding.

"I focus on my little job and leave the bigger things to the educated folks," she says, and then smirks. "I've never known there to be justice in Afghanistan. The poor always lose."

Children kick a soccer ball around inside the women's section of Karbul's notorious Pul-e-Charkhi prison, a penitentiary of doom built decades ago by the French and filled with political prisoners, serial killers, and terrorists. The torture chambers of Pul-e-Charkhi are etched in the collective memory of educated Afghans imprisoned during the Communist invasion. A guard inside the men's section of the prison says he can hear ghosts moaning at night, the souls of the innocent who suffered and died here. I enter the prison after a major riot in which there is a shootout between guards and inmates and several men die. I walk slowly through the concrete grounds, wondering if my paternal uncle who disappeared during the Soviet invasion spent time here.

The women's section of the prison is a separate structure a few yards distant from the main building. It's separated by high walls and a large door. The women incarcerated here can keep their children with them during their sentence. I stroll through the loud hallways. A woman with a boy's short black haircut, her hair sticking

out in different directions, walks around with a boom box playing
Ahmed Zahir's songs.

> Tell the heavens
> To deliver my heart's desire to my lover.

A few women sing along, while others sway from side to side as
they do their chores. The women roam freely inside this building,
which resembles a college dormitory. They even have a television
set to watch the local stations. It's near lunchtime and the sound of
the pressure cooker competes with the music. An aroma of rice and
bean stew wafts down the hallway. These are not the conditions I
imagined at Pul-e-Charkhi, but the guard tells me the men's section
is "really a jail. This is more like playland."

The prison may seem like a playland, but when visitors' hours
end, the guards can do what they want. In 2004, women in the central Kabul jail (not Pul-e-Charkhi) waiting for their cases to be heard
staged a riot. I listened outside the walls of the small jail on the
government grounds in downtown Kabul as they screamed and
shouted words I could not hear. They were protesting being raped
by the guards. More than half of the women in Afghan jails are
serving sentences for moral crimes, such as running away from
home, often from forced marriages.

Totakai is not one of them. She is one of seventy women in jail
here, and one of five women convicted for drug smuggling. When I
walk in, she is lying on a bunk bed. She sits up and spreads a blanket
over her legs. Her eyes are sunken and her creased brown skin is
sallow. "I've been here for six months and I haven't really eaten for
three of those months," she explains.

She is a forty-year-old widow with four daughters and one son.
Her son is fifteen and the family breadwinner, with a small shop

that sells gum and drinks in Nangarhar province. He has also been convicted for drug smuggling, as an accomplice to his mother.

She wears a purple velvet dress and a silver ring on her finger with fading henna on the tips of her fingers and fingernails. "I didn't do it," she says, without any inquiry from me. "I was framed. Somebody put the sack of heroin under my feet in the station wagon. I had gone for a holiday from Nangarhar to Peshawar and on my way back, we decided to pass Nangarhar and go south to Ghazni for a pilgrimage. We took a taxi with six other passengers and when we stopped for a bathroom break, a man brought a bag and put it under my feet."

"Why did you let him do that? Didn't you want to know what was in it?" I ask.

"I was too tired from all the traveling."

Totakai is from Shinwar, Nangarhar, an area infamous for heroin laboratories. The counternarcotics police routinely fly in helicopters and travel through the mountain passes of Shinwar to blow up the labs. All they usually find are empty pots and pans.

Totakai pleads ignorance about the laboratories and how many kilos of heroin the police found on her. "I don't know these things," she says. "I just sit here and cry and pray that I can go home soon."

"But you've been convicted of heroin smuggling. You're going to be here a while. Do you know how long?"

"No. The defense attorney told me she can get me out soon."

"Where's your family? Do they visit you?"

"They don't know I'm here. They would kill me if they find out. It's better if they think I'm dead," she says, lying down and crawling under her blanket.

Totakai is one of several women I interview in Afghan jails charged with narcotics smuggling, and she is representative of most who end up in jail. They are usually poor women without the contacts or the money to bribe their way out. She may lose her health being incarcerated, and I think about putting her in touch with Zainab. The two women are both widows with children, and the heads of their households. Perhaps the compassionate Zainab can overlook Totakai's small crime and find a way to reunite her with her family. I hope that something more powerful than money—empathy from a woman in the government—can rescue this inmate.

Later I explain Totakai's story to Zainab on the phone at work, and she says she has little power but will bring the case up with her superiors. I leave the matter to the two women and go in search of a female trafficker who's still actively working.

I sit on a lone chair inside an empty office in Pul-e-Khumri, a luscious city in the northern province of Baghlan, famous as a vacation spot before the wars, and listen to Haroon. Baghlan produces pistachios and has a copper mine, but it is becoming a drug trafficking center as well. Haroon is an intellectual from a reputable family who works for a cultural organization. He also happens to have many friends who are drug traffickers. He claims absolute innocence, but possesses a wealth of information about the business in his province. I tell him I would like to meet a woman trafficker. He has one in mind, but informs me that I can meet her only if I pretend to be a buyer.

"In order for the transaction to go through, you must provide them with a hostage. They will release the hostage when the meeting is over. They want six hundred dollars up front before the meeting, just for the opportunity to talk to them. They think you're big because you're a foreigner, and that's where the market is. They said they have a ton [of opium] to sell.

"Conditions include no discussion except for the price and the purity of the product. The other woman will bring a sample for you to try, and you're not allowed to take a notebook, pen, map, or any weapons with you. They will pick you up from the town center and take you to the destination. I can be your escort but I cannot be part of the transaction.

"Ready to do it?" He looks at me, expecting an excited yes.

"The question is do I have to actually buy the opium?"

"Probably a few kilos to show them you mean business and then tell them you'll buy the rest later," Haroon says matter-of-factly.

"Who do they think I am?" I ask.

"I told them you were a writer researching a book on women and didn't have the money to publish it. And you hang out with hedonist foreigners who like to use drugs for recreation. As soon as I said 'foreigner' and 'drugs,' they got excited.

"My head's on the line, because they're trusting you because of me," he says sternly. "So when should we go through with it?" he impatiently asks.

"I'll get back to you," I reply. I walk out of his office and never see him again.

THIRTEEN
Adventures in Karte Parwan

General Asif, head of the National Interdiction Unit, tells me I can join them on a drug raid if I agree to watch from afar. The raid is going to take place in my old neighborhood, Karte Parwan. The NIU agents are going to surround the drug dealer in his shop on the main street of the neighborhood and search his place, where they expect to find opium and hashish. Then they will arrest him. I am ordered to position myself across the street like a bystander.

"It's a shop with seven or eight people," Asif explains. "We have an informant inside who tells us the shopkeeper is selling dope. Today we're finally ready to do a raid on the shop. That entire bazaar has an underground network of small dealers and we want the small dealers so we can capture the bigger ones."

The general and I have been meeting for weeks and discussing the perils of the drug trade. It has taken time for him to open up to me. But recently Asif, a former math and physics teacher, had a scolding from his bosses to be more discreet about the level of corruption in the government and the involvement of high officials in narcotics. He's obeying, but with pent-up frustration. "I can't talk about it," he says with a sigh when I ask if his team is wasting their time arresting culprits who will simply pay a bribe to be freed again.

Robust in size and character, he seems to genuinely care about his team and his job, spending hours at the office or on operations. He wears big watches and earth-tone suits and carries a pistol hidden beneath his jacket. He treats his team like his children, especially the women. Protecting them seems at times to be more important to him than confiscating narcotics and capturing criminals. With each meeting, we form a bond, and he speaks to me in the same fatherly tone I hear him using with the NIU women.

"Fariba Jan," he says in Farsi with an endearing Pashto accent, "you can't show yourself to these men, because they can hurt you if they see you on the street without our protection. You must stay to the side and pretend you know nothing."

I nod my head in agreement. An hour later, in a striped black pant suit and black head scarf, I am squished in a Russian Jeep among Asif, a white-bearded prosecutor who's here to witness the bust and gather evidence, and several uniformed and plainclothes officers with AK-47s. There is an informant on site who will purchase opium from the shopkeeper and whom the agents will arrest while in the act. We drive toward the Baharistan bazaar.

Asif receives a call from the narc near the shop. He responds in Pashto and then tells the driver to go slower. He looks at me and says, "The owner we want to bust has left the shop and left his young son in charge." He looks worried.

"So what happens now?" I ask.

"We wait and see," he responds, annoyed.

The prosecutor, who does not want to be named, tells me he's anxious for the special counternarcotics court to open. "It's the only way we can keep these guys in jail," he says. "In the meantime, we capture them by day and they're out by night."

His candidness surprises me. The group in this Jeep do their job knowing that their efforts are futile. "We do it for the income and for the hope that things could improve," the prosecutor explains.

I look at the men in the Jeep and wonder if any of them is a double agent, taking cuts from drug barons while arresting the smaller dealers. In Afghanistan, civil servants and government officials are perceived as guilty (not by the law but by the people) until proven innocent. Whether this is unfair pessimism or justified doubt, I have been indoctrinated here to distrust anyone in power.

Asif receives another call, and the driver speeds up. He drops me off a couple of hundred yards away. The uniformed and plainclothes agents jump out around the corner from the shop. I begin walking toward the shop hoping no one recognizes me. I've bought my groceries and sweets in this bazaar. I had no idea the shops were riddled with drug pushers.

A year before, I still lived in the Karte Parwan neighborhood, which is perched on top of a hill, with angled streets that remind me of San Francisco. It is ten degrees colder than the rest of the capital. The two-story house rented by the aid organization I work for looks kempt and swanky from the street. It has four bedrooms, a large living room, a dining space, three bathrooms, and a kitchen awkwardly situated upstairs. We also have water tainted with feces, electricity for only a couple of hours a night, and no proper heating. In the winter, my gas heater catches fire and is destroyed. I have to wear four layers of clothing and sleep with three blankets to keep warm. The olive oil and bottled drinking water we keep on the kitchen counter freeze from the below-zero Kabul temperatures.

Pajhwok, the Afghan news agency I'm working for, is in its infancy and is supervised by a British NGO. The NGO has spent thousands of dollars installing barbed wire and safeguarding the house and has built a wooden booth for a guard to protect us around the clock. The guard booth in other foreigner-occupied houses is outside the walls of the house, but ours was built inside our small front yard. That means my two housemates and I have little privacy. Before the wars the neighborhood was considered upscale. Now it is filled with commanders loyal to the late Massoud and their kin from the Panjshir Valley. Plenty of children with white skin and green eyes, features common to Panjshiris, play on the street. At the end of our block is a mosque with a green-lit minaret, and every Friday, the resident mullah gives a sermon damning hedonism and excess. The message is typical of every sermon I have heard in half a dozen Muslim countries I've visited. I don't take it too seriously—in the beginning.

My previous trips to Afghanistan took me to Herat, where I stayed with relatives, but in Kabul, I live without any family. I've moved to the capital with hope for change and a job that gives me a view into the lives of moderate and somewhat educated men and women who want to be part of a more liberal and democratic Afghanistan. One of the women I'm training in journalism is Lailuma Sadid. She's a twenty-five-year-old fashion diva and one of the hardest working reporters on staff. She has lived through the years of war without ever leaving the country. With chic short hair and a petite, well-proportioned figure, Lailuma wears clothes that rile some of the more conservative men in the office—tight jeans and a head scarf that sits more on her shoulders than around her head.

This wife and mother scoffs at the men who disapprove of her appearance. "If my husband doesn't mind my clothes, it's none of your business," she tells one of the male editors who openly criticizes her. Behind every woman testing boundaries in Afghanistan seems to be a man who supports her. Qudrat, Lailuma's husband, takes care of their five-year-old daughter and the household. He's a taxi driver, and his hours are flexible. They're a rare modern couple—in my eyes, a model for urban Afghans.

One evening a bomb explodes, shaking the windows of the news agency in the new city of Kabul. Lailuma is the only reporter in the newsroom, with a few of the foreign trainers. Five months pregnant with her second child and wearing three-inch heels, she jumps into one of the agency vans with me and a couple of other trainers and we head to the bomb site, where the police are already clearing the dead. The roads are blocked; vehicles cannot drive through. She and I must run half a mile through shattered glass and debris to get close to the site of the explosion. The smoke from the blast is smoldering and people are running in all directions. Lailuma writes down what she observes and holds out her tape recorder to anyone willing to talk. It's the first time she's covering a bomb explosion, even though she has lived through dozens of them in her lifetime.

Lailuma was born shortly before the Soviet invasion and has no memories of a peaceful Afghanistan. But she's determined to improve the country's conditions, particularly in women's rights and freedom of the press. "We used to think our lives were in someone else's hands," she tells me. "Now I think I'm a new woman. I have the right to say what I want and do what I want." It's Afghans like her who inject me with optimism.

My plan in Kabul is to live like a local woman and respect the culture. I do not go out too often at night. I dress conservatively, and I fast during Ramadan. But as time passes and I become a resident instead of a visitor, I lose tolerance for the misogyny and tradition-alism. I realize that I cannot be a local Afghan woman no matter how hard I try. I talk back whenever a man on the street gives me a lustful stare or makes an inappropriate comment. One afternoon my Indian friend Aunohita and I hail a taxi. The driver notices my red-painted toenails beneath the straps of my summer sandals. He assumes I'm a foreigner and requests an exorbitant fare to take us to the Intercontinental Hotel, his eyes traveling up and down my fully covered body.

"That's too much money," I tell him. "I'll pay you fifty rupia [one dollar] or we can get another taxi."

"Fine, get in," he says.

As he drives, he doesn't look at the road. He keeps turning to stare at my friend and me.

"Where did you learn to speak Farsi so well?" he asks, revealing his yellow teeth in a sordid smile.

"I'm Afghan. Can you please look at the road and not us," I demand.

He's offended by my abruptness and begins to career around corners and speed through the traffic in his clunker. I'm frightened but I don't show it. I ignore him and chat with Aunohita in English. He brakes suddenly in front of our destination, and we get out. I throw the money at him, and he curses at me as he drives away.

Living in Afghanistan forces me to fight the patriarchy and to rebel, enjoying the freedoms that other expatriates do, but I pay the price with constant harassment.

The families in Karte Parwan know one another and do not like having foreign occupants in the neighborhood. When they find out that there's an Afghan girl living with a British man, my sixty-year-old housemate, Martin, it arouses anger and suspicion. One night Martin and a couple of American male friends who have come over for dinner are lured by the mild summer weather up to the roof to have tea. Women are dancing in the courtyard of one of the neighboring houses in celebration of a wedding. Out of curiosity, Martin and the other men look down at the celebration. I know this could have grave consequences and ask them to step away. It's too late.

The next day, one of the unscrupulous former mujahideen commanders in the neighborhood, Arif, knocks on our door and tells our guard that if the men ever go up to the roof again he will blow up our house. When I go to work that day, Qadeer, Pajhwok's operations director, calls me in to his office.

"Your neighbors have complained to the mullah at the mosque about you living with Martin," Qadeer says in a tone sympathetic to my neighbors. "They don't understand how an Afghan girl could live with a foreign man like this. It's dishonorable to them. I told the mullah that they should consider you as a foreigner, not an Afghan. They don't care about the other woman living with you, because she is American. It's dangerous for you. I'm not asking you to change your lifestyle, but please be aware of the things that offend people."

I'm livid, but I have been expecting the official complaint. I knew that having male friends over for dinner, living with a man not related to me, and working for a foreign aid organization were all taboo for me in this neighborhood. I pushed the boundaries as far as I could, but now I have to stand back and be more practical. Local Afghans are confused by Afghan girls who come from abroad, because they do not know what standards to hold them up to—they give foreign women the same freedoms as men, and local Afghan women have their own set of stifling rules. But girls like me are an enigma, and often the confusion over this turns into hostility.

We stop going up to the roof, and our dinner parties become few and far between. My Westernized lifestyle only hurts local Afghan women, because their neighbors will accuse them of becoming loose from working with women like me. It's not my battle to fight; it's Lailuma's. Local women must struggle against the rules that confine them. Only then will the changes be considered legitimate and permanent. Women like me are a passing phase, not yet part of the mosaic of Afghanistan. Our feminism is out of place and still too foreign to take root.

After my assignment with Pajhwok is complete, I move to another neighborhood.

From across the street at the Baharistan bazaar I watch the NIU snitch buy a cassette from a shopkeeper. Then the NIU police surround the small music shop and Asif goes inside. He comes out with the shopkeeper a few minutes later. The police climb into the Russian Jeep with the shopkeeper, Asif, and the prosecutor. I take a cab back to the compound where the shopkeeper will be questioned.

Fatah, the shopkeeper and an accused drug dealer, sits on a chair in Asif's office and nervously crosses one leg over the other several times. He cracks his knuckles with his uncuffed hands as Asif writes something in a report. The shopkeeper's pupils are pinned and his hair is long and disheveled. He wears sneakers and a Pakistani *pirahan tomban* that is too large for his gaunt build. The snitch bought two dollars worth of opium from him. The NIU agents say they also found drugs wrapped around his left leg under his *tomban.* One of the uniformed agents brings in the two packets of opium and five sticks of hashish discovered on him. They also found about $120 in his shop. He looks at me like a puppy dog, as if pleading for forgiveness. "I'll cooperate however you want. I have eleven kids at home; eight are two of my brothers' orphans. I'm the breadwinner for all of them. Give me three days and I'll find you the original seller," he begs Asif.

Asif ignores him and continues to take notes. Fatah asks if he can make a phone call to his son to tell him he's okay. "Yes, wait a minute," Asif responds cordially.

"How did you start selling drugs?" I ask the man.

"All the music sellers in Baharistan sell. A man on a bicycle named Jabar comes and sells us the drugs. I opened my shop six months ago and I was an addict. So I began selling while smoking at the same time.

"I charged five dollars for five grams of opium. What I make feeds the kids and my wife. One of my brothers died in a rocket attack during the mujahideen attacks, and one of them died of a disease. I have three of my own kids and the others are theirs. I lived in Pakistan for many years and when we moved back, I opened the cassette shop and wasn't making enough money with the music. This is the only business that's available for someone like me to make money."

I feel sorry for the man and wonder if all the effort and manpower by the NIU over such a small dealer is worth it. It seems hard to believe that he knows or has evidence against the bigger traffickers. Fatah's arrest only hurts a family of thirteen. What is the point of counternarcotics when the millions of aid dollars spent on it are producing more drugs and more drug dealers? I begin to feel the same skepticism that is creeping into the Afghan psyche in Kabul. The initial faith I had in the new government and its foreign backers is dissipating as I watch Afghanistan fall again. But I refuse to let the negativity take over.

By May 2005 the increasing population in Kabul—villagers leaving the countryside en masse in search of work in the capital—is taxing the city's resources. Power and water are rationed, and the worsening pollution is causing some Afghans to wear surgical masks as they ride to work on their bicycles. Of the eight million workers in the country, three million are unemployed and many flock to the capital for jobs. Prices for food and fuel are rising, parallel with crime rates. The piled-up garbage and the sewage in open ditches paint a vivid picture of what Kabul has become. The once-serene, green, and clean capital is turning into a chaotic urban sprawl like its neighboring cities Tehran and Karachi. When the U.S.-led coalition threw out the Taliban in 2001, Afghans dreamed of a pristine Kabul where food would be plentiful, jobs available, and the streets safe. It's now four years later, and the country is headed backward. "You smell the terrible odor emanating from the streets here?" a jewelry store owner tells me as I look at his ruby necklaces. "That's how much our new government stinks, and so do the Americans and British supporting them."

His metaphor demonstrates the growing resentment against the corruption being unveiled in the Karzai government. From bribery to drug dealing, many government officials and foreign contractors are profiting from the billions of dollars in aid money that's pouring in to Afghanistan. In the United States, Afghanistan is absent in the headlines as the Iraq war rages. Afghans' discontent is overshadowed by comparisons that Iraq is the losing battle and Afghanistan is the model war.

The international community is focused on the five-year Bonn Agreement that cobbled together the Karzai-led government in Germany in 2001. The plan is being implemented on time. Seventy percent of registered voters cast a ballot in the country's first democratic elections in 2004, and the next step is for the Afghan government to write and approve a constitution through a grand assembly with international support. Then come parliamentary elections. The aid community and returning Afghans like me see the implementation of the Bonn Agreement as a sign of progress, despite the setbacks.

"It takes time to make sweeping changes in a country that has been at war for decades. We can't expect immediate results," I tell another journalist friend who voices pessimism about the government. Meanwhile, the Taliban and al Qaeda have regrouped, retrained, and returned with ferocity from across the Pakistan border. Their new and effective weapon: suicide bombings. They do not have local support in most of the country yet, but the graft, the return of the warlords, and the lack of jobs will soon send more Afghans into the arms of the insurgency.

The biggest sector of the economy is still illicit narcotics. And one of the biggest accused kingpins is General Asif's boss, General Daud Daud, the former chief of counternarcotics. (Daud was killed in a suicide attack orchestrated by the Taliban in Takhar in May 2011.)

In June 2005 the counternarcotics highway police (separate from NIU) intercept at least 183 kilos of pure heroin on the road from Kabul to Jalalabad. The drugs belong to Sayyed Jan, who shows the police a signed letter from their boss Daud addressed to all government security forces in Lashkargah, Helmand: "Haji Sayyed Jan from the interior ministry has thirty people with him and is conducting an operation against drug trafficking and narcotics. He has the decree and permission to go ahead with his duties. Please assist him and do not stop him." Documents such as this letter imply that Daud writes protection letters for traffickers, who give him a cut of their profits. Those who have worked with him in the Afghan government say he receives $50,000 for each shipment and $100,000 for each protection letter. The antidrug czar denies any involvement in the drug trade.

Daud is an infamously mysterious man in the Afghan government. He has led the counternarcotics police since 2004 from the interior ministry, and insiders in the ministry have long accused him of helping drug smugglers transport narcotics and receiving huge cuts for his efforts. Other officials in the Afghan government say he's not just assisting the traffickers, but is a kingpin who controls the drug trade in the north of the country. Insiders say Karzai and his foreign backers deliberately hired Daud knowing he was involved in drugs in the hope that he would reform and rein in the traffickers under him—or keep the trade unified to prevent the business from falling under the control of smaller bandits.

The Karzai government demands hard evidence to investigate Daud or Wali Karzai, the president's half brother, who is accused of being an influential player in narcotics in Kandahar and Helmand. Daud, a native of the northern Takhar province, is a former member of Massoud's mujahideen group. He was rewarded with his high position in the government in part because he helps the Americans fight against the Taliban. In his hometown in Farkhar, Takhar, people recite poems in his honor. He can mobilize up to six thousand troops in forty-eight hours. But his appearance belies his power. He is a Tajik with soft manicured hands and a well-groomed beard framing handsome features. He's not a typical mujahideen. He speaks English, writes e-mails on a laptop, and has become media savvy with training from the American public relations firm The Rendon Group. He has two wives; the second is an American citizen.

Shortly after Daud is appointed as the antidrug czar, Lailuma and I interview him for a Pajhwok story about police officials involved in drug smuggling. I tread lightly when posing questions that might be seen as accusing him of any wrongdoing.

"How do you plan to root out these police smugglers?" I ask.

"We'll have a new accountability unit," he says. "We're hopeful that we can get rid of them. We won't solve the problem as long as there are corrupt police in the government, so dealing with these insiders is part of the policy."

The next time I meet with Daud is after the *Los Angeles Times* runs a story quoting one of his provincial deputies, Lieutenant Nya-matullah Nyamat, saying that his boss and his boss's brother Haji Agha protect traffickers. In the same article, a trafficker claims that Daud helped him secure a large shipment of drugs through the Salang Tunnel, the road that connects the north to Kabul.

It's unclear if Daud has mistaken me for a *Los Angeles Times* re-porter or thinks I can write a rebuttal. He's angry and accusatory as I walk into his office.

"You realize that you reporters are writing lies all the time," he scoffs.

I look at him confused. I'm aware of the article, but I've come to discuss a different matter.

"You need to write the truth," he insists. "Nyamat apologized to me for lying to the reporter about me. He will tell you that and swear by it. You need to write that and make sure people know I'm not a drug smuggler."

I nod my head and say nothing. Daud grabs a phone and calls Nyamat. There's no response.

"I'll get you in touch with him later. If you're a good reporter you will follow up on this."

I agree, and on another day when I call Daud, Nyamat is sitting in his office and Daud hands him the phone. The deputy hurriedly spews a practiced speech about Daud's innocence and how the *Los Angeles Times* misquoted him.

"Daud Sahib is innocent. He has nothing to do with the drug trade," Nyamat says. I am surprised the deputy still has a job, but he's no longer based in Kunduz province, which is part of Daud's turf. Briefly after the *Los Angeles Times* article is published in May 2005, Nyamat went missing. Daud secretly ordered his arrest, but British advisers persuaded the chief to release him. Nyamat is assigned a post in Bamiyan, a province in central Afghanistan and the least active area in drug trafficking.

Sayyed Jan, whom the smuggler police catch with heroin and the letter from Daud, is jailed, but he bribes his way out and is reported to be dealing drugs in Pakistan. Daud tries to free him at first, but later sides with the prosecution. Jan's relatives claim that Jan paid $50,000 to be allowed to traffic a convoy through Daud's zone. Jan is from Helmand and buys protection from government officials to run his heroin refineries and safely smuggle out his drugs. Daud is one of his most expensive protectors, but his letters are effective.

The letter Jan presents to the police is one of several paper documents leading to Daud, and his story only one of the dozens of other anecdotes detailing Daud's involvement in the drug trade. In another story counternarcotics agents capture a fuel tanker containing 1,540 pounds of opium and, after the driver makes a phone call, Daud's own bodyguards show up to free the shipment. The tanker and drugs are taken to the counternarcotics headquarters in the interior ministry.

I decide to make a trip through the Salang Tunnel to Daud's home province Takhar.

FOURTEEN

Raids in Takhar

I have come to Takhar, General Daud's turf, because the vendors here deal in heroin. Many of the smugglers are former mujahideen and current government officials. Before he was appointed the counternarcotics chief, Daud was governor of Takhar. The Taliban killed Daud's leader, Massoud, in Takhar. The province borders Tajikistan and is a transport route from other provinces to Central Asian countries and Russia, one of the largest markets for Afghan opiates. Competing with the Turkish and Albanian mafias for Afghan drug profits in Central Asia is the Islamic Movement of Uzbekistan (IMU), an extremist group aligned with al Qaeda and operating from Pakistan's tribal territories. Yet even in Central Asia and Russia, the mafia has powerful partners in the government who facilitate the transport of drugs. These groups have Afghan counterparts in Takhar.

I hire a local Takhar driver who owns a Toyota Corolla that is not capable of going more than twenty miles per hour on the unpaved plains and mountains.

"We have to go to Rustaq tonight. Don't worry. It's safe," my guide, Baktosh, a twenty-three-year-old Kabul university student, promises me. Baktosh also decides to give two of his relatives a ride without asking me. I sit in the front, and they bunch together in the backseat. Our driver isn't talkative or friendly. He stops the Toyota several times en route to take care of personal business in different homes. When he parks at a rest stop for dinner, I am fed up. It is pitch black and I am not hungry. We've already driven eight hours from Kabul to Takhar's capital, Taloqan. Rustaq, Baktosh's home district, is another five hours of driving. "Can't we keep going? It's midnight and I'm the only woman here."

"There are good commanders here who don't harm innocent people," Baktosh shoots back. "Good commanders" is an oxymoron in Afghanistan, but with the power vacuum left by the central government, it is the commanders who have brought a sense of security. The Kabul government has little control here. Local warlords divide up the turf by ethnicity. Mujahideen commanders Piram Qul, who's Uzbek, has controlled Rustaq district, and Amer Bashir, a Tajik, has reigned over Chahab district—both were unchallenged dictators for thirteen years, until the first parliamentary elections in 2005. Tajiks dominate Takhar, with Uzbeks as the second largest group. Pockets of Pashtuns and Hazaras also live here. These former mujahideen commanders have been in power in northern Takhar since 1992. The Kokcha River circles Rustaq and branches out to the Amu River, which divides Afghanistan and Tajikistan. The Taliban seized Takhar up to the Kokcha, but they have not been able to cross the river to capture the northern part of the province, which borders Badakhshan province. These commanders, under the leadership of Massoud, repelled the Taliban until the latter were ousted by the United States in 2001.

The commanders have solidified their power base at the expense of civilians, but the local population has begun to fight back. In May 2005, a year before my visit, thousands of people rose up to call for the removal of the "good" commanders, in demonstrations that killed a few people and injured dozens. When I arrive in 2006, the province is relatively calm. Rows over drugs are the main cause of insecurity.

The province is considered middle class by Afghan standards. The 830,000 residents have access to irrigated and rain-fed land on which they grow mainly rice and wheat. Poppy production makes up 3 percent of agriculture. The opium produced in Badakhshan is transported to Takhar for trafficking to Central Asia. Takhar also has two factories and is rich in minerals: gold, coal, salt, and gems. About 16 percent of the people are literate, and 32 percent of the children attend school.

Marco Polo traveled in Takhar in 1275. He described the region as fine and fruitful, with a great corn market and lofty hills, and he was impressed with the salt mines. "They all consist of white salt, extremely hard, with which the people for a distance of thirty days' journey round come to provide themselves, for it is esteemed the purest that is found in the world. It is so hard, that it can be broken only with great iron hammers. The quantity is so great that all the countries of the earth might be supplied from thence." Now Takhar is known mostly for drug trafficking.

At the rest stop, the men leave me alone in the car and go in search of dinner at a nearby restaurant. I need a few minutes alone. I get out to stretch my legs and dust off my clothes. I can see the stars, but it's too dark to see anything on the ground clearly. I hear the sound of a waterfall or a river. It's familiar; it is the Kokcha, I realize. I close my eyes and take in the fresh air, soothed a bit by the sound of water. I walk toward the river I traveled across in Badakhshan, hoping to wash my hands and face in its white water. In the darkness, I bump into a truck full of what looks like flour sacks. I can hear the men dining in a restaurant nearby, smell the hot plates of rice and kabobs being served. I continue to walk in search of the Kokcha. Suddenly the sound of a deep male voice stops me. In front of me is a Russian Jeep with the English word *Police* written across it. A man sits inside, handcuffed. Two other men in uniforms stand outside in intense discussion. I can make out a few words, but the conversation is garbled. I am sure I hear "powder," which is the local term for heroin. I don't want them to see me; I hide behind the truck. My fidgeting makes a cracking noise on the gravel, and the men stop their discussion and look in my direction. I hear them walking toward me, and my heart starts to pound. The police here are often the criminals. What are they going to do to me? I wish I could somehow disappear under the truck or among the sacks of flour. My breathing is loud and I am trying hard to be silent. I feel paralyzed. The men's footsteps get closer.

They walk right past me.

I wait until I can no longer hear them walking and then I head back to the car.

A day later, safe at Baktosh's uncle's house in Rustaq, I find out that the trail of the heroin bust I witnessed involves an intricate rivalry between the federal secret police, called Amniat, and the local police. In June 2006, a month before I visit Takhar, Amniat raided two heroin labs in Bekha village in Rustaq district and arrested two men who were making heroin in abandoned village homes. Rustaq was devastated by an earthquake in 1998; five thousand were killed and thirty thousand became homeless. Bekha was destroyed, and its few survivors moved to Rustaq town center. Still left in Bekha are dozens of crumbling mud-brick shacks, ideal for setting up heroin labs.

One of the Amniat agents who made the arrest tells me the labs were operating with impunity from the Rustaq police, who were receiving kickbacks from the heroin profits.

"There were ten to twelve of us on the job on a Sunday night about two AM. We filled up two Datsun Jeeps from Taloqan to head for Bekha," the agent begins. "It's a mountainous village near Badakhshan. Badakhshan's where most of the heroin labs are in the north of the country. We had information from insiders of two locations in Bekha; they were two hours apart. There are no paved roads up there. We were heavily armed because we didn't know what we were up against. Sometimes the labs are guarded by armed uniformed policemen.

"At one location we found one man who claimed to be from Nangarhar [province]. It's usually Pashtuns from Nangarhar or Pakistanis who are experts in heroin making. It's hard to tell the difference, since both groups speak similar Pashto and look alike.

"One man, the one who was the chemist, wasn't there. We captured his assistant with two pots the size of oil barrels and a container for storing opium. He's just a boy and has an artificial leg. He had four Kalashnikovs, which we took, but he didn't fight back. They had set up big gas stoves, which they used to cook the opium. At the second location, we captured a guy doing the same thing. He had a boxlike machine that makes twenty percent heroin."

"What's the process in refining opium to heroin?" I ask the agent. We sit in a room at the secret police offices eating fresh melons with our hands. Outside the room, sitting in the sunlight, are the rusting silver-colored pots they seized from the bust. Shouldn't they be sealed and hidden? I think, then realize that this evidence is outside to be displayed for the media. It's a picture of a seizure that officials can show to the public to prove that police are actually fighting drugs rather than dealing them. The truth is more complicated.

"They boil the opium and let the gunk rise to the top," the agent answers. "They take what's left at the bottom and mix it with carbon, acid, and other chemicals. They can make it for different levels of purity. We captured ninety-one kilos of opium, which can be turned into about thirteen kilos of heroin. But they had already refined sixty-seven packets [kilos] of heroin that we also seized."

The two men captured from the two labs are still in jail. The agent says he doesn't know if they will provide more information about whom they worked for or if they will even be prosecuted.

I ask him the same question I asked Asif's NIU team in Kabul.

"What's the point of the capture if they walk free and don't give you any information?"

The agent raises his shoulder in defeat. "The local prosecutor was upset with us for arresting them. I did my job. I'm not sure what will happen next. We have a long way to go."

"Did General Daud have anything to do with these labs?" I ask suddenly.

The agent looks taken aback. "Uh, uh, I would not know that. And if I did, I could not tell you."

The first drug lab in Afghanistan was set up in Nangarhar province in 1971 by a rogue chemist from Germany—a German first created the morphine base for heroin in Germany in 1803, and an Englishman in Britain first synthesized morphine into heroin in 1874. Heroin became a drug of choice on the hippie trail in the 1960s and

'70s after Pashtun tribes in Pakistan's tribal territories recognized the demand for narcotics and began opening labs with the help of Western-educated chemists. By 1995 there were hundreds of heroin labs in the Federally Administered Tribal Areas (FATA) of Pakistan bordering Afghanistan. The Pakistani government has limited control over FATA, but that same year, it executed a massive antidrug operation, destroying two hundred labs. Downsizing poppy cultivation and drug processing in Pakistan propelled the business inside Afghanistan, a country in the grip of war and with no functioning government to fight drugs.

Matt DuPee, an Afghan security specialist at the Naval Postgraduate School in Monterey, California, has done extensive research into drug labs in Afghanistan. He says Nangarhar's first lab was rudimentary, but that members of the Shinwari and Afridi tribes there have now become experts in the business, and the province still boasts the most high-tech labs. According to DuPee's research, labs in Afghanistan burgeoned in 1986 in mujahideen-held territory. The mujahideen had discovered that processing the drug domestically was much more profitable. Prior to 1986, Burma held the record for the biggest producer of poppy, but that year Afghanistan's output surpassed Burma's, and Burmese chemists later traveled to Afghanistan to transform opium into heroin. They showed the Afghans the technique with basic equipment.

The two-thirds of opium refined domestically are done so in facilities capable of making a simple morphine base, the first of eight forms of the narcotic; the eighth form is the purest heroin. In Afghanistan the purest form is called crystal, and in the United States it's China White, the most potent and expensive form of the drug, and the one that gives the most intense impact when injected. On the streets, dealers and addicts cut heroin with adulterants ranging from something as benign as baby formula to caustic substances such as Ajax cleaning powder, to maximize the amount and profit.

The profits are ten times higher, and more traders will come to farms to buy, if the farmer turns the opium into a morphine base. To do so is fairly simple. An opium farmer can use a wood-fired stove, a pot, big barrels, and cheesecloth as a sieve. The farmer also needs some easily available chemicals, such as ammonias and slaked lime, also known as calcium hydroxide, often used in cement and fertilizer. Slaked lime is legal to import. The most important ingredient for turning opium into morphine, however, is water—it takes twelve to fifteen gallons of water to make two kilos of heroin.

DuPee says the facilities become more sophisticated if there's a gas stove to cook large quantities in single batches, and if they're stationary. These "processing workshops" are usually situated in sparsely populated areas in homes or mountain caves. Mobile labs can make pure heroin, but in small amounts. The numbers vary as to how many labs exist in Afghanistan. The United Nations estimates seventy-five to seventy-eight heroin labs, a figure that seems to refer to the most advanced, those that can produce large quantities of China White. But the Tajikistan government estimates that close to its border, in Badakhshan alone, there are at least four hundred labs. The three provinces with the most labs are Badakhshan, Nangarhar, and Helmand, but such facilities are in operation in most Afghan provinces, except for a few in central Afghanistan.

The key ingredient used for China White is the illegal precursor chemical acetic anhydride (AA). Traffickers import the chemical from South Korea, India, and China to Afghanistan, where it arrives by the truckload, says DuPee. "When I was in Baghlan province, you could see a lot of trucks on the highway with blue chemical jugs going through. Locally, they call it water, because it's as important as water. There's no one to stop the trucks because nobody has any idea, even the American military, as to what they're looking at."

The people who man the labs are mostly Afghans, but to produce China White, chemists from Turkey, Burma, Pakistan, and
Iran are hired. The chemicals can be explosive if mishandled by
amateurs. The Afghan workers are men, but according to DuPee,
during the Taliban years, because they were forced to stay indoors,
more women joined the work in the south. Labs are in closed com-
pounds, and the process involves cooking, a task considered suitable
for Afghan women. It takes from eight to twelve workers to run a
large lab, plus twenty to thirty security guards.

"The guards are needed to protect the products from competi-
tor traffickers but mostly from the police, who can seize and sell
it, not confiscate it," DuPee says. "It's accepted that seizures will
lead to skimming by police, but the local perception is that good
police skim small amounts and the bad police will horde large
quantities."

The destruction of these labs does little to fight the drug trade,
since the labs can be set up easily again. The counternarcotics agents
find out the locations sometimes with intelligence help from the
Americans or British, and at times from civilians. Counternarcotics
agents enjoy the spectacle of shooting at pots and pans and blowing
up the labs. Members of the NIU team tell me it's their favorite part
of fighting drugs. But most of the time they don't arrest anyone.
Double agents tip off lab workers, who are able to pack up and leave
before the NIU arrives. From 2003 to 2008, authorities destroyed 527
labs, but DuPee concedes that many of them were empty of personnel and drugs. Only equipment was seized.

The two labs raided in Takhar are considered advanced. The boxlike equipment the Amniat agent described as being seized there are
most likely industrial-size car jacks that can lift fifteen-ton trucks.
Car jacks are used as presses in drug labs.

The capture of the two men in Rustaq was considered a victory for counternarcotics because it could lead to more raids and arrests. And it did.

In July 2006, an Amniat agent named Atiq was arrested with six kilos of heroin reported to be skimmed from the stash seized in Bekha. He was caught with the powder in a Jeep marked *Police* near the Kokcha River in Rustaq.

I was a witness.

One of the uniformed men who walked past me that evening when I hid near the river was Khaleeq, the Rustaq police chief. Khaleeq was angry with Atiq for two reasons. "A few months back, Atiq arrested Khaleeq with a stash of powder, and Khaleeq had to pull many strings and pay off a lot of people to get out," says a Rustaq man close to Khaleeq.

Atiq, a nonthreatening bureaucrat in a suit, allegedly seized from Khaleeq thirty kilos of heroin worth $30,000. The federal agent kept twenty-five of the kilos and filtered the heroin to increase the amount.

"Then you know about the labs in Bekha," the Rustaq man continued. "Khaleeq had a big cut in those labs. Atiq was one of the Amniat men who raided the labs. But of course, he had to take something for himself. It's the norm here.

"Khaleeq didn't need evidence that Atiq had taken a few kilos. He just assumed, and he got lucky when Khaleeq stopped Atiq's car on the Kokcha. Six kilos from the Bekha stuff, the pure heroin, was found in his car. It was sweet revenge for Khaleeq."

"Amniat told me that Atiq was working undercover trying to infiltrate a drug mafia. The drugs were for the job. How true is that?" I ask the man.

He laughs incredulously. "How can Atiq go undercover here when we all know his face? That's the explanation for the media."

The man's account is corroborated by several other Rustaq officials, including at the counternarcotics directorate.

When I go to the Amniat offices to find out what happened to Atiq, the agent who described the labs to me says, "He was freed. He wasn't guilty. He was just doing his job undercover. The Rustaq police didn't know. We seized the drugs found on him and sent him back to Kabul to continue doing a good job."

The culture of drug trafficking in the north, unlike in the south, is not tied to tribal loyalties. Anyone in a position of power can deal drugs and benefit from it. Whether it's ignoring the illicit activity, taking kickbacks, or being directly involved, counternarcotics agents tell me the majority of high-ranking police and former mujahideen commanders and their cohorts are dealing drugs. "From the youngest to the oldest are involved in this, from the farmer to the intellectual," says Abdul Hakim, the counternarcotics chief in Rustaq. "People buy their positions. That's obvious. They are completely illiterate but they work as big guys in the government here."

"You're not illiterate but you're a big guy in the government," I say, smiling. "So, by that account, are you involved?"

Hakim laughs and says firmly, "No."

I give him a list of names of officials I've been told are drug traffickers and ask him if the list is accurate. The last name on the list is Daud's. Hakim gets uncomfortable. "I know who's involved but I cannot tell you. I just can't. I can share with you when I know I can be protected."

In the lower ranks, betrayals, greed, and double crossings occur often among corrupt officials. They implement the law when it serves them, either in revenge or for profit. Higher-ranking men write protection letters in exchange for thousands of dollars in cash. The corruption reaches all the way up to Karzai, who has been protecting his brother Ahmed Wali and others in his administration from arrest. In April 2009 he pardoned five convicted traffickers, one of whom was related to his campaign manager. His interior minister, Ali Ahmad Jalali, resigned in 2005 because Karzai refused to rid the government of drug dealers.

The political divisions are of little concern to traffickers. "Smugglers couldn't care less about who is Pashtun or Tajik or what language the man speaks," says a U.S. embassy official in Kabul. "The Northern Alliance guys will fight Taliban drug dealers one day and negotiate drug deals with them on another."

There might be only a few clean officials in Rustaq, but nationwide there are thousands of respectable policemen who make an honest effort to fight the trade. Still, the consequence of being clean can be deadly.

"If a police officer refuses to allow a drug deal to go through, he can be fired, beaten, killed, or simply his superior will receive thousands in cash to replace him," says one Amniat agent in Kabul. "In some cases, clean cops are forced to become dirty."

What draws me to Takhar is Daud and heroin, and to find out how the two are related. But I discover that Daud's dealings are a well-kept secret in his home province. I speak to more than two dozen people involved in narcotics or counternarcotics and more than a dozen have a similar reaction: they look surprised, they pause, and then they say, in various ways, that they are too afraid to talk about him.

In September 2010, Karzai reshuffles the interior ministry and Daud is transferred as the chief of counternarcotics to become police chief for the northern region. His transfer is among many others and no official reasons are given for the changes. But the shift in position does not take away Daud's power to influence the drug trade. It's not a demotion and it allows him to solidify power over the north.

FIFTEEN

Uprisings Against Warlords

Amer Bashir, the commander who rules Chahab, a district two hours from Rustaq, leads a caravan of sixteen cars to a village at the edge of the Amu River, in Takhar. Across the river is Tajikistan. Bashir is campaigning to become a member of Parliament, to represent the district he has controlled for more than a decade. It's a muggy Friday afternoon and most of the men in the village of Samti are walking to the mosque for Friday prayers. A thick-necked, balding man of forty-five years, Bashir is feeling confident and practicing his speech in his head en route to the mosque when a group of men stop his caravan.

One of the men, Haji Abdul Rahman, a native of Samti, shouts, "We know you. You don't need to campaign here. Go back the way you came!"

Bashir, startled, stays inside his SUV but rolls the window down and shouts back, "I have the power and will remain in power!"

The men stand together to form a barricade against the caravan. Bashir orders one of his guards to fire at Rahman, but the bullet misses him and injures a young man standing next to him. The echo of gunshots draws more men to the scene. They pick up stones and break branches from trees to use as weapons.

The pioneers of the booming heroin business are the former mujahideen, and their alliance with the United States and NATO has allowed them to solidify their hold on the business and their power over entire regions of the country. They form a loose hierarchy of authority, with leaders such as Daud at the top and smaller commanders such as Bashir and Piram Qul as middlemen. But at the same time that foreign intervention has helped them maintain their dominance, the West's promise of democracy has instilled confidence in Afghan civilians to rise up against the smaller commanders who terrorize them.

The natives of Samti are poor farmers who have been terrorized under Bashir's dictatorship. Most are Farsi-speaking Tajiks. Bashir was a mujahid they cheered on during the Soviet invasion, but much has changed in the last twenty years. Chahab residents tell colorful stories of Bashir and his militiamen.

"One of Bashir's commanders forced a white-haired elder to carry him from one village to another," says Mohammed Azam, a teacher, farmer, and respected resident of Chahab district. "He would force shopkeepers to give him a ten percent tax, even if they didn't make any profits. He ran the heroin trafficking that crosses the river to Tajikistan from Samti." Azam is also a former Communist who was district governor before Bashir seized power. He says Bashir considers him his archrival. After the Communists fell from power, Bashir took charge of Chahab and imprisoned Azam, but later released him. Still, Bashir attempted to kill Azam several times after his release. Azam shows me the bullet holes in his guesthouse, where he plays chess with a friend. "I was just sitting here like I am now and his men climbed the wall of my house and began shooting. I crawled to my backyard and made it out alive, but I know he will get to me eventually. I have nowhere to hide."

Azam, who lives in Chahab town center, describes Bashir as a ruthless tyrant who murdered his own family members to maintain control. "Bashir financed his army of twenty-five hundred men with heroin money. Jeeps full of heroin would come to Samti. Bashir gave fifty dollars to fifty men, one dollar for each man who agreed to be a courier to and from Tajikistan. He would load each person with fourteen to twenty kilos to transport and include a few armed militiamen with each group of men. They had rockets, RPGs, Kalashnikovs, and a Thuraya [satellite] phone. They boarded boats made of cowskin, and each one had to be a good swimmer in case the boat sank. They used certain areas of the river to cross, not more than fifty to one hundred meters. Russians watched the Amu from their post. The smugglers communicated with their Tajiki counterparts, telling them on satellite phones that they were going to deliver how much heroin to what location. They spoke to each other in code. Houses, villages, and mountains where they were to meet and deliver the heroin had number codes."

"What were their chances of getting caught?" I ask.

"People would drown or get shot by the Russians on the other side. Now the Tajikis themselves are in charge, and they don't shoot, so the chances of survival are better. It's an open border for trafficking."

"Who were the couriers?"

"Samti villagers who know the river well. Bashir controlled them. Their wives and daughters belonged to Bashir and his men.

They would go to a house, send the men out to work, and force their women to do what they wanted. That was the last straw for the people. That kind of dishonor, *binamosy,* cannot be tolerated by our people."

"Did Bashir do anything for the people?" I ask.

"Bashir tried to build a water dam, which was never finished. He repaired a water storage tank, but used it only to water his own land. The people who worked on these projects were not paid. The reason Bashir stayed in power this long is because he is protected by a drug mafia."

Yet even the mafia distanced itself from Bashir.

In May 2005 one of Bashir's militiamen, Commander Mahmoud, was accused of raping a girl from Samti shortly before Bashir began campaigning. The villagers, perhaps two thousand of them, were livid.

Bashir was warned by his advisers not to go to Samti, but he is genuinely surprised to see a mob headed toward him. "What are they doing?" he asks one of his bodyguards after the bodyguard wounds the young Samti man with his gun. Bashir cannot believe that people have the gall to stand up to him.

"They're upset because of the girl. I think we should leave," the guard tells Bashir.

"Let's head back to Chahab center," Bashir orders.

His skillful driver quickly makes a U-turn, honking. Bashir's guard points his gun out the car window. People clear the way for Bashir but break his car windows and damage six of the other cars in his caravan. Women stand on the roofs of their houses throwing rocks. The mob of men stops one of the cars, pulls out the passengers, beats them, then holds them hostage for two days. No one is killed in Samti, but other villages hear of the uprising and they take to the streets chanting against Bashir. "Death to Amer Bashir!" they shout. "We want justice!"

Bashir hides in a village along the mountains of Chahab while the central government in Kabul tries to defuse the situation. The Chahab district governor and police are frightened of the people and of Bashir. Kabul sends a delegation to talk to the villagers. NATO sends planes to monitor the protests from the air. The villagers show up at the town center, the *chowk*, in anticipation of seeing Bashir and hearing the government promise to try him in court for his crimes.

"The government lied to us," says Azam. "Bashir paid everyone off in the government and never faced the public. He tried to escape a few days later, but people found out and attacked his car. But this time the central government guarded him. There was a shootout between the police protecting him and his rivals, and some people got injured. Then Bashir left. He went to Kabul and escaped justice."

Bashir lost his campaign for Parliament.

"Who runs the drug business now?" I ask Azam.

"It's not centralized so much anymore. Anyone with a gun and power can do it."

Azam is a lively storyteller, but I'm wary of his Communist past and the bias he holds against the mujahideen. He offers to take me to Samti to talk to the villagers. "They should tell you about the things Bashir did to them."

During the riots in Chahab a dispute heats up in Rustaq. The director of education, a follower of Commander Piram Qul, and a teacher's recruit are accused of stealing money from students. The students call for the educators to be transferred from their district. Piram Qul, who is also campaigning for Parliament, stands behind the director and the recruit. The people of Rustaq hear about the uprisings in Chahab. Communists, rival commanders, and those who have suffered under Piram Qul for the last thirteen years become inspired. Piram Qul is accused of crimes similar to Bashir's, including heroin trafficking. The fever of demonstrations spreads rapidly as thousands of men gather at the Rustaq *chowk* with a loudspeaker. They demand Qul's removal from elections and the disarmament of the local commanders. "No more guns. We want law!" the demonstrators chant.

Piram Qul is much more powerful, clever, and articulate than Bashir, and he can point to a few development projects—schools built by NGOs and a health clinic—to show for his years in control. He has a solid constituency of supporters, who come out to defend him in the demonstrations.

The weeklong standoff among the people of Rustaq ends violently. Two people are killed and thirty-three injured.

The people of Takhar tested the boundaries of the nation's nascent democracy in 2005. The demonstrations, albeit disorganized, were a plea for a modern form of justice, a chance to free people from a system ruled by strongmen and corrupt police funded by drug money. Although Piram Qul was elected to the lower house of Parliament, and now travels between Kabul and Rustaq, Bashir was driven out temporarily, and the director of education in Rustaq was transferred to another district. But these short-term victories would entail deadly consequences for the people of Takhar.

It's ten in the morning and the nippy March cold lingers, the stubbornness of a Takhar winter prevailing against the blossoms of spring. The donkeys, which hee-haw throughout the day as they transport melons and other fruits and vegetables, are unusually quiet. The bells around the necks of the sheep crossing the rocky alleyways interrupt the silence of the morning. Two six-year-old boys, Yosuf and Feraidoon, who are neighbors and close friends, hug themselves to ward off the chill, their light sweaters not warm enough. The boys walk toward their school, both holding empty plastic containers. Today the two first-graders are off from school, but their mothers have sent them to bring clean water for drinking and cooking from the fountain near the school. The majority of homes in Takhar do not have running water; they depend on well water. The boys' fathers, Halim and Najib, are also good friends. When the adults meet for tea and conversation, the boys run around and play soccer. On this morning there are no other adults with the boys except a few shopkeepers on the block, who barely notice the children. Yosuf and Feraidoon twirl open the tops of their containers and take turns filling the two gallons with the icy water. A few drops wet their clothes. Yosuf shivers. When the water overflows, Feraidoon seals the cap and tries to lift his container. It's too heavy, but he pulls it up with all his might.

The boys are interrupted by the sound of screeching brakes. They look up to see a four-door black Jeep come to a sudden halt. It's Feraidoon's maternal uncle Haji Ainuddin, with a man they do not know.

"*Salaam Maamaa*," Feraidoon says, greeting his uncle. Haji Ainuddin smiles at Feraidoon and offers his nephew and Yosuf ice cream.

"Get in the car and I'll buy you whatever you want," Haji Ainuddin tells Feraidoon.

"Really? Come on, Yosuf, we'll come back soon so you don't have to tell your mom," Feraidoon convinces his friend.

The boys excitedly board the Jeep. It's the last time they are seen alive.

———————

My sister and me in Herat before the Communist coup.

Families rent private vineyards to swim, eat, and relax on weekends in Herat.

My family—me on the left at age nine, my mother, my sister Faiza, and my father—waits in Islamabad, Pakistan, for a visa to either the United States or Germany in 1982.

Me at age seven in Herat during the Soviet invasion.

Shortly after the Communist coup, my brother Hadi escaped from Afghanistan to Hamburg, Germany.

These girls climb through a window dividing their homes in Ghoryan. Extended families in Afghanistan can live on the same plot of land divided by mud-brick walls.

Aabi, Gandomi's daughter, and her son Maqsud in a moment of happiness.

The Amu River in Samti district. It divides Afghanistan from Tajikistan, and traffickers with boatloads of heroin cross the river nightly from the province of Takhar into Tajikistan.

Faizabad, the capital of Badakhshan, is located along the Kokcha River.

Under these stones lie two of Gandomi's children in a makeshift graveyard she visits every Friday.

The pots and equipment seized from the heroin laboratory raid in the village of Bekha.

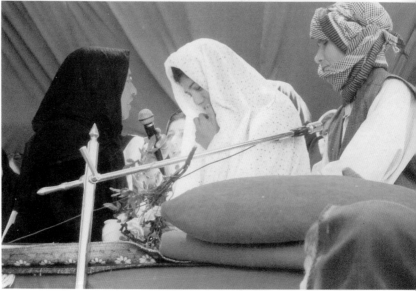

These three girls, one dressed as a man, perform a skit against drug abuse in their high school in Ghoryan.

Some three thousand women gather in Ghoryan High School to protest the penetration of the drug trade in their community.

Drug addicts loiter in the yard of the first addiction treatment center in Herat.

, residents who were washing their dishes in the Kokcha
d Feraidoon's body. None of the men among the coun-
to tell me more about the body or how he was killed. "It's
t to share such gruesome details," one man says.

idoon's father, Najib, is not among the council members. He
rning the loss of his son at the hands of his wife's brother.
the council members do not tell me is that Najib owed Ainud-
0,000 in drug money. Assadullah Walwaluji, a native of Takhar,
mber of the Afghanistan Independent Human Rights Com-
sion, and a critic of Piram Qul, says that Najib did not have the
ney to pay back Ainuddin. "He tried everything to get his money
ck from Najib, but he didn't get it so he resorted to kidnapping his
wn nephew. Halim's innocent in all this. As far as I know, his hands
cannot reach the drug trade. Halim's son might've been targeted because of Halim's role in the demonstrations."

"Is Piram Qul involved in all this?" I ask.

"Piram Qul is the one who ordered the boys to be killed," Walwaluji says. "That would leave no proof. The kidnapping was supposed to pressure Najib to pay off his debt, but when he wasn't able
to, the children became a liability."

The men and women I talk to about Bashir and Piram Qul have
rivalries or loyalties to each, and I search to find a neutral voice. At
Concern, an Irish-based NGO that has been active in Takhar since
the 1998 earthquake, I meet two aid workers, a Bangladeshi man and
an Afghan man, who judge Piram Qul and Amer Bashir in a larger
context of Afghanistan's current history. The men want to remain
anonymous.

"All these commanders are killers," says the Bangladeshi man,
who has spent the last three years in Rustaq. "There's no argument
there, but so are members of the current government. You have to
consider these men in perspective. They bring security to the area,

On the highway from Kandahar to Helmand in 2002, our driver smokes
hashish as he smoothly navigates the bumpy road.

A laborer toils in the fields for
many hours oozing out the opium
gum from poppy bulbs in Argu,
Badakhshan.

The woman hides her face from the
camera, saying she's ashamed to have
to work in the poppy fields.

In Herat, Afghans prepare for Eid guests after a month of fasting during Ramadan.

Me sitting on the steps of my maternal grandfather's orchard home on my first trip back to Herat in eighteen years.

Four months after the kidnappi[ng] [...] in a large, sweltering room on the [...] center. Halim, forty-one, is among a [...] bers of the Citizens' Council, a group [...] tions in Rustaq in 2005. The men eage[r] [...] complaints against the commanders in the [...] still involved in the drug trade. Piram Qul a[nd] [...] Qul, are the targets of their anger. Many of the[m] [...] of land seizures and harassment. Few of them ca[...] Halim expresses.

Heroin is the root cause of his boy's kidnapping[...]

"Relatives told me that Yosuf, my youngest son, w[...] that afternoon. I have three daughters and now two boys[...] third son who completed my family. I don't have much [...] Yosuf's alive. Ainuddin is Piram Qul's father-in-law. I'm su[re] Qul's involved in the kidnapping. He came at eleven PM the n[ight] the kidnapping from Kabul, when Ainuddin was arrested by Am[...] I went on Ariana Television and told the media that Piram Qul's [fa]ther-in-law had kidnapped the boys. A few nights later, eight arme[d] men who work for Piram Qul stopped me. They told me that my child is alive. 'If you want this type of exposure, then he will also die.' I knew then that they had killed Najib's son," Halim says. He busies himself fixing his turban and lowers his eyes to hide the tears.

"Why would Ainuddin or Piram Qul kill your son?" I ask.

"Because I'm the head of nine villages of Uzbeks in Rustaq who do not support him," Halim says. "He considers himself the Uzbek leader here, and I as an Uzbek want to distance myself from these ethnic loyalties and support someone who follows the law. I was a leader in the demonstrations against him last year. Now he's getting his revenge on me."

Yosuf is still missing, but thirteen days prior to my meeting

On the highway from Kandahar to Helmand in 2002, our driver smokes hashish as he smoothly navigates the bumpy road.

A laborer toils in the fields for many hours oozing out the opium gum from poppy bulbs in Argu, Badakhshan.

The woman hides her face from the camera, saying she's ashamed to have to work in the poppy fields.

In Herat, Afghans prepare for Eid guests after a month of fasting during Ramadan.

Me sitting on the steps of my maternal grandfather's orchard home on my first trip back to Herat in eighteen years.

Four months after the kidnapping, I sit with Halim, Yosuf's father, in a large, sweltering room on the second floor of the Rustaq town center. Halim, forty-one, is among a hundred men who are members of the Citizens' Council, a group formed after the demonstrations in Rustaq in 2005. The men eagerly and openly voice their complaints against the commanders in the district, who they say are still involved in the drug trade. Piram Qul and his deputy, Subhan Qul, are the targets of their anger. Many of the men here are victims of land seizures and harassment. Few of them can feel the pain that Halim expresses.

Heroin is the root cause of his boy's kidnapping.

"Relatives told me that Yosuf, my youngest son, was kidnapped that afternoon. I have three daughters and now two boys. He was my third son who completed my family. I don't have much hope that Yosuf's alive. Ainuddin is Piram Qul's father-in-law. I'm sure Piram Qul's involved in the kidnapping. He came at eleven PM the night of the kidnapping from Kabul, when Ainuddin was arrested by Amniat. I went on Ariana Television and told the media that Piram Qul's father-in-law had kidnapped the boys. A few nights later, eight armed men who work for Piram Qul stopped me. They told me that my child is alive. 'If you want this type of exposure, then he will also die.' I knew then that they had killed Najib's son," Halim says. He busies himself fixing his turban and lowers his eyes to hide the tears.

"Why would Ainuddin or Piram Qul kill your son?" I ask.

"Because I'm the head of nine villages of Uzbeks in Rustaq who do not support him," Halim says. "He considers himself the Uzbek leader here, and I as an Uzbek want to distance myself from these ethnic loyalties and support someone who follows the law. I was a leader in the demonstrations against him last year. Now he's getting his revenge on me."

Yosuf is still missing, but thirteen days prior to my meeting with Halim, residents who were washing their dishes in the Kokcha River found Feraidoon's body. None of the men among the council want to tell me more about the body or how he was killed. "It's better not to share such gruesome details," one man says.

Feraidoon's father, Najib, is not among the council members. He is mourning the loss of his son at the hands of his wife's brother. What the council members do not tell me is that Najib owed Ainuddin $30,000 in drug money. Assadullah Walwaluji, a native of Takhar, a member of the Afghanistan Independent Human Rights Commission, and a critic of Piram Qul, says that Najib did not have the money to pay back Ainuddin. "He tried everything to get his money back from Najib, but he didn't get it so he resorted to kidnapping his own nephew. Halim's innocent in all this. As far as I know, his hands cannot reach the drug trade. Halim's son might've been targeted because of Halim's role in the demonstrations."

"Is Piram Qul involved in all this?" I ask.

"Piram Qul is the one who ordered the boys to be killed," Walwaluji says. "That would leave no proof. The kidnapping was supposed to pressure Najib to pay off his debt, but when he wasn't able to, the children became a liability."

The men and women I talk to about Bashir and Piram Qul have rivalries or loyalties to each, and I search to find a neutral voice. At Concern, an Irish-based NGO that has been active in Takhar since the 1998 earthquake, I meet two aid workers, a Bangladeshi man and an Afghan man, who judge Piram Qul and Amer Bashir in a larger context of Afghanistan's current history. The men want to remain anonymous.

"All these commanders are killers," says the Bangladeshi man, who has spent the last three years in Rustaq. "There's no argument there, but so are members of the current government. You have to consider these men in perspective. They bring security to the area, and Piram Qul has pride, capacity, and understanding that he's a leader. However, he has illegally captured land, kept women captive, and killed people. But he's a force that has good potential and he's still a war hero among the mullah population. He supports NGO work and wants to promote women's rights and education."

The aid worker says the demonstrations against Piram Qul had an ethnic bias—the Tajiks wanted the educators removed simply because they were Uzbek and they wanted Tajiks to replace them. He says the Citizens' Council includes corrupt commanders and former Communists who have also killed people and who oppose Piram Qul for being more powerful than they are.

The Afghan aid worker agrees that in a time of anarchy after the Soviet war these commanders served a purpose and may still be a better option than the ragtag corrupt officials in the government. "There's no documentation that the commanders are involved in the drug trade, but they must know about it. The police installed by the current government deal more in drugs than these commanders. Each road crossing has specific fees that must be paid to the police if a vehicle with heroin is passing through," he says. "Our local economy is directly affected by the price of opium here. If it sells for less, then the value of the dollar goes down, too."

"Aren't the militiamen now the police?" I ask.

"A few, but things were more centralized under these commanders. You need a bit of a dictatorship to get things done here. Bashir did a lot for education, allowing girls to study with boys. Piram Qul's keen on morality. The demonstrations actually strengthened Piram Qul, because it united his supporters and they went out to vote for him. Now that he's in Parliament, no matter what anybody says, he looks the other way."

The aid workers do not provide the neutral voice I was looking for but rather a practical outlook on Takhar's political landscape. I'm uncomfortable with their pragmatism. The assumption that Afghans need an iron fist to be ruled reeks of colonialist racism. But is an iron fist necessary for any country that has been at war for thirty years? For the sake of security and stability, do Afghans have to tolerate a leader who seizes their land, rapes their women, and, like the Taliban leader Mullah Omar, forces an outdated code of justice that invites the public to cheer on executions in sports stadiums? Many of my Afghan colleagues and friends tell me that Afghans are not ready for democracy because they are illiterate and have lived under a monarchy for centuries. A king—who, to them, is akin to a prophet—is needed to control the tribes and ethnic rivalries that divide Afghanistan. I think about this question throughout my travels and come to the conclusion that Afghanistan needs a strong leader, one who has the will and courage to make tough decisions. But that leader can also be a progressive democrat who enforces a federalist system that allows local freedoms. Piram Qul, Amer Bashir, and rulers like them may be a viable short-term fix, but Afghans—no matter how uneducated—deserve a benevolent and fair leader.

Piram Qul is in Rustaq on a break from Parliament when I meet with the Citizens' Council. I ask for a meeting with him and am promptly requested to show up at his guesthouse. We meet in the late afternoon and talk until the sun sets. The man described to me as an unforgiving brute shows me a different side. His expressive eyes sparkle when he talks. He's relaxed and kind and exudes sincerity. His ironed turban perfectly frames his face; his fitted *pirahan tomban* and vest are spotless.

I joke that his wives must take good care of him. "Yes, they do," he replies with a grin. "But I'm not a dictator. I give them freedom."

"How many wives and children do you have?"

"Six wives and twenty-three children: thirteen sons, twelve

daughters. My wives are near my age. The youngest is thirty-five, and I'm forty-five. I want to get all my children educated. My oldest daughter just finished high school. Is there any way you can find for my sons and daughters to get scholarships to study in America?" he asks seriously.

"I can get information on scholarships for you if you'd like," I tell him. I don't point out to him that twelve and thirteen add up to twenty-five, not twenty-three. He says it's hard to remember his children's names sometimes because there are so many of them.

Piram Qul presents himself as a simple, uneducated, honest man of the people who is open to change, women's rights, and democracy. "I'm a populist commander, not a party commander," he says. "I'm not an educated commander. I just knew how to fight and lead a battalion against the Communists. I will fight against the Taliban until my death. I do not believe in their way of Islam. I am a Muslim who believes in progress. I tolerate the current government. I try to be careful that the government will not be unhappy with me. It's a sick government. Everywhere you look, there's corruption. Our enemies won't allow us to be in peace. Pakistan is behind most of our troubles."

"Aren't you part of the corruption and drug dealing?" I ask. "Why are so many people demonstrating against you, and what about this kidnapping by your father-in-law that involves drug money?"

"I become happy that whoever has a complaint against me should have the right to complain. When they catch the person with the drugs, then they can convict him. It's possible that my commanders or relatives do it, but I'm not responsible for their actions. I don't protect those relatives. The law should catch those people and punish them. That's why my father-in-law is in jail now, and he should be tried and his guilt should be proven. Up to now, the international community does not have proof against me."

Piram Qul is well aware that unless the international community presents evidence against him, local complaints from residents he harasses carry no weight. Implicit in our conversation is the understanding that he can continue to exercise his power against whoever stands up to him even while denying being involved in any acts of coercion.

We discuss the impact of war, and he becomes melancholy, then emotional. "War is a disaster. It leads to ignorance and illiteracy. I'm the face of war, and there is much darkness in my heart. We have to get out of this violent cycle."

He claims to have given up the five thousand arms he had left over from the Soviet war to the national disarmament program. "Some of the arms the commanders under me sold to Pakistan on the black market. I don't have the same kind of power now that I used to. I'm no longer a military man. The people here do not realize that, and they still think I run things."

"How common was drug smuggling when you were in charge for more than a decade?" I ask.

"When I was in charge, people could not even plant hashish. I had brought stability. We had an earthquake in 1998. There was stability for NGOs to help the victims."

I hold back my next question: Was the reason that no one could plant hashish or traffic in drugs because you controlled the trafficking that passed through Rustaq? I avoid this question—I want to leave Takhar unharmed.

I take up Azam's offer to go to Samti, a forty-five-minute drive from Chahab center. We've just learned that Amer Bashir has returned after a year away and has made an agreement with the government and NATO to take up arms again and set up a garrison against the insurgency along the Kokcha River. We're driving through the mountains in a Russian Jeep. Our driver says that a few hundred meters below is a valley used as a mass grave for casualties during the wars. I look down. The valley is too deep for me to see anything but a dark abyss. Past this death valley the landscape becomes verdant with pistachio trees, orchards, and melon fields. Then, in the distance, I see a body of water and, across it, black mountains. The water is the Amu, a river engraved in the pages of history. Dividing Afghanistan from the former Soviet Union, the Amu is calm, its water soiled and brown, its banks curved like a maze. Rustaq and Chahab lie between the Amu and Kokcha rivers. The Kokcha's white water is loud and wild.

We arrive in Samti village, a fertile land hugging the Amu. The air smells like morning dew; the place is unusually clean and quiet for a village. A group of young girls sit on the boulders of the riverbank and braid one another's brunette locks. Azam summons three village elders and we all gather in a carpeted room overlooking the river. Azam is somber. He greets the elders as if he has come to a funeral. He introduces me, then lets me tell the villagers that the vicious commander they had risked their lives to drive away a year ago has just returned.

"Bashir's back," I say quietly. "Just today."

The tribal elders pause for a moment and put their teacups down. Haji Habib, the eldest, tries to speak, but his voice cracks and his hand shakes. The silence speaks of fear and hopelessness. I do not push them to talk. I compliment them on the beauty of their village and the courage of the villagers. Azam asks them to tell me what crimes Bashir committed against them, but they remain silent. "We'd rather just forget those events and move on—but how could he come back?" Haji Habib finally says. "The Karzai government promised us that he would stay in Kabul."

"The government is full of lies," Azam responds.

The elders invite us to stay for lunch. "But I don't think you should ask too many questions about Bashir if he's back," Haji Habib says. "We will be punished if we answer them."

When Azam and I return to Chahab, he steps out of the Jeep behind a shop so that no one can see us together. He returns home, and I call Amer Bashir on my cell phone to ask for a meeting. He agrees.

Bashir's house is the only painted concrete structure in the district. The other homes are one story and made of bare mud brick. When I arrive, Bashir greets me with an awkward handshake in front of the house, surrounded by his bodyguards, and one of his sons brings a table and chairs so that we can sit out on his lawn.

Bashir is cautious but cooperative with me. He folds one leg over the other and doesn't touch his tea. "I don't know why these people demonstrated against me. I did all I could for them. I built a mosque, I built a school with twenty-nine classrooms for boys, I gave them wheat, I tried to build a dam, but we didn't have the expertise to finish it, and I gave them a paved road. They're so unappreciative."

"Will you meet with them to ask why?" I ask.

"They're not willing to speak to me—not today, not tomorrow. We forgave the Communists. That's the mistake of the mujahideen. We should've let the law punish them. Many of these demonstrators were Communists."

"If the Communists demonstrated because you are a mujahid, then why did the others demonstrate?"

"People now have this democracy and press freedom and it gave them courage," he concedes in his thick, coarse voice.

"So will you apologize to the people?"

"Yes, I'm sorry they're unhappy with me. I want to serve the people here."

"Do you still have an army with weapons?"

"No, I turned in all my weapons, even the antiaircraft missiles. I had a thousand men fighting with me, but now I'm just a civilian."

"How bad is the problem with drug trafficking here?"

"There's no drug trafficking," he says matter-of-factly.

"What do you plan to do here now?"

"I came to make peace with the people. I may leave if they do not want me here. I have no intention of hurting anyone."

During the interview, my legs keep shifting, almost of their own accord. I am ready to sprint away if necessary, but I soon realize Bashir is not a danger to me and is simply trying to get good publicity. I am safe, but I wonder what he will do to the people who rose against him.

Four years later, Azam is the head of the provincial council in Chahab and Bashir has been driven back to Kabul by the people of Chahab. Residents lobbied NATO and the U.S. coalition not to arm him or his soldiers again. International aid money has merely built a school in Chahab town center, while the people of Samti are asking the government to provide access to clean water and health care. Drug trafficking has spread, with General Daud still the alleged kingpin in Takhar. Shipments of heroin across the border to Tajikistan are made without searches or interceptions. In Rustaq district, young Yosuf was never found and is assumed drowned in the river. The man jailed for his kidnapping, Haji Ainuddin, paid a bribe to get out and continues to traffic drugs.

In Takhar, I feel I cannot trust anyone. Every man I speak to seems to have a bloody background mired in drugs. I'm tired of double talk. I'm anxious to return to Kabul, where I know a few clean agents who actually attempt to fight the predators of the drug trade.

SIXTEEN

The Good Agents

The international perspective on the drug trade is that the majority of Afghans are involved in dealing drugs inside the country and it's the Afghans who refuse to give up the illicit trade. Actually, there are Afghans who have given their lives to fight the trade, who cannot be bought off or frightened by drug lords. Idrees and Obaid are two such heroes.

Idrees is a top member of the National Interdiction Unit trained by Blackwater and the DEA. He's a natural policeman with a sense of civic duty and patriotism, an intelligent bodybuilder who enforces law and order both in his family and in his Khair Khana neighborhood in Kabul. He has created a system in which the neighbors on his block pile up the garbage in one area and the city garbage truck takes it away weekly. Idrees's block is one of the cleanest in the neighborhood. At thirty-two, he's one of four brothers and six sisters. He's the sole breadwinner, but his family receives wheat and rice from their fields in Kunduz province in the north. Idrees's parents spend most of their time on their land in Kunduz. He's in charge of his unmarried brothers and sisters. He is married to his cousin Tahmina, and they have a six-year-old daughter, Hellay, and six-month-old twins, a girl and a boy, Sarah and Rahim. Idrees is a loving dad who wakes up in the middle of the night to feed his twins, who laughs and dances with his daughter. But his position as head of the household is never questioned because he has the *siasat* (the discipline) to ensure a timely meal, a clean house, and a moral environment—no cigarettes, drugs, or alcohol. When a member of the family steps out of bounds—for example, by neglecting their homework or chores—he need only frown, and they quickly obey. Idrees is adamant that only he water the plants in the yard.

Idrees normally leaves the house in the morning and comes home after the sun sets. He likes to walk the half hour to work or take one of the two bicycles the family uses for transportation. They do not own a car. Sometimes he gets a call in the middle of the night to come to work, to prepare for an operation. Then he's gone for a couple of days. Idrees does not tell people that he works for the NIU. Only his family knows. Other relatives and friends know him as a simple policeman. Even at home he talks about his colleagues but never about the cases he's working on—it's understood that his job is a secret.

One August night Idrees is watching the news on television while his wife nurses one of the twins. They have eaten dinner and Idrees is relaxing on the *toshak*, his muscular arm resting against a pillow. He's drinking his tea slowly, engrossed in the news, when his cell phone rings. He listens to the voice on the other end.

"I'll be there in thirty-five minutes," he responds. Afghans tell time in intervals of thirty minutes. Mentioning that extra five minutes is a mark of Idrees's promptness and his police training.

His relaxed demeanor suddenly shifts to an urgent strut. He orders Tahmina to bring a washed *pirahan tomban* and his checkered scarf, which he wraps around his neck. He looks in the mirror to make sure his mustache is trimmed. On this pleasant summer night, he puts on his silver watch and his beige vest over his starched outfit and walks to the counternarcotics compound.

Tahmina dreads the late-night calls. She becomes quiet and sad when Idrees leaves for operations. Before he leaves that night he tells his younger brother Zaki, a student at Kabul University, "I'll give you a missed call when I reach the compound. We'll stay the night there and then go on the operation sometime in the morning."

The family waits for the phone to ring. Forty-five minutes later, at 10:45, Idrees lets the phone ring once to signal his safe arrival. Tahmina breathes a sigh of relief and goes to bed.

Idrees sleeps on a cot in the compound, as does his partner, Obaid. In the early morning the two men will embark on their most dangerous assignment yet, to Helmand province in the south, a stronghold of the Taliban and drug smugglers.

The Taliban have made a ferocious comeback. They are better trained and well armed. Helmand is their backyard, supported by powerful drug trafficking networks. The United States, with the help of Afghan authorities, have arrested four kingpins linked to the Taliban, including Haji Juma Khan and Haji Baz Mohammad, but their networks are still active. The networks operate with the Pakistani truckers' mafia, the Quetta Alliance, which smuggles contraband and goods across Afghanistan to Pakistan and Iran and controls a large share of the drug industry coming from the southern Afghan provinces. It is the Quetta

Alliance that helped bring the Taliban to power in 1994. The traffickers pay the Taliban to protect their shipments, and in return the Taliban receive funding and weapons. The most lucrative trafficking route
runs through Nimroz province, west of Helmand; Nimroz is a Baloch
ethnic area that shares a border with both Iran and Pakistan. This tri-
border route provides the shortest way for drugs to be trafficked via
sea, air, or land. The Taliban and these networks have a base in Baramcha district, in Helmand, and Afghans who have been there tell stories
of a village with twenty-four-hour electricity powered by generators
and an underground depot stocked with thousands of tons of opium
and heroin. Neither the Afghan government nor any foreign military
has been able to penetrate Baramcha. This is the Helmand that Idrees
and Obaid are about to enter.

When I enter the counternarcotics compound in Kabul to visit with
General Asif, I notice framed certificates hanging on the wall. On
each certificate is a photo of a man, one with a mustache and one
with a beard. They look like criminal mug shots. The photos on the
wall are of Idrees and Obaid, and the certificates were printed in
honor of their bravery.

I have known General Asif, the immediate head of the NIU,
for a year, and it still takes several cups of tea and chitchat to get a
useful sentence out of him. Today I find he is not his usual hospitable self. "Fariba Jan," he says in his calm Pashto accent, "you have
no idea what I've been through since you were here last. I lost two
of my best boys in Helmand. One of our sources was a double agent,
and now he's fled to Pakistan. We haven't gotten him yet, and who
knows if we ever will.

"These two agents could think on their feet and work indepen-
dently. They were the first two that I thought of for the job," Asif
tells me.

These are the first high-profile homicides in Asif's Western-trained elite unit, and the Afghan authorities have teamed up with the DEA, the British, and the Pakistani police to capture the people responsible.

For the operation in which Idrees and Obaid were involved, the British worked with an Afghan informant who provided intelligence on drug dealers. That information was then shared with the Afghan government selectively. The informant worked with another man from Helmand, Shah Wali, who was connected to Gulbuddin Hekmatyar's former mujahideen party, Hizb-e-Islami. Hekmatyar was a known trafficker in 1979 when the CIA began funding his faction through Pakistan's ISI. He was largely responsible for the destruction of Kabul during the civil war in the 1990s and had teamed up with the Taliban against the U.S. coalition. Hekmatyar was involved with large narcotics smuggling rings in the eastern part of Afghanistan and tribal areas of Pakistan.

Shah Wali told the British informant that two tons of opium were stashed in a house near Grishk district, in Helmand. Idrees and Obaid were to be sent to check out the location of the house. If the information was accurate, they were supposed to quickly drive away. Then a government raid would take place.

The two men were physically fit. Each wore a badge to show to other government forces if they were stopped, and each had a nine-millimeter pistol and a cell phone tucked away. Shah Wali accompanied them in a taxi from Kabul to Kandahar, where they spent the night. They then hopped in another cab and drove toward Helmand. At about six PM Shah Wali made his call. He told his contacts that the NIU agents were on their way.

It was a setup.

Four to six men on motorcycles stopped the men's car, dragged them out, tied their hands, blindfolded them, and drove them to a house sixteen miles away in Gaz, a hotbed of Taliban support. Taliban commanders Mullah Khaliq and Mullah Manan met them there. Obaid began crying, begging them not to kill him. He was poorer than Idrees, and the breadwinner for a family of twenty. He pleaded that his family had no one to take care of them if he was dead. Idrees yelled at him to stop begging. He knew he and Obaid would be killed. It happened almost immediately.

One of the commanders shot Idrees first, then Obaid, multiple times in the chest and head. The bodies were left where they were killed, by the side of the road. Shah Wali had hoped that Americans or the British would come, because then there could've been a ransom. But the bodies of foreign-trained Afghan police were good enough to send a message: the Taliban and their drug lord friends ruled this area and they'd kill whoever got in their way.

Shah Wali and the other killers crossed the Afghan border to Pakistan, but the Helmand governor, Sher Mohammad Akhunzada, also an accused drug dealer opposed to the Taliban, turned over Abdul Malik, Shah Wali's son-in-law, who was present at the executions. Abdul Malik, who was small fish in this high-profile murder, became the fall guy while the masterminds of the homicides walked away. The British protected their informant, who remained unnamed and unharmed. "The drug lords in the south are much harder to fight than those in the north of the country," an official in counternarcotics tells me. "In the north, drugs are commerce, and loyalties can be easily bought. The southerners are tied to tribal loyalties and antiforeign ideologies. They justify their drug dealing politically and convince many younger men to participate by manipulating religion. Twenty kilos of opium for a foreigner's head—that's about a six-thousand-dollar reward offered to fresh recruits of the insurgency."

Two months after Idrees's murder, I visit his family at their Khair Khana home. The cemented front yard is decorated with more than a dozen plants. I can smell rotting garbage mixed with the aroma of fresh adobe after a light rain. My shoes feel heavy from the mud I collect as I walk to the door. I knock, and a young girl in a head scarf answers. I hear a baby crying. "That's my little brother, Rahim," the girl chimes.

"What's your name?" I ask.

"Hellay," she says shyly. She's Idrees's oldest child. She leads me to the living room, where I meet her grandmother, Idrees's mother, Jahan.

"Welcome," she says. We kiss three times on the cheek, and I sit in a sparsely furnished room warmed with a wood heater. Jahan orders one of her daughters to bring tea and then turns her rosary. (Muslims recite verses from the Quran as they finger each bead on the rosary.) I explain my visit. "I want to give my condolences because of your son. I also want to know how the family is doing."

"Not a minute goes by that I don't think about him," Jahan says, her voice thick with authority. She has General Asif's sweet Pashto accent when she speaks Farsi. "We were kings before my son died. Now the flowers are all dead and the house is empty without him." There are no tears in her eyes, no sign of emotion, except for hollow pain. A toddler walks in the room and sits on her lap. Jahan holds her and kisses her head. She sighs.

"This is his youngest daughter, Sarah. Her twin brother is with her mother. She's cooking *nazr* [food for religious offering]."

"How is their mother?"

"She has become very sensitive. She would get upset if she knew I was talking about her with you. She loses her patience and hits the kids. Instead of nursing them, she hits and slaps them, and I'm scared of her anger. She's a widow. God give her patience. We tell her not to hit. If their father was here, he would become very upset. He didn't believe in beating."

"Were they happy together?" I ask.

"Yes, they were good friends. They were first cousins and lived as husband and wife for nine years. Tahmina is only twenty-five years old," Jahan says.

Idrees's sister Khadija brings tea and joins the conversation.

"My brother was the person we all looked up to in this house," she says. "He taught me different ways to decorate the sweets for Eid [a feast after Ramadan]. He had a woman's taste and a man's authority. I water the plants now, but they're dying." Her voice trails off as the tears run down her face.

I have moved into a newly constructed apartment complex in the Project Taimani neighborhood with a good friend. Patricia Omidian is an American anthropologist in her fifties who is well respected for her work and charity among Afghans. We live by ourselves on the third floor in a two-bedroom apartment at an intersection with a mosque, a wedding hall, and welding shops. I have to learn to fall asleep to the muezzin's call to prayer fused with Afghan disco pop music bursting through the wedding hall until two AM. Most expatriates live as a group in large guarded guesthouses in wealthier neighborhoods, as I did in Karte Parwan. Among the foreigners live the drug lords, in opium palaces, or they rent out their houses to foreigners. A *Washington Post* article about opium palaces describes them best: "For rent on Street 6 in the neighborhood of Sherpur: a four-story, eleven-bedroom dwelling of pink granite and lime marble, complete with massage showers, a rooftop fountain and, in the basement, an Asian-themed nightclub. Price: $12,000 a month." The foreigners in Kabul stimulate the drug economy just by renting.

Patricia and I want to keep a distance from the foreigner-occupied neighborhoods. We think it's safer to live a quiet life among Afghans. We have no guards, no cooks, and no foreign guests. We have a woman come once a week to clean the apartment. The neighbors here are a mix of ethnicities and languages. They do not bother us, and I do not try to befriend or antagonize them.

"How can you live there?" an Afghan American friend in Fremont asks me during a phone call. "I mean, you don't have reliable power, clean water, or the right to wear or say what you want. Why keep going back when the situation is getting worse? All of you guys who've gone back to rebuild the country have made it worse."

It's a question I've answered dozens of times, but the longer I stay in Afghanistan, the more complex my answer becomes.

"Because every morning I wake up, there's a surprise: a new person I meet, a new experience I'm told about, a new discovery about myself, about the people here," I tell her. "In college, when I insisted that I would come back someday, an American friend scoffed at me and said I wouldn't be able to adapt. The Afghanistan of the past was gone and the new one would not welcome me. I wondered the same thing myself. But that's not the case.

"It's true I came here to make peace with the past, and that journey is ongoing. Perhaps I never will. But I'm on a new journey here and I'm finding out things about myself that I never would in the U.S.," I tell her, impassioned.

"Like what?" she asks sarcastically.

"Like I can use just a bucket of water to shower, like I can eat potatoes every day for five weeks and be fine, like I can have a deep conversation with an Afghan man who has four wives and makes a living dealing drugs."

"I think you're still romanticizing it," she insists.

"Sweetie, I'm not going to lie to you. It's awful on some days. I'm learning to live beyond my nostalgic dreams. I hate the misogyny, the corruption, the greed, and the mistrust of so many here. But with it there's resilience for survival and love," I explain to her as I make sense of my own mixed feelings. "People here still can love you despite what they've been through."

"I guess," she says. "Whatever makes you happy, but I think you're wasting your time. Afghanistan's doomed to fail."

"That's like saying your family's sick and doomed to die. I guess you just don't feel the personal ties I do with this place," I say. We end the phone call on a polite but tense note.

My friend's cynicism reminds me of my father's attitude. I can understand him because he's old. But I'm angry with my friend for her willingness to give up on her former country, to disconnect herself from a place that needs young dreamers.

I'm frequently traveling around the country, but in Kabul, where I spend the majority of my time, I find a microcosm of all the issues linking narcotics that I am investigating in the provinces. I live in a city that has become home to countless dealers, corrupt officials, bartered brides, and addicts. The stories of those of us who live here are intertwined in that we are all part of the polluted metropolis that has become Kabul. My mother's Kabul is unrecognizable.

Millions of people in the capital still do not have reliable access to services such as water and electricity, even though $10 billion in international aid has been spent on reconstruction since Karzai declared peace in 2001. Few of the ministries have regular power, water, sewage, or sanitation. If residents have the money, they can afford a generator and dig a well, but there is no water treatment plant in the country. The underground aquifers in Kabul are drying up because too many people rely on well water. Sewage wells are

already contaminating well water. There is no government resource
to store rainwater or collect river water. As for power, neighboring
countries sell electricity to some bordering Afghan cities, but the
capital relies on dams. In the spring and summer, the snow melts on
the mountains, feeding water to the dams and giving people more
hours of electricity.

While Kabul has been the beneficiary of much money, Afghanistan as a whole has seen little change. One in four children still dies
before the age of five; about 3.5 million people still rely on food rations. Dozens of private clinics have popped up with phony doctors
and fake medicines, partly because the Western-backed government
has not been able to build enough genuine clinics to provide basic
health care. Many foreign-funded structures have had severe problems. Roads, hospitals, and schools are crumbling. The Taliban take
advantage of the people's discontent with the Karzai government and
its foreign backers. Suicide bombings shot up 600 percent from 2005 to
2006. The rising anger in Kabul explodes in the spring of 2006.

On the afternoon of May 29, 2006, I fly from Herat to Kabul and
find the airport nearly empty and quiet at a time when crowds and
porters usually leave little room for walking. The parking lot where
dozens of taxis pick up passengers is vacant. The roads are full of
foreign troops with guns. It is one of the most violent days in the
capital since Karzai took control. I share a cab I find on the street
with a few other passengers. The driver tells us the city was on fire
a few hours ago. "An American military truck coming from Bagram
lost control and killed and injured several civilians near Kotal Khair
Khana. Some people think the truck killed the Afghans deliberately.
So they started a protest."

The number of rioters was small, in the hundreds, but the
damage done was bloody: at least seventeen people were killed and

dozens of buildings, mostly the homes and offices of foreigners, were looted and set ablaze. The rioters chanted, "Death to Karzai, death to America." Peacekeepers—the U.S. military, along with the Afghan police and army—worked for hours to restore order.

I go out the next day, following the whiff of soot, to talk to Afghans who witnessed the burnings. Some say they understand why the violence occurred but they do not support it. "People are frustrated because they have no jobs and don't feel safe anymore. Their lives have not improved, so they took it out on the foreigners, who are innocent," a shopkeeper tells me.

On many nights, I escape my apartment to stay with friends, foreign consultants who live in one of the houses in the high-class neighborhood of Wazir Akbar Khan. They work for an American company assigned by the U.S. government to revamp the Afghan financial system. The company rents eight houses, paying up to $8,000 a month for the house used by the highest-ranking company official. The area has become a fortress for international consultants, diplomats, and the American military, with nearly all the streets blocked from normal traffic for safety reasons. Inside the homes, aid money has paid for all the luxuries of Western life, including twenty-four-hour electricity provided by truck-size generators, a cook to prepare three meals a day, and access to satellite television and the Internet. I'm not selfless enough to avoid these luxuries and indulge in the amenities offered at the house.

On the first anniversary of Idrees's death, I visit his family again in Khair Khana. The twins are playing in the yard with their older sister. The plants have been removed from the yard. Hellay takes me to the same guest room, and this time I meet Zaki, Idrees's younger brother, and Idrees's widow, Tahmina. They stand up to greet me.

Zaki seems anxious to talk. He is studying Sharia law at the university and will graduate in a month. He wants to get a job and contribute to his family income. They have another brother, in Austria, who sends some money, but it's not enough for the thirteen members of the family. Their youngest brother is in high school. The family still receives the $200 monthly income with which Idrees used to support them. They can maintain their lifestyle for another few months, until that income stops. The American embassy and the Afghan government have promised to compensate the family with $20,000 for Idrees's sacrifice. (The financial loss has affected the family the least.)

Tahmina, a thin, petite woman, sits cross-legged, her twin toddlers circling her. She doesn't speak Farsi, but even when Zaki asks her a question in Pashto, she mumbles a barely audible answer. She stares at the wall as Zaki, an earnest man with solemn eyes and a beard, shares the details of Idrees's life and death. Zaki was the first to find out that his brother had been murdered and the last to see him alive.

"That night he left for the compound, I walked him to the door and locked the gate behind him. I said the travel prayer for him to return home safe. Four days later, somebody came from NIU to the door and asked for me. He said Idrees and Obaid had been imprisoned in Helmand. My heart stopped for a second. I went with him to the compound to get more details. I told him that the drug dealers in Kandahar and Helmand are wild and that Idrees and Obaid should have never been sent there, because they were not from the area. His colleagues became emotional and upset. I became more suspicious. Their reaction told me something I didn't want to hear. The world went dark. I imagined horrible things happening to my brother. Even a poet cannot describe the pain of a close one's murder. His superior called my name and told me with regret that Idrees was killed."

Tahmina begins to whimper, covering her eyes with her glittery head scarf. Zaki turns his head toward her to soothe her, but he breaks down, too. He holds his head in his hands and sobs. Then he lifts up his head and continues to tell me the story, choked up.

"I lost my color. I had no tears then. I was just angry. 'Where is he?' I demanded. The deputy said the bodies are coming about one PM and we can take Idrees when we're ready to bury him. We didn't have to wash the body because he was a martyr. Martyrs are clean from their sacrifice.

"Then I called people, our neighbors here in Kabul, and my cousin in Kunduz. I told him to keep the news until I prepared the family. When I got home, the family wasn't aware yet, but my sister Khadija, who was very close to him, was suspicious. This was the first time he had been gone for so long. Our youngest brother, Ansar, who's in high school, figured it out after a neighbor began crying in front of him. We turned our guests away and I told the family that a distant uncle had died in Kunduz and we had to drive there for the funeral."

In Afghanistan, the closest people to the deceased, especially women, are protected from news of a death until the last possible minute, when the body is buried. Women are discouraged from attending burials, to protect them from the emotional pain. Afghans find it cruel when I tell them that in the United States a person dying of cancer is the first to know, then the closest family members. When an Afghan is diagnosed with cancer, the doctor does not immediately share it with the patient. Zaki's effort to hide the death of Idrees was a desperate attempt to delay his family's grief.

"The family left," he continues. "My parents were already there. I stayed behind to go on the plane with the body. The foreigners gave us a thousand dollars for the burial. I saw his body in a coffin for a minute. He had been in the morgue for five days. His scarf was over his face where they had hit him. His silver watch was still on. I finally believed he was dead.

"When we arrived in Kunduz, at about six PM, my mother asked, 'Where's my son?' She fell apart and insisted on seeing his body at the burial. There were too many men around for her to see. About five hundred people came to the funeral."

"How do you feel now?" I ask.

"I'm angry at the NIU for sending him there and I want to do my own investigation into what happened. There are too many unanswered questions. I want to know if the government is protecting one of their own men for this, was it a small-time informant or someone higher up? Is the governor of Helmand a suspect and is he under investigation?"

The Afghan counterterrorism directorate is also investigating the case, and an official there tells me that the trail of the criminals has gone cold. "They're most likely in Quetta. We know Shah Wali's there but we don't know where exactly. He has a couple of wives and a house in Kabul, and we're watching the house to arrest him if he returns. Until then, there's nothing that can be done. The other side of the border belongs to the Taliban."

I leave Idrees's home sad but inspired—the death of the two honorable agents will go unreported while news of drug dealers, corrupt officials, and the growing unrest in Afghanistan will make news headlines across the world. I wish I had known Idrees, had at least talked to him. After speaking to dozens of greedy, lying, self-serving drug smugglers and law enforcement agents, I find that Idrees's commitment and belief in the law have given me faith in a system tainted with double agents, double crossings, and shifting loyalties. I hope his sacrifice will not be forgotten.

SEVENTEEN
In Search of Darya

The trip I have dreaded for six months is approaching. It's time to find Darya. I have many thoughts of pulling out. Too many violent nightmares, too many risks involved. I have traveled to the north and the west without much fear, because I speak Farsi, the most common language in those regions. Now I am going to unknown territory, where Afghans who speak Pashto dominate. I know I have to go, to tell the full story of my country's relationship with opium, and to try to find the shivering little girl who tugged on my coat and asked me to save her from being enslaved to a man thirty-four years older than she. Darya would be fourteen years old now. I wonder if her eyes still flash with anger the way they did two years ago. Is she still forgetting her slippers and walking barefoot in the sand? She must have reached puberty and become a stunning young woman. I have been thinking about her throughout my travels in Afghanistan. Her pleading eyes are a lasting image in my mind. All I know is that she lives in Helmand, the most dangerous province in the country.

The capital of Helmand, Lashkargah, was called Little America when my family lived there in the 1970s. My father was an administrative manager of the fertilizer company and received a comfortable government salary. My mother says the four years we lived in Lashkargah were the best times of her life. I recall the dinner parties my family threw for their friends and neighbors: men and women gathered together playing music and eating kabobs and *palau* rice. My brother, Hadi, was a university student in Kabul, and when he visited on holidays, he displayed his musical talent playing the harmonium and singing while someone played the *tabla*. I would dance, twirling coquettishly around the living room while the guests clapped. On warmer days, we would take trips to the ancient castle of Qala-e-Bost on the Helmand River, the longest river in Afghanistan. We would fish, then barbecue in the verdant riverside. I have no memory of linguistic or ethnic rivalries. We socialized with everyone on the block—Pashtun, Tajik, Baloch—but I was a little girl who paid no attention to such divisions or to the darker history of Little America.

After World War II, King Zahir had a surplus of cash and he wanted to use it to modernize Afghanistan. In the 1950s he hired the U.S. company Morrison Knudsen, the builder of the San Francisco—Oakland Bay Bridge, to construct a modern city modeled on an American suburb. The project was part of a greater mission by the U.S. government to build capitalistic societies in developing countries and to discourage the spread of communism. The king's foreign advisers chose Helmand because of its river. They gave parcels of land to nomadic Pashtuns to settle and begin farming. The Little America project included a hydroelectric dam and an extensive irrigation network, as well as suburban houses with tree-lined paved roads and green lawns without the usual walls that Afghans erected around their homes. American engineers and American-educated Afghans poured into Helmand to implement the project, but after the first test of the water and soil, they discovered that there was too much salt and that the ground had become waterlogged from the canals they'd built. The experts warned both governments that if they continued building canals and constructing the dam, the river could dry up. The warnings were ignored. It became more important to show short-term results than to consider long-term consequences—a repetitive folly of American policy in Afghanistan. The dam project was abandoned during the Communist takeover, and most of the engineers and technocrats fled the country, but the damage was already done. The soil was so eroded that orchards disappeared and the only harvest yield was from grains and poppy. Hence, American aid played a key role in Helmand's transformation into the largest poppy producing province in Afghanistan.

During the Soviet-Afghan war, Mullah Nasim, commander of the mujahideen in Helmand, issued decrees for farmers to cultivate poppy, and he brought in chemists to process the opium. The farmers stopped growing grains and obeyed Nasim, who taxed their harvest to fund his guerrilla war.

After the Communists seized power, my family left Helmand for Kandahar.

I first returned to Helmand six months after the Taliban's fall, in the summer of 2002. I was with two other colleagues driving cross-country through the southern belt. We turned from the main high-

way on to a dirt road into desert, following the tire tracks toward
Lashkargah. The tree-lined streets were gone, the roads had deteriorated to cracked gravel, and the Helmand River where I used to
fish with my father was lifeless and shallow. The people all wore
traditional Afghan garb, and we saw few women in public. The men
smiled at us, but there was a look of distrust in their eyes. This was
not the Helmand my family had left behind.

Three years later, I am traveling to a much more hostile Helmand,
where NIU agents Idrees and Obaid were shot dead on the side of
a road. The Taliban are gaining ground against the British military.
Helmand farmers have become experts at poppy farming, and drug
lords often clash with one another and their government counterparts in competition for the best deals. The population of 1.5 million is dependent on profits from poppy cultivation to survive; they
say they will stop farming if they have alternatives. But some of
them are being forced into farming poppy by the Taliban, and alternative programs are being sabotaged by a lack of security. For decades Pakistan's poorest province, Balochistan, bordering Helmand,
has been a breeding ground for smuggling. The Balochis, like the
Pashtuns, live on both sides of the border and feel marginalized
and discriminated against by both the Afghanistan and Pakistan
governments.

I decide to wear a burqa and work undercover.

Haji Sufi, Darya's husband, is a poppy farmer in one of the districts here. He took his opium bride a year after I left her in Ghoryan begging to be freed of him.

The last people to see Darya whom I know are the Afghan photographers I work with, Massoud and Farzana. They visited Ghoryan
to take pictures of her. Darya and her mother, Basira, met them in
Darya's grandmother's house. Darya and Basira wore black chadors

for the photos and Darya "showed only her eyes and covered the rest of her body when she caught me taking photos of her," Massoud says. "Both Darya and her mother wanted us to help them free her of the smuggler husband. They blamed the marriage on her father, who was no longer at home. I told them I would report it to the human rights commission in Herat. I did, and the commission did nothing about it."

Finding Darya will not be easy. I have no proper address and no invitation from her husband. As far as I know, he is a Taliban sympathizer who will not welcome me into his home. He may think of me as a loose foreign woman. Still, I was taught that, in Pashtun culture, even if the hosts do not like their guests, they will feed and house them. I am hoping that Haji Sufi's sense of hospitality will be stronger than his anger toward me as a foreigner interested in the well-being of his second wife.

All I have is the name of a district in the province where Haji Sufi has lived—an area where opium is sold openly and the Taliban and their sympathizers rule. Information coming into Kabul about the area suggests that foreigners are generally not welcome there and will likely be kidnapped or killed. I carry a photo of Haji Sufi that I took two years ago. I plan to show it while going door to door until I find Darya. I am betting on the popular notion that there are only two degrees of separation between Afghans, and most often we all know each other.

Some months before, I visited Ghoryan during Eid-al-Fitr, the feast after Ramadan. The district was changing. The road from Herat city to Ghoryan was paved, and it took only an hour, instead of three, to reach the town center. More residents had access to power and water, and more schools had been built in the remote villages of the district.

My former guide, Saber, came to the city and we rode to Ghoryan together, heading directly to his house, where we were welcomed with an elaborate lunch of meat and rice. I was a special guest—my six-week stay in their home a year before had solidified our bond. We had kept in touch in the months I had been away. Saber was working odd jobs, and he was eager for his wife, Tarana, to become pregnant. His sister Tina was still single and tending to their household meticulously. But the opium tragedy had infected his family, too, as one of his younger brothers had become addicted in the last year. Saber didn't want to talk about his brother. "The whole district is still suffering," he told me, "and when you came, the business was divided among a few drug lords. Now more and more people are getting involved and addicted as refugees keep returning from Iran."

After lunch, I insisted on seeing Darya. Saber gave me a mournful look.

"She's gone," he said, pausing for my reaction. "He took her."

I felt a surge of panic. My hands became clammy and my throat knotted.

"What about her sister Saboora?" I asked. "Did her drug dealer husband ever show up?"

"No, he's probably dead. She's still with her mother."

"Let's go see them."

The family now lived in the grandmother's house. Basira came out in her colorful Eid clothes with her youngest daughter, Hana. She kissed my cheek and motioned me to climb a mud-brick-cobbled stairway to a small room. Saboora, who had been hostile every time I visited previously, was standing at the top of the stairway. But she was cordial this time, smiling as her mother led me to the guest room. The room was adorned with Eid sweets—dried fruit, nuts, cakes, and cookies—and fresh pots of green tea. The family seemed better off than when I last visited them, but then again, it was Eid, a holiday when Muslims push away their sadness, dress up, clean their homes, and find their festive mood.

I asked Basira about Darya.

"She finally went with him three months ago," she said. "Her father came back and convinced her to go. We all went to Helmand for her wedding. It was a simple event—no music, no festivity. She was not allowed to wear makeup. No one danced. It was just a bunch of women, and we were fed a meal and told to go home.

"She still had not had her period yet," Basira added. "She had to go. She had no choice. But she insisted that her brother Aman stay with her, because she didn't want to be alone." Aman was ten. I shuddered to think of what was being done to a handsome boy like him. Afghan commanders are infamous for fighting over young boys they want to rape and keep as prizes.

"Aman is so young. Now he has my son and daughter," Basira says, referring to Haji Sufi, "and I haven't seen either for months. Can you go find them and tell him to send my son back?" she pleaded with me like a beggar.

I promised her I would visit Haji Sufi and relay her message.

Basira thinks I'm doing her a favor, but she doesn't realize that, in some ways, finding Darya is my salvation—one that is perhaps as illusory as my nostalgia for the homeland of my childhood—but the trail has grown colder as the months have gone by.

On the night before my trip to the south, I sleep three hours. In those hours, I dream of walking on a river, floating on top of the waves. All around me is green grass, and the air is clean. Then, suddenly, I start to sink, unable to swim, gasping for air. I jolt awake to the phone ringing; it is my driver, Jawid, saying he is waiting outside to drive me to the bus depot. It is four thirty AM and the sun has not come out yet. There is no going back now.

The public bus headed to Kandahar leaves from the crowded bus station in Kabul. The sun is coming up and I am already feeling the oncoming heat as I board the bus. Kandahar is the safest route to Helmand by road and a city in which I spent a year of my childhood during the war. Kandahar is the base of the Karzai clan and the birthplace of the Taliban movement. It's also one of Afghanistan's ancient and strategic cities, where empires have risen and fallen. Like Herat and Kabul, Kandahar is located in a province with the same name. The United States and NATO have set up a base at the city's airport. It borders Pakistan's Quetta province, where the Taliban, al Qaeda, and major drug smugglers have safe haven. Kandahar is a trade route in the region. The province used to produce dried fruit, grains, cotton, silk, and wool, but after the Soviet invasion farmers turned to poppy, and so did the traders. Some of the major Afghan drug kingpins hail from Kandahar.

The three outfits I've packed for my trip are full-skirt knee-length dresses with long pajama-like pants. I take along large head scarves that will not slip and will cover every strand of hair. With my scant knowledge of the Pashto language, it won't be easy for me to fit in, but the clothes will help me resemble a liberal girl from Kabul. The south has become hostile to Westerners or anyone working with international aid agencies or the media. The news headlines from Kandahar, Helmand, and Uruzgan commonly contain the words *killed, kidnapped, bombed,* or *injured.* I must pass through Kandahar by road in order to reach Helmand from Kabul.

I wear my green outfit with the burqa and sit next to Zabi, a friend from Kabul, who will be my traveling partner for the next eight hours, until we reach Kandahar. I carry a plastic bag containing bottled water, small juice boxes, pistachio nuts, and cookies. We pass dust-covered apple orchards, fields of wheat, and nomads with camels walking along the side of the highway. This is my second road trip to

Kandahar and I know the greenery will not last. It is a quick glimpse before the endless desert encroaches on the pleasant view.

The bus stops at a checkpoint. The counternarcotics police step on board. A woman dressed all in black, a round scarf pulled up above her nose, precedes the men. With her black-gloved hands, she frisks the women, lightly patting their burqas and hand luggage. She sees me watching her. I can tell she is diligent in her job, because she is sniffing as she searches. The smell of opium can be overpowering. Her eyes are dark brown. When she reaches me, she somehow knows I do not fit in. She looks at the old, dusty local sandals on my feet as if to say, "I know those shoes are a front," and motions me to open the bag holding my laptop case. She is right. Women going to Kandahar on public buses don't usually carry laptops. Before anyone else can see, she closes the bag and walks to the front to tell her supervisor the women are clean. She seems to understand that I'm trying to fit in and doesn't want to blow my cover. The passengers go back to what they were doing, and the driver blasts the upbeat Pashto music as loud as it was.

Eight hours later, the lively streets of Kandahar city greet us: rickshaws, overcrowded buses, donkeys, and horse wagons compete for space with pedestrians. A few women in blue burqas stand out in the crowds. Nearly every man sports a beard and wears the *pirahan tomban*. It's spring, but the summer heat has already come to Kandahar. I'm boiling under the polyester burqa. It was this hot in the spring of 1979, when my family lived here during the Communist era. The sight of flies buzzing around a sheep carcass in a butcher shop takes me back twenty-six years.

Shortly after the Communist coup, the American aid project in Helmand disintegrated as foreign consultants escaped the country and Afghans, such as my father, moved to other locations. He stayed with the fertilizer company but was transferred to Kandahar, where we spent a year.

We shared a two-family home in the Manzil Bagh neighborhood. The living room windows faced a major thoroughfare and I used to sit on the windowsill to watch the cars pass. There was regular power and running water, but there were no more mixed-gender dinner parties, fishing trips, or dancing. I stayed home with my mother, while Faiza attended high school. She had to wear a chador, and one of my parents had to escort her to the stop where she caught the public bus to reach her Farsi-instruction school. Kandahar offered Pashto-instruction schools with a subject in Farsi, and Farsi-instruction schools with a subject in Pashto. Kandahar has a considerable Farsi-speaking Tajik population—mostly Shiites, who live in relative harmony with the Pashtuns. With few friends and no family, we felt like immigrants in the city.

"Initially, we could go to the bazaars and visit the shrines and have a normal life," my mother tells me. "But as the war progressed, it became harder and harder to leave the house."

It was in Kandahar where we learned that the secret police had taken my paternal uncle Fazel Ahmed Ahrary from his Kabul University office. He disappeared like thousands of other innocent intellectuals. The secret police rounded up and arrested dozens of people at a time, sent them to Pul-e-Charkhi, and then executed them in the military training fields behind the prison. Some were buried alive. Survivors tell tales of torture and brutality. The first time I saw my father cry was in Kandahar.

"Agha, why are you crying?" I asked him.

"Because Fazel Ahmed died for nothing," he said, holding my hand and explaining. "No justice. None."

"But we don't know he's dead," I insisted.

"You're too young to be exposed to these things. Go play," he ordered me.

The government was particularly suspicious of thinkers from Herat because of the first uprising there. During his last semester at the university, my brother, Hadi, was also being watched. When he finished his degree in English literature, he came to Kandahar to visit us and consulted with my parents about leaving the country. The mass exodus of educated Afghans had already begun.

In December 1979, during Hadi's visit, the Soviet Union invaded the country. I sat on the windowsill, hugged my legs with my chin perched on my knees, and watched a caravan of Soviet military trucks, tanks, and Jeeps drive by our house for an hour. I was six years old and trying to understand the concept of war and death. I didn't ask my parents my usual array of questions, but I wondered silently where those trucks were going. My father walked over to me, touched my shoulder, and answered my unspoken question.

"They're going to the countryside. They're not going to bother us," he reassured me.

Hadi left Kandahar for Kabul, took two of Uncle Fazel's sons with him, and they fled to Pakistan, to await asylum in either Europe or the United States.

"We gave him a carpet to sell and fund his trip," my mother remembers. "I cried so much when he said good-bye casually, as if he were going back to school. I didn't know if I would ever see my son again."

It didn't take long before the war reached the city. My sister's memories of Kandahar are vivid. "During recess time in school, we could go in the shops and have fun, and then come back. There were four of us shopping around and we saw this guy holding maybe a five-year-old girl. He passed by me and the next thing we know, he was shot in the head. I just heard the gunshot. We hid in a stationery store for a while and then got out. Everybody was running. When we looked behind us, some men were running after us as if they wanted to hurt us. They didn't catch us because we were way ahead of them. We ran to school and the school had a lockout."

On the day the war broke out in the city, my father and his colleagues at the fertilizer company heard that rioters were attacking anyone working for the government. They left work immediately to seek refuge in their homes. They jumped in a company car but didn't make it far before they were under attack. The rioters threw sticks and stones at their car. My father ducked and ran into a residential home. His hosts, complete strangers, gave him a *pirahan tomban* and a turban to wear. (His slacks and collared shirt would have made him a target, since that was the style of dress for civil servants.) He rode the bus home and frightened my mother. "I was cooking and suddenly I could see a man appear from the corner of my eye," my mother says. "I thought he was there to attack me. I screamed and your father took off his turban and smiled. I had never seen him dressed in traditional clothes before."

Shortly thereafter, my father requested a transfer back to his birthplace, Herat, where the uprisings had been crushed and the war had reverted back to the countryside.

Kandahar city had become a front line.

The afternoon sun fades with evening prayer time and I can feel a light draft sneak in through the closed window of my room. I'm staying at an Afghan NGO that is helping farmers maximize their incomes. The management is taking a big risk hosting me—if the locals find out there is a single Afghan woman without a *mahram* inside a house full of men, they might attack the NGO. They allow me to stay here because I've asked for their help. Afghan NGOs offer the same hospitality the Afghan people do. I can see a colorful garden through the mesh of my burqa, but I am not allowed to sit outside. They give me a room facing a wall and send a Farsi-speaking engineer named Kazi to watch over me. He is dreadfully scared that protecting me will cost him his life.

"It's very unusual for me to come here and talk to you like this. It's dangerous," he says.

"You can leave if you're more comfortable," I respond.

"I can't do that. I'm responsible for you here. I'm not sure whether you're brave or stupid for coming here like this, without any guards or family."

When I speak on the phone in the room, he warns me not to laugh too loud or speak English too loud, because the people on the street might hear my feminine voice.

I tell him the truth about my reasons for traveling to the south, but few others know. My official story is that I am going to Helmand in search of my cousin Darya, whose mother has lost touch with her and wants me to reestablish contact. If I admitted that Darya's not related to me, then I would have to reveal more details, which would endanger both of us. I decide that maybe a hotel room in a quiet part of the city would be safer than the NGO.

The staff at the hotel where I've relocated knows I'm headed to Helmand the next day. One of them stops me on my way to my room. "*Hamshira,* this week the Taliban killed five Afghan aid workers who were trying to get rid of opium in Helmand," he warns me. "Then they killed six other men who were driving the body of one of the men killed in Helmand to Kabul for burial. They ambushed their car and just shot them on the way in Zabul province. I don't think you should go."

"I'll be fine," I reply coldly. "I have to go."

"The Taliban will kill you if they find out you're a journalist," he insists, trying to convince me. "Whatever it is you want from there, it's not worth it."

"Yes, it is, very much so."

I walk into my room and shut the door.

EIGHTEEN

Through the Mesh

The taxi driver, Samay, will not look at me, even in my burqa. But Imran, my guide, is more than eager to look. The three of us are driving across a rugged desert, over thorns and pebbles. I look for red painted rocks, a marker of mines, but I don't see any. We pass the shrine of Malalai, an Afghan heroine who died in battle against the British in the nineteenth century. The men in the car speak Pashto together; I can make out that it is small talk. They do not know each other, but they have one goal on this trip: making sure I come back from Helmand alive.

Samay has five children and one wife. A diminutive man in his thirties, he was recommended to me by a couple of local journalists in Kandahar who said I could trust him with my life. Apparently

Samay's loyalty to his passengers is unmatched in the city. He is also a cheap ride compared with the other drivers catering to foreigners. I've convinced him to drive Imran and me for five hours on the rough desert to the district of Sangin, in Helmand, for fifty dollars a day. Other drivers would charge at least double that.

Samay knows the road well. I cannot figure out how he knows which direction in the desert to go. Each way looks the same, with endless sunny skies, rocks, and sand. The only signs are the tire tracks along which his yellow Toyota chugs as fast as it can, at speeds of thirty to forty kilometers. He doesn't smoke hashish on the drive like the last driver I hired in Kandahar, and he keeps his eyes on the road instead of in his rearview mirror to peek at me.

Imran is my friend's relative. He is from the district of Grishk, Helmand. When my friend insisted he become my guide, he left his family business, wife, and children in Grishk and rushed to Kandahar to assist me. His family is prosperous from running a soft drink business. They are part of the minority of Farsi-speaking Shiites who have survived in the south over hundreds of years. I am amazed at how the Taliban, who disapprove of Shiites and believe they are infidels, have allowed this community to survive. Imran's religious sect and language may be different at home, but in public he fits in with other men, minus the turban and beard. Instead, he sports a mustache and talks like a businessman—a bit too smooth for my taste. He stares at me, not for sexual interest but to read me. He keeps asking me the same question in roundabout ways.

"Why are you really here? I mean, what's the real reason you're looking for this girl?"

"I'm obeying her mother's wishes to find her, and I care to know how she is," I say.

That response isn't good enough.

"*Rasti* [really]?"

His suspicion is clear, so the fact that he continues to take this risk for me is puzzling.

The unforgiving desert wind blows the flowing fabric of my burqa through the open window and I feel relief from the breeze. I have a photocopy of Haji Sufi's picture in my bag. First Imran is going to visit the contacts he has and show them the picture. The photo is of a man sitting on a mat drinking tea, his legs crossed, his turban looking too big for his head. He looks into the camera lens uncomfortably, as if this picture will be used against him at some point. This photo of Haji Sufi is the only clue I have to finding Darya. Her mother told me she lived in Sangin district, in a home located on an orchard near the homes of Haji Sufi's two other brothers.

I will find Darya. I have to. Her quavering voice echoes in my head: "Please don't let him take me."

If I find her, at least she will see that I cared enough to come back; she will know that she matters and isn't a slave. I want her to know that she can fight back and change her life. Most important, I want her to know that there's someone out there who will listen to her and who is concerned about her. I also want to know her more: What is her favorite subject in school? Does she like to dance? Does she resent her father for what he did to her? What does she want to be when she grows up? Is she anything like me?

We finally arrive in Sangin. It is a district with high mud walls, colorful metal doors, and a silence that reminds me of the Taliban years. There are no women outside, only men with kohl-lined eyes and black-and-white-striped turbans. They look at the taxi with suspicion, not with the usual welcoming smile I encounter in villages. I was told to be as I am, a visitor, and not to pretend to be anything else. I have the same strange sense of empowerment wearing the burqua as I did during the Taliban years, when I first returned to Afghanistan—that I can see them and they cannot see me.

Imran and I walk to the village bazaar, which is made up of mud huts with small wooden doors. It looks like any other Afghan village bazaar, except that instead of selling rice and cooking oil, most of these tiny shops look empty and dark. Karzai's government has no presence in this village, as far as I can tell, but the official ban on opium seems to have taken the sale of narcotics underground. This isn't like Badakhshan, where the shopkeepers sat between a scale and bags of heroin with crisp dollar bills in their hands. I ask Imran what these shops sell.

"Opium," he replies as if I should know better than to ask.

"Is there a storage space they put it in, because the shops are empty?"

"No, they just make the deals here and then, if someone wants to buy, they bring it from their homes or wherever they have it stashed."

I asked why it is so secretive when no one here is opposing it.

"These people are former Taliban and they think they'll be attacked at any point, so they cover their tracks."

We arrive close to noon, when families are preparing lunch. Imran orders me to stay at his aunt's house while he shows the picture of Haji Sufi around. Inside the courtyard, the women and children in his family welcome me, bringing tea and fresh bread. This familiar kindness relaxes me a little. They want to know why I am here, where my *mahram* is, and how I am related to Imran.

"Imran is a relative of a friend, and I am searching for my cousin Darya."

"I know a girl from Herat married to an old man. Do you have a photo of her?" Imran's aunt asks.

I kick myself. I do but I didn't bring it. I did not want to put Darya in any kind of danger. When Imran returns, he looks defeated, until his aunt tells him to try a couple of blocks up their street.

"I showed several shopkeepers, but they do not know too many people by the name of Haji Sufi. That's a generic title. What's his real name?"

I am dumbfounded. I didn't realize he lied to me about his name. When I spoke to Darya's mother about him, we referred to him as the girl's "husband" and nothing more.

Imran sees the disappointment in my face. "People say he looks familiar, but they don't know where he lives or what his name is."

I join him in Sameh's taxi as we stop at each door. Imran goes out under the sweltering sun and repeats the same question.

"Have you seen this man? He's a relative we want to visit."

When he asks a young boy, the boy runs off, probably fearing we might be kidnappers. Only men open doors, and most of them shake their heads when they see the photo. The family that Imran's aunt told us to visit has no Herati girl married to an old man.

Two hours later I end up in another house with womenfolk. Imran stays for a few minutes, then leaves to chat with the men. I am welcomed by the women and barraged with the same questions. They see the concern on my face and ask me why I am here. I try to explain. The wife and mother-in-law speak only Pashto, but we manage to get a few ideas across. I want to ask them how their life has changed since the Taliban left. Are the men in their family opium vendors? Do they know Darya? But I am deprived of words. Learning Pashto has never been a goal of mine, but now I realize how important it is to be Afghan and know both Farsi and Pashto.

Still, I am able to get along with these women. I learn a few words of Pashto from them, and they learn a few words of Farsi from me. I learn that wife is *shazai*, brother is *orror*, and the Taliban are *bad di* (bad). They are so similar to the women in the north. Ethnic, political, and linguistic rivalries seem to play no significant role in their lives, because they are not competing for power or positions. They care for their families and take care of their homes, just like the women in the rest of the country.

Most Afghan village homes have an outhouse with a hole in the ground: don't look, hold your nose, and shoot. These women do not have outhouses. Their bathroom is their front yard. I squat uncomfortably, looking around to see if I am being watched. Two chickens are my only spectators. The women usually clean up the mess with a shovel and throw it in the nearest ditch outside. I do the same.

I want to know how this place can be a central point for drug deals, where thousands of dollars exchange hands every day, and yet suffer from so much poverty that these women do not even have a bathroom. Where does the money go? Sangin, located at the edge of the Helmand River—perfect for a healthy poppy harvest—is near the main highway and offers an easy trafficking route. But it's the higher ranks in the trafficking chain that benefit from the drug, and they do not invest locally—their money is laundered in Gulf countries. The majority of the population here lives poor.

Back in the room with the women, I am waiting for Imran when a round-bellied man enters. He is not friendly but he speaks Farsi. "What is it that you want from here?" he asks me. "You should not be traveling without a *mahram*. Imran is not your *mahram* and you're traveling with him."

I say that I want to find my cousin and that's all. "Her mother has sent me to find her and I mean no harm to anyone."

There is no sympathy. He orders the woman to serve me more tea and dashes off. What is Imran doing? Is he going to protect me from these men who seem to hate me? I really don't know much about him. An hour later, he shows up.

"No luck. We asked every shopkeeper and house in the neighborhood. It'll be dark soon and we'll need a place to sleep," he says sternly. "Let's go to my niece's house. They live better than this, and the men there are powerful in this village. We can ask them."

I jump up, grab my burqa, and kiss the women good-bye. Back in the taxi we all feel dejected. Imran and Sameh are as anxious to find Darya as I am, but they have their own reasons: they want this trip to be over as soon as possible. They are in danger traveling with me, and it seems that people have figured out I am not related to Imran. The fact that we are traveling together is a grave sin in the villagers' eyes. I suspect that the population includes many members of the Taliban and powerful drug traffickers. If they find out that I'm an Afghan American, they could kill my companions and me. The Taliban have said that they hate the Afghans coming from the West and those Afghans from Afghanistan who work with them. We have no ransom or political value to them. But I'm more afraid of being kidnapped than being killed.

We drive for a good hour before arriving in verdant farmland near the Helmand River. Clear water flows in the river and the purple grapes glow amid emerald-green vines. Our car has to roll through mud and water to get to Imran's niece's home.

At the house, Imran gets out to greet a group of men with hugs and kisses on the cheek. I learn later they are his niece's husband and his brothers. They seem delighted to see him. They ask him if I am his wife and I see him shaking his head. There is a pause for a second and no more questions are asked. One of the men is apparently a doctor. I'm not sure how much of an actual doctor he is—if someone knows how to use a needle to give a shot, that person is considered a doctor here—but it's a comfort to know there's a health care worker in the house. There are four brothers living in the same compound. Each has a room, and they all share the courtyard, which they have turned into a garden of roses.

When I enter the courtyard and lift my veil, the women sitting on the patio all get up with curiosity. Mina is Imran's niece; she is the doctor's wife. The striking nineteen-year-old wears a long tunic and loose pants. She looks nine months pregnant as she wobbles toward us, giving her uncle a nod. She says a cold hello to me in Farsi. I know why she is being so uncharacteristically unfriendly. She is thinking, who is this strange woman with my uncle? Where is his family?

"How is the family, *zan kaka* [paternal uncle's wife] and the kids?" she asks him. Then she whispers with concern, "Who is she?"

He looks at me directly and answers her with confidence, "She's my cousin from Iran."

That is not the story Imran and I had agreed to tell people. We agreed to tell anyone who asked that I am a relative's friend from Herat who is looking for her cousin. I don't understand why Imran has changed the story. He tells me later that he forgot our agreement and that this was the first thing that came to mind.

But Mina knows Imran's first cousins living in Iran and the suspicious young bride becomes paranoid. She refuses to serve me the rest of the night and exchanges only a few brisk words with me. She is embarrassed in front of her in-laws that her uncle is shaming their family by bringing a stranger, probably a woman he is having an affair with, into their home.

Mina doesn't have to say anything for me to know her concerns. Her anger is written all over her face. If I tell her that I have no interest in Imran and I am here for another purpose, she probably will not believe me. But she is the only woman who speaks Farsi. Her mother-in-law is a sympathetic talker who has no problem with the fact that I cannot understand her. She speaks Pashto, telling stories about her family. I pick up only that she is ashamed of Mina's inhospitable behavior. She keeps gesturing that her daughter-in-law's mood is due to her pregnancy. The other women are the wives of one of the brothers. One is a heavyset woman with coarse brown skin who wears gold bangles that jingle every time she moves her hand. The other is a pale, thin woman with henna-painted hands. They appear to be happy I'm there, chattering about my presence. One of the wives is absent; she has gone to her parents' house. We all sit on the patio in the middle of the courtyard, surrounded by the scent of roses, which has diffused but not fully disguised the stench from the garbage piled up on the ground below in the courtyard. Each corner of the property has a room, and each brother occupies a separate room with his family.

Imran leaves with the men to talk about finding Darya. I refuse to sit anymore without doing something to help him. I take out my satellite phone and call Saber in Herat to ask him to help me speak with Darya's mother. I will at least find out Haji Sufi's real name. Saber says he'll go to Basira's home and call me back. A few minutes later Basira is on the phone.

"What's his real name? Where do they live?" I ask her desperately.

"Well, the men call him Haji Tor. I'm not sure where they live. I know it was Sangin, Helmand," she yells into the phone. "Thank you so much for doing this for us. May God bless you."

"I don't know if I can find her, Basira Jan, but I'll try my best." The line goes dead.

People locate one another in this part of Afghanistan through family and by word of mouth. There are no phone books or landlines, and cell phones are not in service in the villages in Helmand yet. Villages in Herat, such as Ghoryan, are advancing rapidly, while southern villages lag behind because of violence. I can reach Saber and Basira, who are twelve hours by car from Sangin, but I cannot find Darya, who may be living a few houses from me.

An hour later, Saber calls back to say he was able to find out from Darya's paternal uncle that Darya may have moved from Sangin to another district in Helmand with her husband's extended family.

"Her uncle also told me to tell you that Darya's father [Touraj] found out that you're looking for her. Touraj is going to call her husband and tell him to harm you. They want you to leave her alone, Fariba Jan."

"What's the new address?"

"Marjah district. That's all I have."

I thank Saber and hang up.

This new information is crucial, but it leaves me with little hope. Marjah is five hours from where we are, and it is not a sure thing. I need a more specific address, with at least the name of a village rather than an entire district.

I hear the women arguing among themselves. It seems to be about who I should eat dinner with. They all share a house but not meals or expenses. The mother-in-law is with the brother in the northeast corner of the compound, and Mina is in the northwest. She isn't arguing. I notice that she is no longer sitting with the other women.

Later I learn that Mina called Imran's wife on their satellite phone to ask her who I was, and his wife explained that I was a guest and that she should not worry. Mina thought that Imran had purchased me from Iran and was planning to wed me as a second wife. I am amused at how distrustful she is, but also touched that she was protecting his wife and her honor. I admire her brazenness even though she could have gotten me into a lot of trouble. I am not sure what to say to the other women about dinner. If I choose to eat with one of them, I will be rude to those I reject.

But no decisions are left to me. The two wives married to the same brother win by sheer force. The heavy one throws me over her

shoulder and walks me over to the southeast corner of the courtyard and sits me down on her mat outside the room she shares with
her husband and his other wives. She leaves my sandals on the patio
and later brings them to me. The thin *hambaq* (a woman who shares
a husband with another woman) sits beside her. They prepare salad
in the moonlight and bring orange soda from inside their room.
The main meal is rice and meat, which is cooked on a portable gas
stove.

Unfortunately, I have no appetite. I point to my stomach and
say the word *pain* in Farsi, *dard,* hoping it is the same as in Pashto.
They look at me concerned and seem to understand. But they still
insist I eat. I nibble on the bread and eat a cucumber, then I try to
talk to them.

"What's your name?" I ask the heavyset woman.

"Shabnam Gul," she says with a smile. "This is Turpikay." She
points to the thin woman. "We're happy that you're our guest. We
don't go out much, but we have a family garden with fruit orchards
nearby and we can go there."

"Where is the garden?"

"I'll take you in the morning."

Many words in Pashto and Farsi are the same, such as *bagh* for
"garden," and I am becoming familiar with some of the different
intonations. Our informal sign language seems to be the best form
of communication. Shabnam Gul and Turpikay laugh with me a lot.

"We're all friends with each other," Turpikay says. "But we don't
like our husband. He's mean."

He takes turns sleeping with them in different spots. In the
summer, Shabnam Gul sleeps with him on the roof and Turpikay
sleeps inside the room. The third wife takes another corner of the
room and waits her turn. Their children run around the compound
and sleep wherever they want.

"How do you make a living?" I ask.

"*Tariak*," they answer in unison. *Tariak* is the word for "opium" in Farsi and Pashto.

These women see no reason to hide this fact. Apparently they have farmland in another district that produces enough poppy for sale, so they can be fairly comfortable compared with others in town. I figure that if they have a satellite phone, which costs $1,000 to buy and $1 a minute to use, this family has some money. Shabnam Gul gestures as she talks about her husband. She puts out her left index finger and lays three of the fingers of her right hand on top of it, then moves the bottom finger back and forth. I wonder if she is trying to tell me that they have orgies, because Turpikay is giggling loudly. But in the end I figure out that Shabnam Gul means that all three women are under the husband's control. Still, these women have a raunchy side, and I am delighted at how humorously they can express their complaints.

The fun with the *hambaqs* ends when all the men enter. The two wives run to their room. I stay outside, knowing I don't have to follow their rules. Imran tells me they might have a clue as to Darya's husband's whereabouts. Several men they asked have seen him. He is a poppy farmer and a smuggler. My mind immediately flashes to Darya working in the fields, scoring the opium bulbs under the scorching sun.

The men stand in a circle discussing something animatedly. The conversation becomes loud and aggressive. It is the brother with three wives who is shouting; Imran is trying to calm him down. The word *mahram* flies around several times. When the brother points at me and begins to yell, it becomes obvious that I have become a nuisance. I can pick up that he doesn't approve of my clothes, which I thought would fit in; he doesn't approve of the fact that I am trav-eling without a proper *mahram*; and he certainly isn't in agreement with my search for Darya. To him, I am a liability, a shame to the honor of Afghan women.

The other men exit the courtyard, and only Imran and this man, who wears a black turban, remain. The two wives step back outside, because now they are in the presence of male kin. They've heard the shouting. Shabnam Gul holds my hand in support; she sees that I am frightened. Her hands are coarse but warm. Her husband finally speaks to me in Farsi. The men all seem to speak Farsi, probably because they have access to the outside world.

"Why are you looking for this girl? She has a husband now, and he's her owner. You have no right to be searching for her."

"Her mother asked me to find her and see how she is. She's my cousin." My voice shakes.

Before the man can speak, Shabnam Gul whispers what I take as a rare admonishment to her husband. "The mother loves her child."

The husband ignores his wife. Imran defuses the standoff by touching the husband's arm. "It's time for tea," he says.

After the evening tea, it is finally bedtime. Shabnam Gul asks if I want to sleep next to her on the roof. I decline. The desired place to sleep in the summer is the patio, and I am offered a spot next to the children. Mina comes and throws a big blanket on top of me and wishes me good night. I notice again how ethnic and linguistic tensions do not exist on the surface here because Mina is a Shia Tajik. But she has married into a Sunni Pashtun family and has learned their language and seems to be happy with her husband.

That night I sleep for three hours. I wake up with the sunrise and feel like vomiting. The nervousness and food have not sat well. The two wives who are now my friends bring cookies, home-baked fresh bread, and tea with sugar. I don't touch it. Shabnam Gul sees I am not feeling well. She grabs my hand and puts my sandals on my feet and says, "Garden." I put on the burqa, she puts on an orange chador, and we leave the house to cross an alley. She opens a padlock to a four-walled paradise. The aroma of mint and roses wakes me up. The sight is magnificent. It is a fairly small garden, a quarter of an acre perhaps, filled with cherry, pomegranate, apple, and mulberry trees. On the ground are newly sprouting leaves of mint, eggplant, tomatoes, and colorful flowers—some roses, some tulips—in pink, purple, red, and yellow. A kaleidoscope of butterflies flutters around the greenery. The garden is groomed, but a wilderness coexists with it: overgrown grass and birds chirping in the trees. I forget my ailments and anxiety. I close my eyes and take a deep breath. Shabnam Gul squats down and seems to say that I should not worry, that I will find Darya.

Our moment of peace doesn't last long. The men knock on the wooden door and Imran comes to tell me that their search has led to an impasse. He says we can go to Marjah, the new address, but the chances of finding Darya will be slight. It is my decision.

I think about going door to door myself, but I'm not sure that will make a difference. I will find her, but not this time. I will call people who can find her and tell me how she is so that I can tell her mother. I feel defeated by the men's hostility and by the realization that the men in Marjah may become violent, especially after Touraj talks to Darya's husband about me. The tears are welling up but I cannot cry, not in front of all these men. I squeeze Shabnam Gul's hand.

"Let's go back," I say.

We head back toward Kandahar. With us this time is the brother who has the three wives. He wants to get a ride to the bazaar in town and then he will disappear. I never ask his name, perhaps because he does not deserve one. On the way, he sits in the front and says he is a Taliban member.

"We kidnapped the Italian aid worker," he says, referring to Clementina Cantoni, who was kidnapped in Kabul that spring. The Afghan and Italian governments were negotiating her release when

I left Kabul. "We have her and we're not sure she will get out alive. It depends on what the government offers in exchange for her. If Imran weren't with you, the same thing would happen to you," he roars.

I say nothing. I wonder if he's just trying to scare me to seem powerful.

Later I find out that he was bluffing. He must've heard about the kidnapping on the news, because it turns out the Taliban had nothing to do with it. A band of professional thieves from Kabul kidnapped Cantoni, and she was eventually released after the ransom was paid.

After their rise to power in the south, the Taliban offered the people of Helmand security and complete freedom to grow and smuggle opium. They also protected the Sangin-based Kajaki Dam, which provides power to parts of Kandahar and Helmand. The dam was part of the American project started in the 1950s and then deserted when the Communists invaded. Americans destroyed parts of it with bombs in the 2001 war, but now Louis Berger, an American engineering company, is rebuilding the dam with American aid money.

The new Afghan government in Helmand is corrupt. Not all residents of Sangin want the Taliban back, but the man threatening me claims to be one of them, and it is clear that the cycle of power and corruption will continue here.

"Do you realize how inappropriate it is for an Afghan woman to do this?" he asks me. "Where are you really from? If the Taliban were in charge now, we would've shown you our punishment."

I shiver and hope he doesn't see it. I am glad that I now feel more trust for Imran, but the more I trust him, the less the man attacking me trusts him. He seems to be questioning Imran's loyalty. *It's her or us.* The driver pretends he doesn't hear, and none of us says much. I repeat that I have no bad intentions. Yet I know from that moment that the man's objections are about not just my being a woman traveling alone but my being a threat to him.

Imran informs me a few hours later that the brothers were afraid that I was a spy working for the U.S. government. They feared that I was infiltrating their homes and gathering information about their activities with the Taliban. The U.S.-led coalition conducts regular raids on homes suspected of housing or aiding insurgents, and districts in Helmand have been the focus of many of these raids.

We drop the man off outside Kandahar. Once he's out of the taxi, I thank Imran and Sameh.

"I appreciate both of you risking your necks out here for me."

"I'm sorry we failed to find the girl," Imran laments.

"It wasn't meant to be," I say.

When we reach Kandahar, I feel safe but sick. I have to stop the car to get out and vomit. Imran hands me a bottle of water afterward and suggests we stop at a rural area en route to the city. "This area is famous for drug lords marrying girls they've bought with opium," he says.

Two hours later the taxi halts in front of a large gate. Imran asks a passerby if he knows of any new brides from Herat in the last year. It is a strange question to ask, and the boy gives him a confused look. Imran then shows the photo of Darya's husband. The boy shakes his head and says, "I don't know this man, but there are a lot of Herati girls who are second and third wives to the men here. They are opium brides. Most of them are from the district of Ghoryan."

When Imran translates the information, my jaw drops. I had an idea how common the practice was, but hearing it explained by this boy makes it clear that the link between the drug lords in the south and the traffickers in Herat is probably a multimillion-dollar business bartering women, boys, and drugs—all in one.

We reach the hotel in Kandahar city. I am exhausted. I pay Imran $100 and Sameh $50 and walk to my room. I take a long shower, crawl under the covers of the bed, and try to sleep. I stare at the ceiling for hours.

I feel the failure of not finding Darya looming over me. I will not make a difference in her life. But she has made a difference in mine. A deep sense of loss begins to sink in.

I returned to Afghanistan with a myth, and Darya embodied that myth.

The Western media propagates an image of a romantic Afghanistan, one that cannot be conquered or tamed. Its people are warriors whose only purpose is to resist and fight; they are unruly natives unwelcoming to modern society. Afghanistan is a mystery that no outsider can unravel or know. Western experts warn that just like the British and the Soviets, the United States will fail to pacify Afghanistan. Others believe that Afghanistan may be uncivilized, but that it's the white man's burden to save its people from ignorance and tribalism. They base their judgment on a myth about Afghanistan.

When I met Darya, I held these same beliefs about the country. I was immediately attracted to the young girl because she was a mystery and a victim who needed to be saved from barbaric traditions. I thought it was my job as an outsider from the West to rescue her. But as I traveled and got to know the country, the myth unraveled to reveal a complex nation and people.

Afghanistan is like many other impoverished nation-states that suffer from illiteracy, strife, and instability. But it has had its periods of peace and stability, such as the forty years under King Zahir. Throughout history, conquerors such as Alexander the Great, Genghis Khan, and even the British have influenced the culture and ethnic makeup of the country. The American historian Thomas

Barfield concludes that Afghanistan is not the graveyard of empires but rather the cradle of them. Afghans are diverse as a result of various conquests and their ability to co-opt various cultures.

What makes the country unique and prone to war is its geographic location and its role as a buffer zone. The misery of Afghanistan for the past two hundred years can be summarized as a result of internal neglect and foreign interference. The myth has had its validity at points in the country's history. At times Afghanistan has been romantic and mysterious; its people can be fierce warriors, independent and resilient. But these descriptions should not become fixed ideas invoked to understand or analyze the country. True, Afghans have their cultural characteristics, but their culture and identities are fluid and cannot be categorized with simplistic stereotypes. American and British policies and military strategies have been based on these perceived notions, as if Afghans were not capable of change or progress, as if they were frozen in time and with tribal mentalities.

Darya is no longer a mystery or a victim I must liberate. She's one of thousands of girls bartered as opium brides, a casualty of an international drug problem. I remember all of the people I've met across Afghanistan who were impacted by the opium trade, from the farmer to the addict. Each person helped me understand the effects of the trade in a different way. But Darya had something special about her, a will to resist not just an outsider but also an internal family struggle—the injustice of forced marriage. It is that characteristic that allows me to come to terms with the end of my search. She will rescue herself, perhaps by learning to cope, by standing her ground with her husband, or even by running away. Darya offers hope for change. I will always want to know what happened to her, and perhaps someday I will.

NINETEEN
Letting Go

The Karzai government has lost any legitimacy it may have had among the poor and uneducated. The rising corruption, inflation, and insecurity in Afghanistan are building Taliban confidence. The militia has penetrated all parts of the country, paying its recruits more than what the Afghan police or army receives. The Obama administration has taken a practical approach, deciding to begin pulling out its troops in July 2011, ending ten years of military conflict, the same amount of time the Soviets spent in the country. The Karzai government is holding secret talks with the Taliban in Saudi Arabia to persuade them to join the government. The Taliban demand complete withdrawal of foreign troops, which more than likely will ignite another gruesome civil war.

The Taliban movement has spread beyond the border areas of Afghanistan and Pakistan. Various factions make up the insurgency in both countries, but all of them advocate a radical practice of Islam that advocates the removal of women from public space and no interference from Western governments. Al Qaeda is linked with the Taliban but has its own international agenda. The United States killed its leader, bin Laden, in a raid on May 1, 2011, in Abbottabad, Pakistan. He was living in a mansion in the city known for its government military training school. Pakistan came under attack for protecting him for ten years while the U.S. was hunting him, but the Pakistan government denied the charge. Al Qaeda continues to use the tribal border area in Pakistan for training camps, preparing operations, and recruitment for attacks against the United States and other Western countries, even without bin Laden.

More and more Afghans in the southern countryside are calling for the return of the Taliban. But not the urban educated, who are frightened of a future without economic or educational opportunities. Drugs will become the staple of the economy again. At least with a foreign presence, more schools are being built, women can attend those schools in secure areas, and a sporadic job market and foreign aid and investment support a proportion of the population.

Yet even with the Karzai government, the drug trade is penetrating deeper into all ranks of the government. In 2007 poppy production peaked, with 477,000 acres producing 8,200 tons of opium, half of it in Helmand. The United States and Britain are finally tackling the fact that the Taliban are using drug money to buy weapons, fund logistics, and pay their fighters. The U.S. State Department and the Pentagon have begun to collaborate effectively to fight drugs in Afghanistan, and in 2007 the United States allocated $600 million for the mission. NATO and the U.S. Marines have become directly involved by targeting traffickers, and in 2008, with the help of Afghan police, they assassinated Mullah Osman, a major Taliban smuggler. But the shift in discussion becomes skewed by the politics of war. Until 2007 the United States underemphasized the connection between drug profits and the insurgency. Now policymakers overstress it. The drawback to this is that Afghanistan's government brokers who are involved in the drug trade consolidate their power without much competition. The foreign powers leave them alone, but they target the insurgency's drug profits.

A controversial UN report published in August 2007 states that the counternarcotics strategy worked in central and northern Afghanistan, where, ironically, there is more poverty than in the south. The report concludes that relative security, local leadership, and incentives for farmers reduced poppy farming and that thirteen provinces are poppy free. It claims that the breadbasket of the country, the southwest, which includes Helmand and Kandahar, produced most of the opium, a supply fueled by greed, not need. The report's authors criticize the weak eradication effort—only 10 percent of poppy fields—and advocate an aggressive poppy destruction campaign in the southwest region. The U.S. government backs the report, and Thomas Schweich, the American former counternarcotics coordinator for Afghanistan, publicly emphasizes eradication, claiming that the poor Afghan farmer is a myth.

What the report ignores is that forced suppression has been proven a failure not just in Afghanistan but also in other poppy-producing countries, such as Colombia and Burma. International opinion overemphasizes the Taliban link to drugs to divert attention from the proliferation of drug dealing inside the Afghan government, as practiced by Ahmed Wali Karzai. Sharecroppers in Helmand may be as poor as farmers in Balkh in the north. The local leaders who enforce eradication use coercive methods that disregard human rights. In Balkh province, Atta Mohammad Noor, the mujahideen-appointed governor, successfully eliminated poppy farming and replaced it with cannabis cultivation.

From 2008 to 2010, poppy production dropped 22 percent and twenty provinces in the north were declared poppy free. But this is a temporary fix. The large opium output in 2007 caused a drop in prices because of an oversupply in the market, just as in any other business. Another drought hit, and wheat prices rose nearly 200 percent.

Farmers in some provinces pursue poppy cultivation for simple business reasons. They say they will farm again when opium prices go up and wheat goes down. That trend is confirmed by a 2010 UN opium survey: three of the twenty poppy-free provinces have reverted to opium cultivation.

The serious shift in policy occurred when Richard Holbrooke, Obama's late special envoy to Afghanistan, took charge in 2009. Forced eradication was reduced, and farmers were offered alternative seeds and fertilizer for voluntary eradication. A list was drafted of the fifty top traffickers for the United States to hunt down and execute, and the combined efforts of NATO and the U.S. military with the Afghan counternarcotics agents resulted in large seizures of stash houses and precursor chemicals. The response drove opium markets to operate in secret, the price of precursor chemicals rose—500 percent for acetic anhydride—and processing labs moved to more clandestine mountain hideaways. The drug industry is resilient and adaptable. The withdrawal of foreign troops in Afghanistan, which began in July 2011, will be a setback for counternarcotics efforts.

A sustainable, long-term plan to curtail the drug industry should focus on the bigger issues of stability and security. An emphasis on unity and national identity under a federalist system that does not insist on central control but rather on provincial power may work best in Afghanistan. King Zahir did not force centralization during his forty-year peaceful reign.

Other countries solved their drug problems after establishing a certain level of stability that allowed for alternative economic opportunities. If Karzai and the Taliban reach an agreement on government sharing, the Taliban should receive incentives to stop protecting drug traffickers. The Taliban's relationship with the Quetta Alliance, the powerful Pakistani smuggling mafia, is tricky because the Alliance can easily turn against the Taliban for blocking trafficking routes and form a militia to attack them. But if an international peacekeeping group protects the future Afghan government, which would include the Taliban, the plan could work. Some traffickers, including those in the current government who have shown an interest in being a part of the reconstruction process, should not be assassinated but rather persuaded to negotiate with the government, and their influence should be leveraged. They should reinvest their drug funds in developing Afghanistan in the same manner as Haji Barat of Badakhshan and Gul Agha Sherzai, the governor of Nangarhar province. Sherzai, who has been accused of being a drug smuggler himself in the past, has had success in convincing Nangarhar farmers to curtail poppy growth. Those drug funds are being funneled to the Arab Gulf now.

Voluntary eradication should continue, and forced eradication should target the small number of wealthy landowners. Farmers should continue to receive alternative seeds and fertilizer, but they should also have access to a fair and legal banking system. The *salaam* system they borrow under now treats them like indentured servants; under that system they rarely have enough money to pay back their loans. Once a stable government is in place, perhaps some farmers can produce opium for pharmaceutical opiates under government regulation.

Internationally, the drug trade is propelled by demand, and every counternarcotics agent I speak with says that their law enforcement activities have minimal impact because the answer to reducing drug trafficking lies in demand reduction. More addicts in the world demand more drugs. Addiction rates for heroin are soaring worldwide. The most effective way to deal with addiction in some countries is tolerance, treatment, and legalization. Holland and Portugal have lower addiction rates because they have decriminalized the use of narcotics.

Afghanistan's drug trade can become irrelevant over time, a generation's time. It took Thailand thirty years to solve its opium conundrum. It has taken Afghanistan that long to build a strong opium trade, and it should be expected that it will take the country at least that long to destroy it. There are no short cuts, quick fixes, or shock-and-awe solutions.

It's a sweaty September morning in Kabul, about seven thirty, the hour at which civil servants and law enforcement officials commute to work in their employers' buses or vans, the hour at which Kabul residents expect to hear a bang reverberate through the walls.

The hour when suicide bombers blow themselves up.

It happens: the sound, the cacophony that follows, and then the silence. One big explosion, the third one this summer, the lovely summer of 2007, when the pomegranates on the tree in the front yard are beginning to ripen, when little boys fly kites on their rooftops, when the baby inside me has begun to kick. The summer I bid farewell to Afghanistan.

The explosion is audible but too far away to shake the windows. It's Ramadan, a couple of weeks before Eid. My husband, Naeem, is fasting and busy on his laptop. Naeem, the IT technician I met at UNHCR in Herat, moved to Kabul in the fall of 2005, and after four years of friendship, we decided to get married. I went to Afghanistan in search of my roots and I found the warmth, acceptance, and commitment I was looking for in him. In 2006 we had an Afghan engagement party and *nikah* (Islamic marriage ceremony) in Herat for the standard 850 friends and family. We arrived from the capital to find that my in-laws had seen to all the details and had even made the two gowns I would wear, one pink satin and the other a shimmering baby blue. The female guests remained on the top floor of the wedding hall, and the male guests on the bottom, with only the close male relatives of the bride and groom able to join the women's section. The event, complete with a live band, four-course meal, and videographers, lasted the entire day.

Naeem works for a Danish NGO, which is housing us in a comfortable three-bedroom home with a small garden in Qala-e-Fatullah, a quiet, clean neighborhood in Kabul. I'm lazily getting out of bed. As soon as I hear the bomb, my pace shifts. I slip on my jeans, wrap on a head scarf, and grab my purse. My large suitcase is lying on the floor half full. Today is my day to pack and do one last story, a positive article about a clandestine music school where women are taking voice lessons and learning to play musical instruments. But the plan has just changed. I run downstairs and ask Naeem, "You want to come with me to the bomb site?" It's his day off from work and I don't want us to spend a minute apart, because I'm leaving and he's staying for a few months.

Naeem and I arrive late at the site of the explosion, which is at my old neighborhood in the Baharistan bazaar in Karte Parwan. It's also the market where I witnessed a drug bust by counternarcotics agents. Authorities have cleaned up the bodies and blood from the street, but shattered glass is still strewn across the sidewalk. I

soon learn that the suicide bomber, dressed in Afghan Army fatigues, boarded an Afghan National Army bus while soldiers were
boarding and detonated his bomb, killing twenty-nine people.
Among the sixteen injured are two boys and their father, a sidewalk shoe shiner. The bomber killed sixteen soldiers. The insurgents have been infiltrating the Afghan police and military inside
Kabul simply by wearing army uniforms and then setting off the
explosives strapped to their bodies. I walk around the site in a daze,
interviewing witnesses.

The windows of the bakery where I used to buy bread and
cookies are broken. I kick away some pieces of glass as I enter. The
owner smiles and greets me. He's busy tending to customers who are
buying sweets for Eid. The broken glass is the only reminder of an
abnormal day. I ask him what happened.

"The usual, *khwarak* [sister]," he says. "We're used to this. I have to
pay God knows how much to replace that glass."

I have been feeling guilty for our decision to leave the country,
not knowing when we would return again. But this latest bomb
relieves the guilt. It was the bomb at my school that convinced my
parents to escape from Afghanistan in 1982. My father had nothing to gain in the West but his children's safety. In Kabul, I have a
meaningful career, a house with a garden, a housekeeper and cook,
a driver, and the warmth of a culture that I longed to return to for
two decades. But it is not safe, and soon I'll have a child to care for.
The sight of blood and shattered windows is no longer a thrill for
me. My fascination with war is waning as I get closer to motherhood.
I do not want the children I plan to bear desensitized to violence
like the man in the bakery. The end of my journey in Afghanistan
parallels my parents', but how dare I make the comparison?

I contrast my parents' loss in leaving Afghanistan with mine.
They had to give up their families, jobs, status, homes, and lan-

guage—an entire lifetime—to be transplanted to safety and convenience, an oasis of comfort that's slowly killing them with depression and loneliness. Their grandchildren speak English and get bored when they visit them because the TV programs are in Farsi and there are no computers or video games to play. How dare I compare my situation to theirs? They cannot return because the Afghanistan they left vanished with them.

I can simply resume my suburban life in the United States. I can take my child to Lake Elizabeth in Fremont to play with the ducks and swing in the playground. I can watch a movie in the theater, appreciate twenty-four-hour electricity and sanitized water, be in public with no head scarf and a sleeveless blouse, and enjoy the freedoms I forsook to be back in my homeland. I can return to my parents, lay my head on my father's shoulder, and eat my mother's cooking. I can help them feel less lonely.

The next day, when I get on the plane from Kabul, I fully intend to return with my daughter and husband and can only hope that, by then, the mines will be cleared, health care will be reliable, suicide bombers will be gone, and opium will no longer be the staple crop of the economy. I will return to visit, stay connected, and preserve my rich and diverse heritage. Afghanistan is a part of me, and I no longer fear losing it. I can let go of the nostalgia, the bittersweetness of a gratifying childhood ruptured by war, and supplant it with the memories of the seven years I have spent here in my adulthood. These five years have clarified the country, made it real for me. My evolving relationship with Afghanistan has allowed me to reconcile my two cultures and strengthen my Afghan identity. I no longer need to prove that I'm an Afghan to myself, to anyone.

Naeem is reading *Mullah Nasruddin*, a comical folk tale read in Afghanistan and Iran, to our two-year-old daughter, Bonoo, as she sits on his lap twirling her brunette curls. Her majestic black eyes are fixed on the pages. "Asp," she says excitedly, pointing to the horse Mullah's wrestling with in the book. I have just finished loading the dishwasher. The living room floor is littered with toys in our compact two-bedroom town house in Fremont, the hamper is overflowing with laundry, and the leftovers from the dinner I cooked have to be stored in the refrigerator. I have joined the tired working mothers of America who don't have maids, drivers, or nannies. Leaving the kitchen, I watch my husband reading to my daughter and smile with gratitude.

We live five minutes from my parents, ten minutes from my sister, and fifteen minutes from my brother. It's comforting to be settled near my family after more than a decade of traveling. My parents are thrilled to have a new grandchild, the youngest of six, and they take great joy in playing with her in their seventh-floor apartment overlooking the rolling green hills of Fremont. My father is eighty and suffers from a long list of ailments. After a mild stroke, he's barely able to speak, but he still has the ability to do what he loves: read. I replenish his Farsi book collection from the Fremont library, which offers materials in several foreign languages. My mother continues to be a social butterfly and is taking an English class, again, at the age of seventy-four. Their most time-consuming recreation is still Afghan satellite TV, whose programs include dubbed Indian soap operas and dozens of new Afghan music videos.

On weekends someone in our Herati circle throws a dinner party and we all get together to eat sumptuous Afghan food and talk. The men and women segregate themselves. The men like to talk politics, and the women assemble in the kitchen, where the conversation centers on their children, cooking, and shopping. I usually don't fit in, but I'm too busy running after my toddler to notice who is doing what.

Naeem and I often miss our life in Afghanistan, and we stay in touch with his family in Herat and my friends in Kabul. I'm at times restless to return to the field and work, but then I look at Bonoo and forget those desires. "One day we'll take you back to Afghanistan," I tell her. "Can you say 'Afghanistan'?"

She stumbles on the first two syllables, hugs me, and asks for milk. After I put her to sleep for the night, I check the news online. Afghanistan is often in the headlines. President Obama has sent twenty-one thousand more troops there, and the U.S. Marines have teamed up with the Afghan National Army to attack the last Taliban stronghold, Marjah district, in Helmand province, the place I didn't dare travel to when I went to look for Darya. Marjah's main source of income is raw opium. It has the largest distribution market in Helmand and provides safe haven for hundreds of heroin laboratories. The Taliban receive a tax and kickbacks for protecting trafficking routes and poppy farms. When the military operation began there, the Taliban used women and children as human shields inside civilian homes. Fifteen civilians were killed.

I wonder if Darya is in Marjah. Perhaps I can still find her.

After reading the news about Marjah, I track down Saber, who is still living in Ghoryan with his entire family. It's a delight to hear his tender voice.

"I have two kids and another one on the way. My mother has stomach problems and she went blind, and one of my brothers became a heroin dealer in Iran, but he has promised to stop because my father threatened to disown him. I have no job—my father supports us—but I'm happy that I have these kids," he says quickly, not wanting to hike up my phone bill. "My sister Tina is married to a man who keeps her on a leash, but she's happy with the one daughter she has now."

Saber tells me that Ghoryan town center has developed, the roads are paved, twenty-four-hour power and running water are available, and the farmers who planted poppy have switched to saffron in the last couple of years. Yet unemployment has risen because villagers in the desert have moved to the center of the district. The only jobs that remain are in drug trafficking, which has doubled in the last seven years, and drug lords such as Haji Sardar have become richer with government backing. They launder their money through car businesses. "It's all about crystal heroin now," Saber says. "Opium is for small-timers."

When I ask about Darya, he says her mother is in Ghoryan and she might know her daughter's whereabouts. An hour later, he calls me with Basira's mobile number. My heart is pounding when I dial it. Basira's life must have improved financially for her to have a cell phone. My worst fear is that Darya has self-immolated like so many girls in Afghanistan.

Basira answers with unusual warmth. She tells me that her son Aman, who had gone with his sister, returned safely from Helmand, and that Darya is alive and well. She does live in Marjah. "Every time I hear Helmand in the news, I worry about my baby," Basira tells me. "But her life is there now." She tells me that her oldest daughter, Saboora, is married to a man close to her age, in Ghoryan. The smuggler her father had sold her to never came to marry her.

I ask Basira so many questions that she can't keep up. Darya's eighteen or nineteen now and has a son who's a year old. New brides generally get pregnant as soon as they marry, but Darya did not get her period until two years ago. Her husband consummated their relationship despite her prepubescence.

Basira stayed with Darya in Marjah to take care of her after she had her son. Darya has calmed down now and no longer fights back. Her biggest problem is with her *hambaq*, her husband's other wife, who shares the same yard but lives in different rooms. "When his two wives fight, he beats both of them," Basira says. "But he's a good Muslim. He brings her to visit me every six or seven months." When they visit, they stay for about two months, during which time Darya buys herself makeup and clothes in Ghoryan, which is nearly a city compared with Marjah. "My heart doesn't want me to go back there," Darya has told her mother. "They are all strangers to me."

Basira says Darya's life is poor but tolerable. Marjah has no power or running water, mobile phones, or television signals. Darya and her husband and his other wife live off the land, and Darya spends her time doing housework. She has learned to speak fluent Pashto and translates for her mother. Women do not go outside in

Marjah unless they need to go to the doctor. Darya wears a chador
when she visits the doctor and is accompanied there by her husband. According to Basira, she was cold toward her husband until
she had her son. Now that Haji Tor is the father of her child, Darya
seems to have some affection for him.

"He has sons her age. Why didn't he marry one of them to her?"
I ask Basira.

"It was written in his and her forehead that they would marry
each other. It was their destiny."

I'm angry about her response but I listen, relieved and horri-
fied at the same time. Darya's life doesn't seem any different from
that of the women I met in Sangin, Helmand. She seems to have
learned to cope with the lack of freedom and the distance from her
family. Afghan women's threshold for suffering seems higher than
any Western woman can imagine. The calm, quiet martyr is a good
woman in many Afghan eyes. Basira says her daughter is a "good"
girl now that she has learned to obey. It's this ability to adapt that
keeps Afghan women confined. But it's also how they survive.

I may never find out how Darya learned to cope, how she calmed
the rebel in her. But perhaps I will one day see her again and she can
share her story. I want to believe that the free-spirited Darya I met
still has her defiant zeal, even if it's hidden; that she can defend herself and needs no savior; that she can be herself when she visits her
mother; that she can go out shopping, laugh out loud, and scream
at the top of her lungs.

Acknowledgments

Dozens of individuals helped me complete this book. I'd like to extend my deepest gratitude to those whose names I cannot divulge but who were an integral part of the process. You know who you are. For those I can name, thank you first and foremost to my research partners, Matthew DuPee, Fayaz Siddiqi, Farhad Azad, and Naeem Poyesh, for spending their precious time fact-checking and providing invaluable information. To my family: my parents, my sister and her family, my brother and his family, and the aunts and uncles who endured hours of questioning and prying into their personal lives and our family history. I'm indebted to my mother-in-law, Zahra Azizian, and brother-in-law Younes Azizian for their unwavering support for this book. My agent, Rebecca Friedman, and editors, Allison Lorentzen and Maya Ziv, believed in this book and worked hard to make it happen. Thanks also to Barnett Rubin and the Open Society Institute for the grant that made it possible for me to research the Afghan drug trade. OSI's partner organization in Kabul, the Foundation for Culture and Civil Society, and the FCCS colleagues who helped with research and logistics, Said Niazi and Omar Sharifi, were instrumental in giving me a place to work in Kabul. My editor Cathy Galvin at the *Sunday Times Magazine* in London was the first to give Darya's story a voice by publishing it. Freelance photographers Massoud Hossaini and Farzana Wahidy risked their lives traveling to Ghoryan to photograph Darya and her family at the beginning of their careers, and I'm happy to see them now as two of Afghanistan's renowned photographers, and engaged to be married. Massoud, thank you for allowing your photos to be used on the cover of this book. I'm also grateful to the friends and colleagues who gave ideas, feedback, and support: Khaled Hosseini, Leela Jacinto, Annia Ciezadlo, Mary Rajkumar, Angeles Espinosa, Maryam Miazad, Maneeza Aminy, Yama Rahimy, Fahima Danishgar, Khalid Khaliqi, Manavi Menon, Omar Karim, Anna Ghosh, Esmael Darman, Patricia Omidian, Botoul Maqsodi, Daanish Masood, Hanaa Arafat, Nushin Arbabzadah, Homa Clifford, Pratap Chatterjee, Mir Hekmat Sadat, Katrin Fakiri, Homira Nassery, Nell Bernstein, Joel Hafvenstein, Graeme Smith, Aunohita Mojumdar, Manizha Naderi, and Mahesh and his staff at Suju's Coffee in Fremont. I will always be grateful to Fawzia and Mohammed Y. Akbarzad for taking wonderful care of my daughter, Bonoo, in the hours I wrote this book.

To my husband, Naeem, *tashakor* for being there during all the difficult and grueling moments of writing and research, for your patience and partnership, and for your encouragement and love.

Notes

PROLOGUE

2 A former chief of the U.S. Drug Enforcement Administration: Asa Hutchinson, speech delivered at the Heritage Foundation, Washington, D.C., April 2, 2002, viewed online at www.justice.gov/dea/speeches/s040202.html.

ONE: HOME AFTER EIGHTEEN YEARS

9 The government first jailed him: Author's interview with Fazul Haq Nawa.

10 *The Authorities of Herat*: title translated by the author.

11 The Mongol leader killed thousands: *Lonely Planet*, viewed online at www.lonelyplanet.com/afghanistan/herat-and-northwestern-afghanistan/herat/history.

12 The United States gave weapons: Peter Dale Scott, *Drugs, Oil, and War: The United States in Afghanistan, Colombia, and Indochina*, Lanham, Md.: Rowman and Littlefield, 2003, 29; and Adam Stahl, "Al-Qa'ida's American Connection," *Global Politics*, May 16, 2008, viewed online at www.global-politics.co.uk/issue6/Stahl/.

12 The Afghan Communist government: Edward Girardet, "In the Marjah Offensive of the Afghanistan War, a Reporter Hears Echoes of the Soviet War," *Christian Science Monitor*, March 18, 2010.

18 The four thousand tons of opium produced: John Pomfret, "Drug Trade Resurgent in Afghanistan," *Washington Post*, October 23, 2001, viewed online at www.washingtonpost.com/ac2/wp-dyn/A36532-2001Oct22?language=printer.

18 Until the 2000 opium ban: United Nations Office on Drugs and Crime, *The Role of Women in Opium Poppy Cultivation in Afghanistan*, June 2000.

19 "Call of Love": Eva de Vitray-Meyerovitch, in *Rumi and Sufism*, trans. Simone Fattal, Sausalito, Calif.: Post-Apollo Press, 1977, 1987, 104.

TWO: FOUR DECADES OF UNREST

31 The Durand Line was drawn: Ralph H. Magnus and Eden Naby, *Afghanistan: Mullah, Marx and Mujahid*, Boulder, Colo.: Westview Press, 1998, 36.

32 the United States spent more than $3 billion: Political Freedom Research Institute, country profile Web site, University of Massachusetts, Amherst, viewed online at www.peri.umass.edu/fileadmin/pdf/dpe/modern_conflicts/Afghanistan.pdf.

32 Ronald Reagan's government: Amir Zada Asad and Robert Harris, *The Politics and Economics of Drug Production on the Pakistan-Afghanistan Border*, Burlington, UK: Ashgate, 2003.

32 "The United States was not waging": Peter Dale Scott, *Drugs, Oil, and War: The United States in Afghanistan, Colombia, and Indochina*, Lanham, Md.: Rowman and Littlefield, 2003, 29, 33.

32 The king's motives were twofold: Magnus and Naby, *Afghanistan*, 36, 37.

33 In 1958, King Mohammed Zahir: Martin Booth, *Opium: A History*, New York: St. Martins Press, 1996, 252.

33 Afghanistan produced one hundred: Interview with Matthew DuPee, Naval Postgraduate School.

33 Seeds were loaned: Gretchen Peters, *Seeds of Terror: How Heroin Is Bankrolling the Taliban and al Qaeda*, New York: St. Martin's Press, 2009, 34.

34 American agricultural aid projects: Adam Curtis, "The Lost History of Helmand," *The Medium and the Message* (blog), BBC, October 2009, viewed online at www.bbc.co.uk/blogs/adamcurtis/2009/10/kabul_city_number_one_part_3.html.

34 Mullah Nasim forced farmers: Peters, *Seeds of Terror*, 34.

34 supplies fifteen million addicts: United Nations Office on Drugs and Crime, *Addiction, Crime, and Insurgency: The Transnational Threat of Afghan Opium*, New York: United Nations Publications, 2009, 1, viewed online at www.unodc.org/documents/data-and-analysis/Afghanistan/Executive_Summary_english.pdf.

35 which sells for $3,000: Interview with U.S. Drug Enforcement Administration agent, Kabul, 2005.

38 Pakistan returned Hekmatyar and Massoud: Paul Fitzgerald, Elizabeth Gould, and Sima Wali, *Invisible History: Afghanistan's Untold Story*, San Francisco: City Lights Books, 2009, 126, 127.

38 no tolerance for religious militancy: Magnus and Naby, *Afghanistan*, 46.

39 buried them alive: Interviews with families of Afghans who disappeared during the Communist regime, Kabul, 2007.

39 guided by the Soviet KGB: Interview with Assadullah Sarwari, head of the Afghan secret service in 1978 and 1979, Kabul, 2007.

40 first serious uprising: Interviews with eyewitnesses in Herat present during the 1979 uprising, Fremont, California, 2008.

40 Moscow refused: Gregory Feifer, *The Great Gamble: The Soviet War in Afghanistan*, New York: HarperCollins, 2009, 33.

41 five thousand people died: Ibid., 31.

41 smothered to death with a pillow: Ibid., 48

42 fund heroin laboratories: Asad and Harris, *The Politics and Economics of Drug Production*, 53.

42 the mujahideen found ways to hook: Ibid., 53, 54

43 fake Russian newspaper articles: Ibid., 53

43 CIA executed the plan: Ibid.

43 accounted for 68 percent of employment: Deepak Lal, "Endangering the War on Terror with the War on Drugs," *World Economics*, July—September 2008, 1—29, viewed online at www.econ.ucla.edu/Lal/Lal_World_Economics_vol_9_03_08.pdf.

43 there had been a 45 percent decrease: Ibid.

43 treated as second-class citizens: Interviews with Afghan refugee returnees from Iran, Herat, 2003.

52 had shrunk from ninety thousand: Feifer, *The Great Gamble*, 105.

52 In 1989, with 15,000 Soviet soldiers: Lawrence M. Paul, "Afghanistan: How We Got There," *New York Times*, February 8, 2010, viewed online at teacher.scholastic.com/scholasticnews/indepth/upfront/features/index.asp?article=f020810_afghan.

53 casualties rose to sixty thousand: Danish Karokhel, "Mujahedin Victory Event Falls Flat," Institute for War and Peace Reporting, May 4, 2003, viewed online at www.eariana.com/ariana/eariana.nsf/allDocsArticles/D499F506DA74819687256D1C0046BCC5?OpenDocument.

THREE: A STRUGGLE FOR COHERENCY

56 allegedly masterminded: Tony Perry, "Afghan Commander Massoud, Killed on Eve of 9/11 Attacks, is a National Hero," *Los Angeles Times*, Sep-

tember 22, 2010, viewed online at articles.latimes.com/2010/sep/22/world/la-fg-afghanistan-massoud-20100922.

57 dictate future wars: Samuel P. Huntington, "The Clash of Civilizations?" *Foreign Affairs* 72, no. 3 (Summer 1993): 26.

57 "clash of ignorance": Edward W. Said, "The Clash of Ignorance," *The Nation*, October 22, 2001, viewed online at www.thenation.com/article/clash-ignorance.

67 The extent of Nadeem's understatement: Tom Coghlan, "Mass Grave Plundered at Site of Taleban Prisoners' Massacre," *Sunday Times*, December 24, 2008. Viewed online at www.timesonline.co.uk/tol/news/world/asia/article5391550.ece.

68 thousands in the diaspora: Interviews with Afghans repatriating from the West, Kabul, 2003.

FOUR: MY FATHER'S VOYAGE

70 "Several other travelers and I boarded": Fazul Haq Nawa, "The Continuation of Memories," trans. Fariba Nawa, Ansari Literary Association Publication, September 1997.

78 coercion and bribery: Agence France Presse, "Afghan Warlords Hindering Loya Jirga Process: HRW," June 13, 2002, viewed online at www.rawa.org/warlord4.htm.

78 "Voting for the Loya Jirga": Lakhdar Brahimi, interviewed on ABC News, June 12, 2002.

79 "The former king is not a candidate": Sonali Kolhatkar and James Ingalls, "America's Viceroy," ZNet, May 20, 2009, viewed online at www.zcommunications.org/americas-viceroy-by-sonali-kolhatkar.

79 "we delegates were denied": Omar Zakhilwal and Adeena Niazi, "The Warlords Win in Kabul," *New York Times*, June 21, 2002, viewed online at www.nytimes.com/2002/06/21/opinion/21NIAZ.html.

84 It was a polarized society: Interviews with several Ghoryan natives who are scholars, Herat, 2004.

84 He gave the tribes land: Interviews with tribal elders, Herat, 2003.

FIVE: MEETING DARYA

91 dousing themselves with accelerant: Interview with officials at Ghoryan Hospital, Herat, 2003.

91 With three to six million addicts: A. William Samii, "Iran: Country's Drug Problem Appears to Be Worsening," Radio Free Europe, July 18, 2005, viewed online at www.rferl.org/content/article/1059991.html.

98 the 4.8 million children: United Nations Development Fund for Women, Women in Afghanistan Fact Sheet 2010, viewed online at www.unifem.org/afghanistan/media/pubs/factsheet/10/index.html.

100 between $25 million and $75 million: Alfred W. McCoy, *The Politics of Heroin: CIA Complicity in the Global Drug Trade*, Chicago: Lawrence Hill Books, 2003, 508; and Pierre-Arnaud Chouvy, *Opium: Uncovering the Politics of the Poppy*, London: I.B. Taurus, 2009, 52.

100 teach Ghoryan farmers: Interviews with Ghoryan farmers, Herat, 2003.

100 encouraged unemployed young men: Interviews with Ghoryan couriers, Herat, 2003.

101 more than 3,000 sentenced to death: Antoine Blua, "Kabul Alarmed by Iran's Executions of Afghan Prisoners," Radio Free Europe, October 15, 2010, viewed online at www.rferl.org/content/Kabul_Alarmed_By_Irans_Executions_Of_Afghan_Prisoners/2013239.html.

101 Iranian law states: Iranian law on drug crimes on the Iran Justice Ministry Web site, viewed online at www.dadkhahi.net/law/Ghavanin/Ghavanin_Jazaee/gh_mobareze_ba_mavade_mokhader.htm.

103 The Taliban's ban on opium production: Raphael F. Perl, "Taliban and the Drug Trade," Congressional Research Service Report, October 5, 2001, 2, viewed online at fpc.state.gov/documents/organization/6210.pdf.

105 Afghan girls face forced marriages: United Nations Development Fund for Women, Women in Afghanistan Fact Sheet 2010, viewed online at www.unifem.org/afghanistan/media/pubs/factsheet/10/index.html.

SIX: A SMUGGLING TRADITION

115 opium debts for widows: Interviews with widows in debt in Ghoryan, Herat, 2003.

115 can read and write: United Nations Development Fund for Women, Women in Afghanistan Fact Sheet 2010, viewed online at www.unifem.org/afghanistan/media/pubs/factsheet/10/index.html.

EIGHT: TRAVELING ON THE BORDER OF DEATH

134 With a 40 percent unemployment rate: *The World Factbook 2009*, Washington, D.C.: Central Intelligence Agency, 2009, viewed online at www.cia.gov/library/publications/the-world-factbook/geos/af.html.

134 chain of the narcotics link: Interview with a Drug Enforcement Administration agent, Kabul, 2005.

135 seized Iranian-made weapons: Michael R. Gordon, "U.S. Says Iranian Arms Seized in Afghanistan," *New York Times*, April 18, 2007, viewed online www.nytimes.com/2007/04/18/world/middleeast/18military.html.

135 weapons are disassembled and smuggled: Sayed Yaqub Ibrahimi, "Turning Afghan Heroin into Kalashnikovs," Institute for War and Peace Reporting, July 8, 2008, viewed online at iwpr.net/report-news/turning-

afghan-heroin-kalashnikovs; Matthew DuPee, "Iran's 30-Year War on Drugs," *World Politics Review*, February 10, 2010.

135 caught American private contractors: Gregor Salmon, *Poppy: Life, Death, and Addiction Inside Afghanistan's Opium Trade*, Sydney: Random House Australia, 2009, 214—18.

135 with 50 percent of the drug smuggled: DuPee, "Iran's 30-Year War."

135 drug syndicates, or mafias: Interview with counternarcotics expert Matthew DuPee, Monterey, 2010.

136 DEA says the Quetta Alliance: Interviews with DEA agents, Kabul, 2005.

136 Nigerian drug trafficking organizations: Interview with DuPee, Monterey, 2010.

136 transferred from Afghanistan to the UAE: Dexter Filkins and Mark Mazzetti, "Key Karzai Aide in Corruption Inquiry Is Linked to C.I.A.," *New York Times*, August, 25, 2010, viewed online at www.nytimes.com/2010/08/26/world/asia/26kabul.html.

137 dry lips and dehydrated state: Salmon, *Poppy*, 215.

137 more than a three-hundred-kilometer: Interview with DuPee, Monterey, 2010.

140 Amanullah Khan: Reuters, "Fighting Resumes in North and West of Afghanistan," October 4, 2002, viewed online at www.rawa.org/fight.htm.

141 more than 3,700 troops: DuPee, "Iran's 30-Year War."

141 Iran's intelligence agencies dabbled: Gretchen Peters, *Seeds of Terror: How Heroin is Bankrolling the Taliban and al Qaeda*, New York: St. Martin's Press, 2009, 138.

142 seized a thousand tons of opium: DuPee, "Iran's 30-Year War."

NINE: WHERE THE POPPIES BLOOM

151 the Taliban allowed women to work: United Nations Office on Drugs and Crime, *The Role of Women in Opium Poppy Cultivation in Afghanistan*, Islamabad, June 2000, 37.

151 "not an illicit crop but rather a blessing": United Nations Office for the Coordination of Humanitarian Affairs—Integrated Regional Information Network, "Afghanistan: Interview with Female Opium Farmer," *Bitter-Sweet Harvest: Afghanistan's New War*, August 2004.

156 reduced from two hundred thousand acres: Pierre-Arnaud Chouvy, "Afghan Opium Production Predicted to Reach New High," *Jane's Intelligence Review*, October 1, 2004, viewed online at www.rawa.org/opium6.htm.

156 opium, at $500 a kilo: David Mansfield and Adam Pain, *Counter-Narcotics in Afghanistan: The Failure of Success?* Afghanistan Research and Evaluation Unit, Kabul, December 2008, 8, viewed online at www.areu.org.af/Uploads/EditionPdfs/822E-Counter-Narcotics%20in%20Afghanistan%20BP7%202008.pdf

156 Afghan informants bankrolled: David Gibson, "President Bush Has Made Afghanistan Safe Once Again for Opium Production," *The American Chronicle*, January 23, 2008, viewed online at www.american chronicle.com/articles/view/50029.

157 for $50 million to $150 million: United Nations Office for the Coordination of Humanitarian Affairs—Integrated Regional Information Network, "Afghanistan: Donor-Supported Approaches to Eradication," *Bitter-Sweet Harvest: Afghanistan's New War*, August 2004, viewed online at www.irinnews.org/InDepthMain.aspx?InDepthId=21&ReportId=63019.

157 British compensated farmers $350 for less than half an acre: "Afghan Heroin Trade 'Booming,'" BBC News, July 25, 2002, viewed online at news.bbc.co.uk/2/hi/south_asia/2150580.stm.

157 farmers in Faizabad received: David Mansfield, *Afghanistan: Strategy Study #9: Opium Poppy Cultivation in a Changing Policy Environment: Farmers' Intentions for the 2002/03 Growing Seasons*, United Nations Office on Drugs and Crime, Kabul, May 2003, 1—28, viewed online at www.david mansfield.org/all.php.

158 more than 70 percent of the farmers: Ibid.

158 DynCorp paid five dollars a day: DynCorp official, phone interview with author, March 2006.

158 killing twelve people: Interview with Dyncorp supervisor, Kabul, 2005.

159 a perverse incentive for farmers: Joel Hafvenstein, "Afghanistan's Opium Strategy Alternatives: A Moment for Masterful Inactivity," in Whit Mason, ed., *The Rule of Law in Afghanistan: Missing in Inaction*, Cambridge, UK: Cambridge University Press, 2011.

160 killed eleven Afghan aid workers: Joel Hafvenstein, *Opium Season: A Year on the Frontier*, Guilford, UK: The Lyons Press, 2007, 2.

160 "random, certain and universal": UNOCHA, "Afghanistan: Donor Supported Approaches to Eradication."

160 "establishment of those institutions for formal governance": David Mansfield and Adam Pain, *Alternative Livelihoods: Substance or Slogan?* Afghanistan Research and Evaluation Unit, Kabul, October 2005, 1, viewed online at ageconsearch.umn.edu/bitstream/14650/1/bp05ma01.pdf.

161 "made survival possible for many farmers": Chouvy, "Afghan Opium Production."

167 The United Nations estimates that 245,000: United Nations Office on Drugs and Crime, *Afghanistan Opium Survey 2009*, Kabul, September 2009, 9, viewed online at viewer.zmags.com/publication/f1effeeb#/f1effeeb/1.

TEN: THE SMILES OF BADAKHSHAN

174 bankroll the insurgency: Barnett Rubin, "The Political Economy of War and Peace in Afghanistan," *World Development* 28 (2000): 1795, viewed

online at pdfcast.org/pdf/the-political-economy-of-war-and-peace-in-afghanistan.

174 mineral and gem mines: Ibid.

175 poppy cultivation rose by 43 percent: Jonathan Goodhand, "Frontiers and Wars: The Opium Economy in Afghanistan," *Journal of Agrarian Change*, April 2005, 200.

175 produced the entire 185 tons: A. William Samii, "Drug Abuse: Iran's 'Thorniest Problem,'" *The Brown Journal of International Affairs* 9, no. 2 (Winter/Spring 2003): 285.

176 "When children felt like buying": Associated Press, "Without Opium, Afghan Village Economy Spirals," www.msnbc.com, August, 2, 2009, viewed online at www.msnbc.msn.com/id/32258924/ns/world_news-south_and_central_asia/.

177 largest share of opium addicts: "In Pictures: Life in Badakhshan," BBC News, May 17, 2010, viewed online at news.bbc.co.uk/2/hi/8678388.stm.

177 from fourteen to eighty: United Nations Office on Drugs and Crime, *Illicit Drug Trends in Afghanistan*, June 2008, 15, viewed online at www.unodc.org/documents/regional/central-asia/Illicit%20Drug%20Trends%20Report_Afg%2013%20June%202008.pdf.

177 four hundred makeshift labs: Interview with Matt DuPee, Monterey, California, 2010.

177 processed domestically: UNODC, *Illicit Drug Trends in Afghanistan*, 6.

181 "For most households this expansion": Adam Pain, *Afghanistan Livelihood Trajectories: Evidence from Badakhshan*, Afghanistan Research and Evaluation Unit, Kabul, February 2010, 12, viewed online at www.areu.org.af/EditionDetails.aspx?EditionID-310&ContentID-7&ParentID-7.

ELEVEN: MY MOTHER'S KABUL

184 four million people: Afghanistan Investment Support Agency, provincial demographics chart, viewed online at www.aisa.org.af/english/about.html.

190 heroin users doubled: Agence France Presse, "Afghan Drug Addiction Twice Global Average: UN," June 21, 2010, viewed online at www.google.com/hostednews/afp/article/ALeqM5j7PYiYzBFkt0XCtImz5Yaz-2BU0yQ.

191 police recruits test positive: Rod Nordland and Abdul Waheed Wafa, "Sign of Addiction May Also Be Its Remedy," *New York Times*, May 16, 2010, viewed online at www.nytimes.com/2010/05/17/world/asia/17afghan.html; and Reuters, "Drug Abuse Is a Problem Among Afghan Police Recruits," March 10, 2010, viewed online at www.reuters.com/article/idUS TRE6294ZU20100310.

191 forty-three addiction treatment centers: Niamatullah Zafarzaoi,

"Number of Drug Addicts on the Rise in Kabul," Pajhwok Afghan News Service, June 1, 2010, viewed online at www.e-ariana.com/ariana/eariana .nsf/allDocs/A40BFD1CEF0A580B87257735005FBF64?OpenDocument.

191 increasing number of AIDS cases: "Afghanistan Grapples with Growing HIV/AIDS Problem," 46664.com, October 30, 2009, viewed online at www.46664.com/News/afghanistan-grapples-with-a-growing-hivaids-problem-id=7802.aspx.

195 Russia reported that it had surpassed: Victor Ivanov, "Proposals for the Elimination of Afghan Drug Production," a talk presented at *Drug Production in Afghanistan: A Challenge for the International Community,* June 8—9, 2010, Moscow.

195 90 percent of the heroin in Britain: Mark Townsend, Anushka Asthana, and Denis Campbell, "Heroin UK," *The Guardian,* December 24, 2006, viewed online at www.guardian.co.uk/society/2006/dec/24/drugsand alcohol.drugs.

196 that's 8 percent of the entire U.S. population: National Survey on Drug Use and Health (for 2008), Substance Abuse and Mental Health Services Administration, U.S. Department of Health and Human Services, September 2009, viewed online at www.oas.samhsa.gov/ nsduh/2k8nsduh/2k8Results.cfm.

196 the number of overdoses is rising: Garrett Therolf, "Heroin from Afghanistan Is Cutting a Deadly Path," *Los Angeles Times,* December 26, 2006, viewed online at articles.latimes.com/2006/dec/26/local/me-heroin26?pg=2; and McClatchy Newspapers, "Afghanistan Heroin Finds Way to US Streets," *The State,* January 7, 2007, viewed online at www.rawa .org/temp/runews/2007/01/07/afghanistan-heroin-finds-way-to-us-streets .html.

196 DynCorp company team leader: Richard Lardner and Matthew Lee, "State Department Investigating Death of US Employee Hired to Help Train Afghan National Police," Associated Press, September 16, 2009, viewed online at blog.taragana.com/health/2009/09/16/state-department-investigating-death-of-us-employee-hired-to-help-train-afghan-national-police-12042/.

196 a Dyncorp medic: Ellen Nakashima, "DynCorp Facing State Dept. Investigation," *Washington Post,* April 18, 2009, viewed onine at www.washington post.com/wp-dyn/content/article/2009/04/17/AR2009041703491.html.

196 Australian soldiers: Dan Oakes, "Soldier Found Unconscious After Suspected Drug Overdose in Afghanistan," *Sunday Morning Herald,* June 3, 2010.

196 drugs to Americans at Bagram Airfield: Gerald Pozner, "The Taliban's Heroin Ploy," *The Daily Beast,* October 19, 2009, viewed online at www .thedailybeast.com/blogs-and-stories/2009-10-19/the-heroin-bomb/.

TWELVE: WOMEN ON BOTH SIDES OF THE LAW

205 from $23 million to $250 million: Interviews with DEA, Afghan, and British officials, who gave various figures, and this is the range; Eric Schmitt, "Many Sources Feed Taliban War Chest," *New York Times*, October 18, 2009, viewed online at www.nytimes.com/2009/10/19/world/asia/19taliban.html?_r=2.

206 The intensified focus on the drug trade: Author's interview with Afghan counternarcotics officials, Kabul, 2006. Several agents in the National Interdiction Unit confirmed that more women are hired to fight the increasing number of women traffickers.

206 General Aminullah Amarkhil, the former chief of security: Gregor Salmon, *Poppy: Life, Death, and Addiction Inside Afghanistan's Opium Trade*, Sydney: Random House Australia, 2009.

206 "Do not touch me": Bilal Sarwary, "Afghan Officials Accused on Drugs," BBC News, January 6, 2006, viewed online at news.bbc.co.uk/2/hi/south_asia/4585188.stm.

206 Amarkhil told the press: Ibid.

212 serving sentences for moral crimes: Lyce Doucet, "The Afghan Women Jailed for 'Bad Character,'" BBC *Newsnight*, June 29, 2010, viewed online at news.bbc.co.uk/2/hi/programmes/newsnight/8771605.stm.

THIRTEEN: ADVENTURES IN KARTE PARWAN

225 eight million workers: Voice of America, "Afghanistan Battles Insecurity, Joblessness," December 23, 2010, viewed online at www.payvand.com/news/10/dec/1219.html.

225 Seventy percent of registered voters: Bernard Gwertzman, "Limbo in Afghanistan," *Newsweek*, August 17, 2009, viewed online at www.newsweek.com/2009/08/16/limbo-in-afghanistan.html.

226 biggest accused kingpins: Graeme Smith, "Afghan Officials in Drug Trade Cut Deals Across Enemy Lines," *The Globe and Mail*, March 21, 2009, viewed at v1.theglobeandmail.com/servlet/story/LAC.20090321.AFGHANDRUGS21/TPStory/Afghanistan; Paul Watson, "The Lure of Opium Wealth Is a Potent Force in Afghanistan," *Los Angeles Times*, May 29, 2005, viewed online at articles.latimes.com/2005/may/29/world/fg-drugs29.

226 pure heroin on the road: Smith, "Afghan Officials in Drug Trade."

226 Sayyed Jan: Ibid.

226 "Please assist him and do not stop him": Letters from General Daud Daud written to the Afghan security forces in Helmand, translated by Fariba Nawa and Naeem Azizian.

226 antidrug czar denies: Daud Daud interviews with author, Kabul, 2004, 2005, 2006.

227 control of smaller bandits: Interviews with American and Afghan counter narcotic agents and officials, Kabul and Washington DC, 2006, 2007

227 Wali Karzai: James Risen, "Reports Link Karzai's Brother to Afghanistan Heroin Trade," *New York Times*, October 4, 2008, viewed online at www .nytimes.com/2008/10/05/world/asia/05afghan.html.

227 mobilize up to six thousand troops: Smith, "Afghan Officials in Drug Trade."

227 The Rendon Group: Author's phone interview with John Rendon, head of the Rendon Group, Washington DC, 2005.

228 a trafficker claims that Daud helped him: Watson, "The Lure of Opium Wealth."

228 secretly ordered his arrest: Smith, "Afghan Officials in Drug Trade."

229 fuel tanker containing 1,540 pounds of opium: Ibid.

FOURTEEN: RAIDS IN TAKHAR

232 killed a few people and injured dozens: Abdul Matin Sarfaraz, "Takhar Residents Took to the Streets Against Armed Men," Pajhwok Afghan News, October 2, 2006, viewed online at www.rawa.org/takhar4.htm.

232 makes up 3 percent of agriculture: Afghanistan Ministry of Rural Rehabilitation and Development, provincial profile reports, *Takhar* [n.d.], 7, viewed online at www.mrrd.gov.af/nabdp/Provincial%20Profiles/ Takhar%20PDP%20Provincial%20profile.pdf.

232 "They all consist of white salt": Marco Polo's writings in Nancy Hatch Dupree, *A Historical Guide to Afghanistan*, 2nd ed., rev., Kabul: Afghan Tourist Organization, 1977, 418.

233 Amniat raided two heroin labs: Interviews with Afghan secret police, Amniat, July 2006.

234 earthquake in 1998: Khaleda Atta, "Aid Relief Efforts Made by Afghans in America for Earthquake Victims," *Lemar-Aftaab*, April—June 1998, viewed online at www.afghanmagazine.com/april98/articles/quake.html.

235 synthesized morphine into heroin: "Transforming Opium Poppies into Heroin," *Frontline*, PBS TV, viewed online at www.pbs.org/wgbh/pages/ frontline/shows/heroin/transform/.

236 destroying two hundred labs: David MacDonald, *Drugs in Afghanistan: Opium, Outlaws, and Scorpion Tales*, London: Pluto Press, 2007, 87.

236 Burmese chemists traveled: Interview with Matt DuPee, Monterey, California, 2010.

237 more traders will come: Ibid.

237 The United Nations estimates seventy-five: United Nations Office on Drugs and Crime, *Illicit Drug Trends in Afghanistan*, June 2008, 15, viewed online at www.unodc.org/documents/regional/central-asia/Illicit%20 Drug%20Trends%20Report_Afg%2013%20June%202008.pdf.

238 authorities destroyed 527 labs: Interview with Matt DuPee, Monterey, 2010.

241 pardoned five convicted traffickers: Farah Stockman, "Karzai's Pardons Nullify Drug Court Gains," *Boston Globe*, July 3, 2009, viewed online at www.boston.com/news/world/middleeast/articles/2009/07/03/presidential_pardons_nullify_victories_against_afghan_drug_trade/.

241 refused to rid the government: Interviews with Afghan ministry officials, Kabul, 2006.

241 Daud is transferred: Khwaja Basir Ahmad, "Karzai Orders Huge Shakeup in Ministry of Interior," Pajhwok Afghan News Agency, September 2010, viewed online at www.pajhwok.com/en/2010/09/01/karzai-orders-huge-shakeup-ministry-interior.

FIFTEEN: UPRISINGS AGAINST WARLORDS

245 Mahmoud, was accused of raping: Khalil Ahmad Fetri, "Kingdom of Bandits Prevails in Takhar Province, North of Afghanistan," Pajhwok Afghan News, August 18, 2007, viewed online at www.rawa.org/temp/runews/2007/08/18/kingdom-of-bandits-prevails-in-takhar-province-north-of-afghanistan.html.

247 Piram Qul is accused of crimes similar: Interviews with Rustaq residents, Rustaq, 2006.

247 Two people are killed and thirty-three injured: Sarfaraz, "Takhar Residents Took to the Streets."

SIXTEEN: THE GOOD AGENTS

260 Haji Juma Khan and Haji Baz Mohammad: Interviews with DEA agents, Washington, D.C., 2008.

261 the Taliban receive funding and weapons: Ibid.

261 Baramcha district, in Helmand: *The Pak Tribune*, "Afghan Drug Barons Flaunt Their Wealth and Power," April 9, 2006, viewed online at paktribune.com/news/index.shtml?140142.

262 Four to six men on motorcycles: Interviews with Idrees' brother, General Asif, and an official in the Afghan Directorate of Counter Terrorism.

263 The British protected their informant: Interviews with US and British counternarcotics officials, Kabul, 2006.

265 "Price: $12,000 a month": Karin Brulliard, "Affluent Afghans Make Their Homes in Opulent 'Poppy Palace,'" *Washington Post*, June 6, 2010, viewed online at www.washingtonpost.com/wp-dyn/content/article/2010/06/05/AR2010060502872.html

268 about 3.5 million still rely on food rations: United Nations World Food Program, "3.5 million Afghans face critical shortage of food aid," appeal

to donors, April 5, 2006, viewed online at www.wfp.org/node/573.

268 bombings shot up 600 percent: "Bleeding Afghanistan: Washington, Warlords and the Propaganda of Silence," Democracy Now TV, October
6, 2006, viewed online at www.democracynow.org/2006/10/6/bleeding_
afghanistan_washington_warlords_and_the

SEVENTEEN: IN SEARCH OF DARYA

275 The warnings were ignored: Adam Curtis, "The Lost History of Helmand," *The Medium and the Message* (blog), BBC, October 2009, viewed
online at www.bbc.co.uk/blogs/adamcurtis/2009/10/kabul_city_number_
one_part_3.html.

275 guerrilla war: Gretchen Peters, *Seeds of Terror: How Heroin Is Bankrolling the
Taliban and al Qaeda*, New York: St. Martin's Press, 2009, 32.

EIGHTEEN: THROUGH THE MESH

304 graveyard of empires: Christian Caryl, "Bury the Graveyard," *Foreign Policy*, July 26, 2010, viewed online at www.foreignpolicy.com/
articles/2010/07/26/bury_the_graveyard.

NINETEEN: LETTING GO

305 paying its recruits more: Taliban pay $300 per fighter, according to U.S.
General Stanley McChrystal, *Afghanistan Crossroads*, "Taliban Pay vs.
Afghan Forces Pay," CNN, December 9, 2009, viewed online at afghanistan
.blogs.cnn.com/2009/12/09/taliban-pay-vs-afghan-forces-pay/.

305 holding secret talks with the Taliban: Steve Coll, "US-Taliban talks," *The
New Yorker*, February 28, 2011, viewed online at www.newyorker.com/
talk/comment/2011/02/28/110228taco_talk_coll.

306 The U.S. killed its leader bin Laden: "Bin Laden is Dead, Obama Says," *New
York Times*, May 1, 2011, viewed online at www.nytimes.com/2011/05/02/
world/asia/osama-bin-laden-is-killed.html.

306 poppy production peaked, with 477,000 acres: United Nations Office for
Drugs and Crime, *Afghanistan: 2007 Annual Opium Poppy Survey*, August
2007, IV, viewed online at www.unodc.org/pdf/research/AFG07_ExSum_
web.pdf.

307 United States allocated $600 million: David Rohde, "Taliban Raise Poppy
Production to a Record Again," *New York Times*, August 26, 2007, viewed
online at www.nytimes.com/2007/08/26/world/asia/26heroin.html.

307 a supply fueled by greed, not need: *Afghanistan: 2007 Annual Opium
Poppy Survey*.

307 American former counternarcotics coordinator: Thomas Schweich,

"Is Afghanistan a narco state?," *New York Times Magazine*, July 27, 2008, viewed online at www.nytimes.com/2008/07/27/magazine/27AFGHAN-t .html.

307 International opinion: Associated Press, "U.S. Announces Revamp of Afghan Drug Policy," June 27, 2009, viewed online at www.msnbc.msn .com/id/31580590/ns/world_news-south_and_central_asia/.

308 replaced it with cannabis cultivation: Kirk Semple, "Cannabis thrives in an Afghan province," *New York Times*, November 4, 2007, viewed online at www.nytimes.com/2007/11/04/world/asia/04cannabis.html.

308 dropped 22 percent: United Nations Office for Drugs and Crime, *Afghanistan: Opium Survey 2010, Winter Rapid Assessment*, February 2010, 1, viewed online at www.unodc.org/documents/research/ Afghanistan_Opium_Survey_2010_Winter_Rapid_Assessment.pdf.

308 Three of the twenty poppy-free: Ibid.

308 500 percent for acetic anhydride: interview with DuPee.

309 Gul Agha Sherzai: "Afghanistan's Opium Poppies: No Quick Fixes," *The Economist*, June 19, 2008, viewed online at www.economist.com/ node/11591396.

EPILOGUE: 2010

316 Marjah's main source of income: Saeed Shah, "Afghanistan War: Marjah Offensive Targets Opium Capital," McClatchy Newspapers in the *Christian Science Monitor*, February 9, 2010, viewed online at www.csmonitor .com/content/view/full/279158.

316 Fifteen civilians were killed: Alfred de Montesquiou and Rahim Faiez, "Civilians Used as Human Shields in Marjah Fight," Associated Press, in *San Francisco Chronicle*, February 18, 2010, viewed online at articles .sfgate.com/2010—02—18/news/17926999_1_civilians-afghan-forces-human-shields.

Bibliography

BOOKS

Asad, Amir Zada, and Robert Harris. *The Politics and Economics of Drug Production on the Pakistan-Afghanistan Border.* Burlington, UK: Ashgate, 2003.

Booth, Martin. *Opium: A History.* New York: St. Martin's Press, 1996.

Chouvy, Pierre-Arnaud. *Opium: Uncovering the Politics of the Poppy.* London: I.B. Taurus, 2009.

de Vitray-Meyerovitch, Eva. *Rumi and Sufism.* Trans., Simone Fattal. Sausalito, Calif.: Post-Apollo Press, 1977, 1987.

Dupree, Nancy Hatch. *A Historical Guide to Afghanistan.*, 2nd ed. Afghan Tourist Organization, 1977.

Feifer, Gregory. *The Great Gamble: The Soviet War in Afghanistan.* New York: HarperCollins, 2009.

Fitzgerald, Paul, Elizabeth Gould, and Sima Wali. *Invisible History: Afghanistan's Untold Story.* San Francisco: City Lights Books, 2009.

Hafvenstein, Joel. "Afghanistan's Opium Strategy Alternatives: A Moment for Masterful Inactivity." In Whit Mason, ed. *The Rule of Law in Afghanistan: Missing in Inaction.* Cambridge, UK: Cambridge University Press, 2011.

————. *Opium Season: A Year on the Frontier.* Guilford, UK: The Lyons Press, 2007.

MacDonald, David. *Drugs in Afghanistan: Opium, Outlaws and Scorpion Tales.* London: Pluto Press, 2007.

Magnus, Ralph H., and Eden Naby. *Afghanistan: Mullah, Marx and Mujahid.* Boulder, Colo.: Westview Press, 1998.

McCoy, Alfred W. *The Politics of Heroin: CIA Complicity in the Global Drug Trade.* Chicago: Lawrence Hill Books, 2003.

Peters, Gretchen. *Seeds of Terror: How Heroin Is Bankrolling the Taliban and al Qaeda.* New York: St. Martin's Press, 2009.

Salmon, Gregor. *Poppy: Life, Death, and Addiction Inside Afghanistan's Opium Trade.* Sydney: Random House Australia, 2009.

Scott, Peter Dale. *Drugs, Oil and War: The United States in Afghanistan, Colombia and Indochina.* Lanham, Md.: Rowman and Littlefield, 2003.

ARTICLES

"Afghan Drug Barons Flaunt Their Wealth and Power," *The Pak Tribune,* April 9, 2006. Viewed online at paktribune.com/news/index .shtml?140142.

"Afghan Heroin Trade 'Booming,'" BBC News, July 25, 2002. Viewed online at news.bbc.co.uk/2/hi/south_asia/2150580.stm.

"Afghanistan's Opium Poppies: No Quick Fixes." *The Economist,* June 19, 2008. Viewed online at www.economist.com/node/11591396.

Agence France Presse. "Afghan Drug Addiction Twice Global Average: UN." June 21, 2010. Viewed online at www.google.com/hostednews/afp/ article/ALeqM5j7PYiYzBFkt0XCtImz5Yaz2BU0yQ.

————. "Afghan Warlords Hindering Loya Jirga Process: HRW." June 13, 2002. Viewed online at www.rawa.org/warlord4.htm.

Ahmad, Khwaja Basir. "Karzai Orders Huge Shakeup in Ministry of Interior," Pajhwok Afghan News Agency, September 2010. Viewed online at www.pajhwok.com/en/2010/09/01/karzai-orders-huge-shakeup-ministry-interior.

Associated Press. "Without Opium, Afghan Village Economy Spirals." Accessed at www.msnbc.com, August, 2, 2009. Viewed online at www .msnbc.msn.com/id/32258924/ns/world_news-south_and_central_asia/.

Associated Press. "U.S. Announces Revamp of Afghan Drug Policy," June 27, 2009. Viewed online at www.msnbc.msn.com/id/31580590/ns/world_ news-south_and_central_asia/.

Atta, Khaleda. "Aid Relief Efforts Made by Afghans in America for Earthquake Victims." *Lemar-Aftaab,* April—June 1998. Viewed online at www .afghanmagazine.com/april98/articles/quake.html.

"Bleeding Afghanistan: Washington, Warlords and the Propaganda of Si-

lence," Democracy Now TV, October 6, 2006. Viewed online at www
.democracynow.org/2006/10/6/bleeding_afghanistan_washington_
warlords_and_the.

Blua, Antoine. "Kabul Alarmed by Iran's Executions of Afghan Prisoners." Radio Free Europe, October 15, 2010. Viewed online at www.rferl
.org/content/Kabul_Alarmed_By_Irans_Executions_Of_Afghan_
Prisoners/2013239.html.

Brulliard, Karin. "Affluent Afghans Make Their Homes in Opulent 'Poppy
Palace.'" *Washington Post,* June 6, 2010. Viewed online at www.washington
post.com/wp-dyn/content/article/2010/06/05/AR2010060502872.html.

Burch, Jonathan. "Afghan Opium Crop Falls 22 Percent, Prices Plummet—
U.N." Reuters, September 2, 2009. Viewed online at in.reuters.com/
article/2009/09/02/idINIndia-42159520090902?pageNumber=2.

Caryl, Christian. "Bury the Graveyard." *Foreign Policy,* July 26, 2010. Viewed
online at www.foreignpolicy.com/articles/2010/07/26/bury_the_graveyard.

Chouvy, Pierre-Arnaud. "Afghan Opium Production Predicted to Reach
New High." *Jane's Intelligence Review,* October 1, 2004. Viewed online at
www.rawa.org/opium6.htm.

Coghlan, Tom. "Mass Grave Plundered at Site of Taleban Prisoners' Massacre." *The Sunday Times,* December 24, 2008. Viewed online at www.times
online.co.uk/tol/news/world/asia/article5391550.ece.

Coll, Steve. "US-Taliban Talks." *The New Yorker,* February 28, 2011. Viewed
online at www.newyorker.com/talk/comment/2011/02/28/110228taco_
talk_coll.

de Montesquiou, Alfred, and Rahim Faiez. "Civilians Used as Human
Shields in Marjah Fight." Associated Press, in the *San Francisco Chronicle,* February 18, 2010. Viewed online at articles.sfgate.com/2010-02-18/
news/17926999_1_civilians-afghan-forces-human-shields.

Doucet, Lyce. "The Afghan Women Jailed for 'Bad Character.'" BBC *Newsnight,* June 29, 2010. Viewed online at news.bbc.co.uk/2/hi/programmes/
newsnight/8771605.stm.

DuPee, Matthew. "Iran's 30-Year War on Drugs." *World Politics Review,* February 10, 2010.

Fetri, Khalil Ahmad. "Kingdom of Bandits Prevails in Takhar Province,
North of Afghanistan," Pajhwok Afghan News, August 18, 2007. Viewed
online at www.rawa.org/temp/runews/2007/08/18/kingdom-of-bandits-
prevails-in-takhar-province-north-of-afghanistan.html.

Filkins, Dexter, and Mark Mazzetti. "Key Karzai Aide in Corruption Inquiry
Is Linked to C.I.A." *New York Times,* August, 25, 2010. Viewed online at
www.nytimes.com/2010/08/26/world/asia/26kabul.html.

Girardet, Edward. "In the Marjah Offensive of the Afghanistan War, a Reporter Hears Echoes of the Soviet War." *Christian Science Monitor,* March
18, 2010.

Goodhand, Jonathan. "Frontiers and Wars: The Opium Economy in Afghan-
    istan." *Journal of Agrarian Change*, April 2005.
Gordon, Michael R. "U.S. Says Iranian Arms Seized in Afghanistan." *New York
    Times*, April 18, 2007. Viewed online www.nytimes.com/2007/04/18/world/
    middleeast/18military.html.
Gwertzman, Bernard. "Limbo in Afghanistan." *Newsweek*, August 17, 2009.
    Viewed online at www.newsweek.com/2009/08/16/limbo-in-afghanistan
    .html.
Huntington, Samuel P. "The Clash of Civilizations?" *Foreign Affairs* 72, no. 3
    (Summer 1993).
Ibrahimi, Sayed Yaqub. "Turning Afghan Heroin into Kalashnikovs." Insti-
    tute for War and Peace Reporting, July 8, 2008. Viewed online at iwpr
    .net/report-news/turning-afghan-heroin-kalashnikovs.
"In Pictures: Life in Badakhshan." BBC News, May 17, 2010. Viewed online at
    news.bbc.co.uk/2/hi/8678388.stm.
Karokhel, Danish. "Mujahedin Victory Event Falls Flat." Institute for War
    and Peace Reporting, May 4, 2003. Viewed online at www.e-ariana.com/
    ariana/eariana.nsf/allDocsArticles/D499F506DA74819687256D1C0046BCC
    5?OpenDocument.
Lal, Deepak. "Endangering the War on Terror with the War on Drugs." *World
    Economics*, July—September 2008, 1—29. Viewed online at www.econ.ucla
    .edu/Lal/Lal_World_Economics_vol_9_03_08.pdf.
Lardner, Richard, and Matthew Lee. "State Department Investigating Death
    of US Employee Hired to Help Train Afghan National Police." Asso-
    ciated Press, September 16, 2009. Viewed online at blog.taragana.com/
    health/2009/09/16/state-department-investigating-death-of-us-employee-
    hired-to-help-train-afghan-national-police—12042/.
Lasseter, Tom. "Afghan Drug Trade Thrives with Help, and Neglect, of Offi-
    cials," McClatchy Newspapers, May 11, 2009. Viewed at www.mcclatchydc
    .com/2009/05/10/v-print/67723/afghan-drug-trade-thrives-with.html.
McClatchy Newspapers. "Afghanistan Heroin Finds Way to US Streets."
    The State, January 7, 2007. Viewed online at www.rawa.org/temp/
    runews/2007/01/07/afghanistan-heroin-finds-way-to-us-streets.html.
Nakashima, Ellen. "DynCorp Facing State Dept. Investigation." *Washington
    Post*, April 18, 2009. Viewed onine at www.washingtonpost.com/wp-dyn/
    content/article/2009/04/17/AR2009041703491.html.
Nawa, Fazul Haq. "The Continuation of Memories." Trans. (from the Farsi)
    by author. *Ansari Literary Association Publication*, September 1997.
Nissenbaum, Dion. "Afghan Report Links President's Brother to Illegal
    Land Grabs." McClatchy Newspapers in *Anchorage Daily News*, June 23,
    2010. Viewed at www.adn.com/2010/05/17/1292341_afghan-report-links-
    presidents.html.
Nordland, Rod, and Abdul Waheed Wafa. "Sign of Addiction May Also Be

Its Remedy." *New York Times*, May 16, 2010. Viewed online at www.nytimes.com/2010/05/17/world/asia/17afghan.html.

Oakes, Dan. "Soldier Found Unconscious After Suspected Drug Overdose in Afghanistan." *Sunday Morning Herald* (Sydney), June 3, 2010.

Paul, Lawrence M. "Afghanistan: How We Got There." *New York Times*, February 8, 2010. Viewed online at teacher.scholastic.com/scholasticnews/indepth/upfront/features/index.asp?article=f020810_afghan.

Perry, Tony. "Afghan Commander Massoud, Killed on Eve of 9/11 Attacks, is a National Hero," *Los Angeles Times*, September 22, 2010. Viewed online at articles.latimes.com/2010/sep/22/world/la-fg-afghanistan-massoud-20100922.

Pomfret, John. "Drug Trade Resurgent in Afghanistan." *Washington Post*, October 23, 2001. Viewed online at www.washingtonpost.com/ac2/wp-dyn/A36532—2001Oct22?language=printer.

Powell, Bill. "Inside the Afghan Drug War: The Strange Case of Haji Bashir Noorzai," *Time*, February 19, 2007.

Pozner, Gerald. "The Taliban's Heroin Ploy." *The Daily Beast*, October 19, 2009. Viewed online at www.thedailybeast.com/blogs-and-stories/2009-10-19/the-heroin-bomb/.

"President Bush Has Made Afghanistan Safe Once Again for Opium Production." *The American Chronicle*, January 23, 2008. Viewed online at www.americanchronicle.com/articles/view/50029.

Reuters. "Drug Abuse Is a Problem Among Afghan Police Recruits." March 10, 2010. Viewed online at www.reuters.com/article/idUSTRE6294ZU20100310.

Reuters. "Fighting Resumes in North and West of Afghanistan," October 4, 2002. Viewed online at www.rawa.org/fight.htm.

Risen, James. "Reports Link Karzai's Brother to Afghanistan Heroin Trade." *New York Times*, October 4, 2008. Viewed online at www.nytimes.com/2008/10/05/world/asia/05afghan.html.

Rohde, David. "Taliban Raise Poppy Production to a Record Again." *New York Times*, August 26, 2007. Viewed online at www.nytimes.com/2007/08/26/world/asia/26heroin.html.

Rubin, Barnett. "The Political Economy of War and Peace in Afghanistan." *World Development* 28 (2000). Viewed online at pdfcast.org/pdf/the-political-economy-of-war-and-peace-in-afghanistan.

Said, Edward W. "The Clash of Ignorance." *The Nation*, October 22, 2001. Viewed online at www.thenation.com/article/clash-ignorance.

Samii, A. William. "Drug Abuse: Iran's 'Thorniest Problem.'" *The Brown Journal of International Affairs* 9, no. 2 (Winter/Spring 2003).

———. "Iran: Country's Drug Problem Appears to Be Worsening." Radio Free Europe, July 18, 2005. Viewed online at www.rferl.org/content/article/1059991.html.

Sarfaraz, Abdul Matin. "Takhar Residents Took to the Streets Against Armed

Men." Pajhwok Afghan News, October 2, 2006. Viewed online at www
.rawa.org/takhar4.htm.

Sarwary, Bilal. "Afghan Officials Accused on Drugs." BBC News, January 6,
2006. Viewed online at news.bbc.co.uk/2/hi/south_asia/4585188.stm.

Schmitt, Eric. "Many Sources Feed Taliban War Chest." New York Times, October 18, 2009. Viewed online at www.nytimes.com/2009/10/19/world/
asia/19taliban.html?_r=2.

Schweich, Thomas. "Is Afghanistan a Narco State?" New York Times Magazine, July 27, 2008. Viewed online at www.nytimes.com/2008/07/27/
magazine/27AFGHAN-t.html.

Semple, Kirk. "Cannabis Thrives in an Afghan Province." New York Times,
November 4, 2007. Viewed online at www.nytimes.com/2007/11/04/world/
asia/04cannabis.html.

Shah, Saeed. "Afghanistan War: Marjah Offensive Targets Opium Capital."
McClatchy Newspapers in the Christian Science Monitor, February 9, 2010.
Viewed online at www.csmonitor.com/content/view/full/279158.

Smith, Graeme. "Afghan Officials in Drug Trade Cut Deals Across Enemy
Lines." The Globe and Mail, March 21, 2009. Viewed at v1.theglobeandmail
.com/servlet/story/LAC.20090321.AFGHANDRUGS21/TPStory/Afghanistan.

Stahl, Adam. "Al-Qa'ida's American Connection." Global Politics, May 16, 2008.
Viewed online at www.global-politics.co.uk/issue6/Stahl/.

Stockman, Farah. "Karzai's Pardons Nullify Drug Court Gains." Boston Globe,
July 3, 2009. Viewed online at www.boston.com/news/world/middle
east/articles/2009/07/03/presidential_pardons_nullify_victories_against_
afghan_drug_trade/.

"Taliban Pay vs. Afghan Forces Pay," Afghanistan Crossroads, CNN, December
9, 2009. Viewed online at afghanistan.blogs.cnn.com/2009/12/09/taliban-
pay-vs-afghan-forces-pay/.

Therolf, Garrett. "Heroin from Afghanistan Is Cutting a Deadly Path."
Los Angeles Times, December 26, 2006. Viewed online at articles.latimes
.com/2006/dec/26/local/me-heroin26?pg=2.

Townsend, Mark, Anushka Asthana, and Denis Campbell. "Heroin UK," The
Guardian, December 24, 2006. Viewed online at www.guardian.co.uk/
society/2006/dec/24/drugsandalcohol.drugs.

"Transforming Opium Poppies into Heroin," Frontline, PBS TV. Viewed
online at www.pbs.org/wgbh/pages/frontline/shows/heroin/transform/.

Voice of America. "Afghanistan Battles Insecurity, Joblessness." December 23,
2010. Viewed online at www.payvand.com/news/10/dec/1219.html.

"Warlord or Druglord," Time, February 8, 2007. Viewed at www.time.com/
time/magazine/article/0,9171,1587252—1,00.html.

Watson, Paul. "The Lure of Opium Wealth Is a Potent Force in Afghanistan." Los Angeles Times, May 29, 2005. Viewed online at articles.latimes
.com/2005/may/29/world/fg-drugs29.

Zafarzaoi, Niamatullah. "Number of Drug Addicts on the Rise in Kabul." Pajhwok Afghan News Service, June 1, 2010. Viewed online at www .eariana.com/ariana/eariana.nsf/allDocs/A40BFD1CEF0A580B87257735005 FBF64?OpenDocument.

Zakhilwal, Omar, and Adeena Niazi. "The Warlords Win in Kabul." *New York Times*, June 21, 2002. Viewed online at www.nytimes.com/2002/06/21/ opinion/21NIAZ.html.

REPORTS

Afghanistan Ministry of Rural Rehabilitation and Development, provincial profile reports, *Takhar* [n.d.]. Viewed online at www.mrrd.gov.af/nabdp/ Provincial%20Profiles/Takhar%20PDP%20Provincial%20profile.pdf.

Caulkins, Jonathan, P. Mark, A. R. Kleiman, and Jonathan D. Kulick. *Drug Production and Trafficking, Counterdrug Policies, and Security and Governance in Afghanistan*. New York: Center on International Cooperation, New York University, June 2010. Viewed at www.cic.nyu.edu/Lead%20 Page%20PDF/sherman_drug_trafficking.pdf.

Mansfield, David. *Afghanistan: Strategy Study #9: Opium Poppy Cultivation in a Changing Policy Environment: Farmers' Intentions for the 2002/03 Growing Seasons*. Kabul: United Nations Office on Drugs and Crime. May 2003, 1—28. Viewed online at www.davidmansfield.org/all.php.

Mansfield, David, and Adam Pain. *Alternative Livelihoods: Substance or Slogan?* Kabul: Afghanistan Research and Evaluation Unit. October 2005, 1. Viewed online at ageconsearch.umn.edu/bitstream/14650/1/bp05ma01.pdf.

———. *Counter-Narcotics in Afghanistan: The Failure of Success?* Kabul: Afghanistan Research and Evaluation Unit. December 2008, 8. Viewed online at www.areu.org.af/Uploads/EditionPdfs/822E-Counter-Narcotics%20in%20 Afghanistan%20BP%202008.pdf.

Pain, Adam. *Afghanistan Livelihood Trajectories: Evidence from Badakhshan.* , Kabul: Afghanistan Research and Evaluation Unit. February 2010, 12. Viewed online at www.areu.org.af-EditionDetails.aspx?EditionId=310& ContentId=7&ParentId=7.

Perl, Raphael F. *Taliban and the Drug Trade*. U.S. Congressional Research Service Report. October 5, 2001, 2. Viewed online at fpc.state.gov/ documents/organization/6210.pdf.

Political Freedom Research Institute country profile Web site. University of Massachusetts, Amherst. Viewed online at www.peri.umass.edu/file admin/pdf/dpe/modern_conflicts/Afghanistan.pdf.

Substance Abuse and Mental Health Services Administration: U.S. Department of Health and Human Services, *National Survey on Drug Use and Health (for 2008)*. September 2009. Viewed online at www.oas.samhsa.gov/ nsduh/2k8nsduh/2k8Results.cfm.

United Nations Development Fund for Women. Women in Afghanistan Fact Sheet 2010. Viewed online at www.unifem.org/afghanistan/media/pubs/factsheet/10/index.html.

United Nations Office for the Coordination of Humanitarian Affairs— Integrated Regional Information Network. "Afghanistan: Interview with Female Opium Farmer." *Bitter-Sweet Harvest: Afghanistan's New War.* August 2004.

United Nations Office on Drugs and Crime. *Addiction, Crime and Insurgency: The Transnational Threat of Afghan Opium.* New York: United Nations Publications, 2009, 1. Viewed online at www.unodc.org/documents/data-and-analysis/Afghanistan/Executive_Summary_english.pdf.

———. *Afghanistan Annual Opium Poppy Survey.* August 2007. Viewed online at www.unodc.org/pdf/research/AFG07_ExSum_web.pdf.

———. *Afghanistan Annual Opium Survey 2009,* Kabul, September 2009, 9. Viewed online at viewer.zmags.com/publication/f1effeeb#/f1effeeb/1.

———. *Afghanistan Annual Opium Survey 2010, Winter Rapid Assessment.* February 2010. Viewed online at www.unodc.org/documents/research/Afghanistan_Opium_Survey_2010_Winter_Rapid_Assessment.pdf.

———. *Illicit Drug Trends in Afghanistan.* June 2008, 15. Viewed online at www.unodc.org/documents/regional/central-asia/Illicit%20Drug%20Trends%20Report_Afg%2013%20June%202008.pdf.

———. *The Role of Women in Opium Poppy Cultivation in Afghanistan.* Islamabad, June 2000.

United Nations Office for the Coordination of Humanitarian Affairs— Integrated Regional Information Network. "Afghanistan: Donor Supported Approaches to Eradication." *Bitter-Sweet Harvest: Afghanistan's New War.* August 2004. Viewed online at www.irinnews.org/InDepthMain.aspx?InDepthId=21&ReportId=63019.

ONLINE ONLY

"Afghanistan Grapples with Growing HIV/AIDS Problem." 46664.com. October 30, 2009. Viewed online at www.46664.com/News/afghanistan-grapples-with-a-growing-hivaids-problem-id=7802.aspx.

Afghanistan Investment Support Agency. Provincial demographics chart. Viewed online at www.aisa.org.af/english/about.html.

Asa Hutchinson, Director of the U.S. Drug Enforcement Administration. Speech delivered at the Heritage Foundation. Washington, D.C. April 2, 2002. Viewed online at www.justice.gov/dea/speeches/s040202.html.

Curtis, Adam. "The Lost History of Helmand." *The Medium and the Message* (blog). BBC, October 2009. Viewed online at www.bbc.co.uk/blogs/adam curtis/2009/10/kabul_city_number_one_part_3.html.

Kolhatkar, Sonali, and James Ingalls. "America's Viceroy." ZNet, May 20,

2009. Viewed online at www.zcommunications.org/americas-viceroy-by-sonali-kolhatkar.

Lonely Planet. Viewed online at www.lonelyplanet.com/afghanistan/herat-and-northwestern-afghanistan/herat/history.

United Nations World Food Programme. "3.5 Million Afghans Face Critical Shortage of Food Aid." Appeal to donors. April 5, 2006. Viewed online at www.wfp.org/node/573.

The World Factbook 2009. Washington, D.C.: Central Intelligence Agency, 2009. Viewed online at www.cia.gov/library/publications/the-world-factbook/geos/af.html.

Index

women *(cont.)*
  as opium addicts, 190—95
  as poppy farmers, 149—56, 160—62, 163, 209
  prisons for runaways, 125
  protection from news of death, 271
  in Pul-e-Charkhi prison, 211—15
  in the Rapid Reaction Force, 207—11
  requirement for male travel companions, 6—8, 18—21, 22, 27—29, 121, 298—99
  self-immolation as protest, 89, 91, 114, 122, 164
  Taliban controls on, 5—7, 18, 21—23, 26, 28, 46, 76, 80, 88—89, 93, 125, 284—86, 306
  Taliban dress requirements, 7, 21—23, 28, 46, 93, 186, 280—81, 285, 289, 293, 299—300

Taliban fear of, 8
World Trade Center
  predictions for future attack, 56—57
  September 11, 2001 attacks, 4, 12, 55—58, 75, 179

Yosuf (kidnap victim), 247—50, 257

Zabi (travel partner), 280—81
Zahir, Ahmed, 62, 189, 211—12
Zahir, King Mohammed, 33, 35—36, 78—79, 189, 274—75, 303, 309
Zainab (policewoman), 207—11, 214
Zakhilwal, Omar, 79
Zikria (retired opium smuggler), 132—34
Zir Koh district, 140
Zulaikha (wife of great-uncle), 21, 25—26